Managing Effective
Relationships in Education

Education at SAGE

SAGE is a leading international publisher of journals, books, and electronic media for academic, educational, and professional markets.

Our education publishing includes:

- accessible and comprehensive texts for aspiring education professionals and practitioners looking to further their careers through continuing professional development

- inspirational advice and guidance for the classroom

- authoritative state of the art reference from the leading authors in the field

Find out more at: **www.sagepub.co.uk/education**

Managing Effective
Relationships in Education

Carol Cardno

Los Angeles | London | New Delhi
Singapore | Washington DC

SAGE Publications Ltd
1 Oliver's Yard
55 City Road
London EC1Y 1SP

SAGE Publications Inc.
2455 Teller Road
Thousand Oaks, California 91320

SAGE Publications India Pvt Ltd
B 1/I 1 Mohan Cooperative Industrial Area
Mathura Road
New Delhi 110 044

SAGE Publications Asia-Pacific Pte Ltd
3 Church Street
#10–04 Samsung Hub
Singapore 049483

Library of Congress Control Number: 2011930845

British Library Cataloguing in Publication data
A catalogue record for this book is available from the British
Library

ISBN 978-1-4462-0303-3
ISBN 978-1-4462-0304-0 (pbk)

Typeset by Dorwyn, Wells, Somerset
Printed in India by Replika Press Pvt Ltd
Printed on paper from sustainable resources

CONTENTS

ABOUT THE AUTHOR

Carol Cardno is Professor of Educational Management in the Department of Education at Unitec Institute of Technology, Auckland, New Zealand where she was the Head of Department for a number of years. She was formerly the principal of Waitakere College, a large co-educational secondary school in West Auckland before taking up an academic career. Carol teaches and supervises postgraduate students in the field of educational management and leadership and presents workshops on managing dilemmas through productive conversation both nationally and internationally. She is the author of several books including *Collaborative Management in New Zealand Schools* (Longman, 1990) and *Action Research: A Developmental Approach* (New Zealand Council for Educational Research, 2003). She has also co-authored three books on performance appraisal. Her publications include many papers in scholastic journals on topics related to her research interests which are educational leadership and management, leadership development, staff appraisal, organisational learning, the management and resolution of leadership dilemmas, team learning and strategic leadership. Her work is internationally acknowledged and she has been invited to present keynote addresses in several countries, including Australia, Cyprus, South Africa and Sweden. She is a Fellow of the New Zealand Association for Educational Administration and Leadership and a Fellow of the Commonwealth Council for Educational Administration and Management. In 2007 Carol featured in the Queen's Birthday honours list and was made a companion of the Queen's Service Order for services to educational administration and management.

ACKNOWLEDGEMENTS

The author and publisher would like to thank the following for granting permission to use copyright material:

SUNY Press for Figure 1.1 – illustration of administration and management from C. Hodgkinson (1991) *Educational Leadership: The Moral Art.*

Emerald Publishing Group for Figure 5.2 – illustration of model of holistic professional development from C. Cardno (2005) *International Journal of Educational Management,* 19(4).

Harvard Business Review for Figure 6.1 – adaptation of illustration of continuum of leadership behaviour from R. Tannenbaum and W.H. Schmidt (1973) *Harvard Business Review,* 51.

McGraw-Hill for Figure 6.2 – adaptation of illustration of zone of acceptance from W. Hoy and C. Miskel (2001) *Educational Administration: Theory, Research and Practice;* and Figure 6.3 – adaptation of illustration of Vroom-Yetton decision-making tree from R.G. Owens (2004) *Organisational Behaviour in Education.*

Peters, Fraser and Dunlop Publishing for Figure 7.1 – illustration of elements of teamwork leadership from J. Adair (1986) *Effective Teambuilding.*

R.A. Napier for use of material in Reflective Exercise – understanding your leadership behaviour from R.A. Napier and M.K. Gershenfeld (1988) *Making Groups Work: A Guide for Group Leaders.*

Little, Brown Publishers for Reflective Exercise – self-assessment of emotional intelligence domains adapted from D. Goleman, R. Boyzatis and A. McKee (2002) *The New Leaders: Transforming the Art of Leadership into the Science of Results.*

Pearson Education for Figure 8.1 – illustration of a model of the elements of strategic management from G. Johnson and K. Scholes (2002) *Exploring Corporate Strategy: Texts and Cases.*

Open University Press for Figure 8.2 – adaptation of illustration of choosing a strategic framework from S. Murgatroyd and C. Morgan (1992) *Total Quality Management and the School.*

FOREWORD

There are many books on educational leadership and management. These range from guides intended for practitioners to theoretical texts aimed primarily at academics and research students. Carol Cardno's new book bridges this divide by stressing both the concepts underpinning practice and the need for school leaders to acquire a specific set of leadership skills to carry out their activities successfully. She argues that theory is demanding but essential in resolving complex problems.

The chapters in this book weave together several central strands of educational leadership and management. She begins by tackling the semantics of the field and the meanings given to three overlapping terms; educational administration, educational management and educational leadership, which collectively define the field. She rightly focuses on the leadership of teaching and learning, which is widely regarded as the most important task facing school principals. She links this to notions of organisational learning. Schools ought to be the ultimate learning organisations, as that is their central purpose, but achieving this is not straightforward, as Carol shows in this part of her book. Subsequent chapters address issues of managing dilemmas through dialogue, performance management, collaborative decision-making and teamwork. The final chapter brings these ideas together in a powerful discussion of strategic leadership and management. She argues that school-level strategy is inevitably constrained by the policies prescribed by governments but it is also true that leaders often fail to exploit the discretion which is available to them. Interpreting, and not simply implementing, government policy is essential if school principals are to be leaders and not simply administrators of central policy.

Carol draws on her extensive experience, as a school principal and a professor, to bring together theory and practice in a novel way. She eschews esoteric theory, intended only for academic debate, and focuses on showing how concepts can illuminate practice and lead to better outcomes for all who work within, or care about, educational organisations.

Tony Bush
Professor of Educational Leadership,
University of Warwick, and the University of the Witwatersrand,
Johannesburg

INTRODUCTION

In this book I have woven the idea of the importance of establishing productive relationships through each of the chapters to show how effectiveness can be enhanced when complex problems are openly, collaboratively and trustingly resolved. The chapters are all interrelated and have connections to other chapters. This creates a holistic approach to what I believe is a core body of knowledge that can be drawn on to understand the expectations of effectiveness.

In educational organisations, a relationship is productive when the interactions between those who lead and manage and the people they work through and with to achieve organisational goals, produce results which are desirable in terms of serving those who benefit from the organisation's endeavours. In this sense productive relationships are the antithesis of defensive relationships which in many situations are unlikely to produce outcomes that solve problems. Ultimately, a productive relationship is forged beyond the bounds of any personal relationship issues because the paramount concern is not about being nice or sociable or comfortable but about being accountable.

Leaders and managers in educational organisations are accountable to multiple stakeholders and invariably there are very many educational purposes to be achieved. This inevitably leads to situations of problem complexity – an unavoidable challenge for those charged with resolving educational problems. In their problem-solving efforts leaders encounter values and beliefs (their own and others') that guide their approach and attempts to problem solve. When relationships are defensive, problems are hardest to resolve.

In the course of attempts to achieve productive relationships there are many challenges that need to be recognised, confronted and overcome. The book is unique because it conveys a 'tough message' about adopting a particular attitude to problem-solving. The message is tough because it reiterates a need to know the theory base *and* the need to learn a particular set of

1

skills which enable the theory of productive problem-solving to be put into practice. Practice (which can mean failure) reveals that the theory is demanding intellectually and behaviourally, and requires change at three levels: the intrapersonal level, the interpersonal level and the organisational level. The change demanded can often be disquieting but the gains can be of considerable benefit to those served by the organisation. It is achieved through a praxis of knowledge and action that involves skilled theory application.

Every topic in the book indicates an area in which effective leadership and management should be developed. Every topic is related to other topics in the book through the theme of the power of productive relationships in solving complex problems. This power of productive relationships is presented as a necessary condition for the achievement of effectiveness.

> **Effectiveness** itself is presented as the ability to solve complex problems so that they remain solved, and the organisation learns how to achieve this.
>
> **Organisational learning** is an essential condition which builds a foundation for the management of leadership dilemmas.
>
> In **leading learning and teaching**, the condition that enables change is the leader's ability to model and teach others to recognise dilemmas and conduct productive dialogue. This then establishes trust in order to improve the quality of teaching and learning.
>
> **Effective performance appraisal** rests on open and honest evidence-based feedback which can be achieved when dialogue is productive and this, in turn, informs effective planning for professional development.

Productive dialogue both relies upon and builds a culture in which collaborative decision-making can foster productive relationships to produce desired results. Without productive relationships, teamwork lacks a critical condition for effective, collaborative task achievement, and collaboration in formulating and implementing strategy is essential.

A productive relationship relies on collaboration and trust, openness and dialogue that is productive. It is a leader's responsibility to influence others in ways that create these conditions for learning, change and effectiveness. Productive relationships are established when the culture of an organisation makes it possible for leaders to resolve complex problems in ways that openly deal with the defensiveness that is usually present in situations that are fraught with tension. Leaders have little difficulty in working collaboratively and harmoniously with colleagues when issues do not create conflicted situations. In an organisation where there is a high degree of motivation to achieve common goals, where there is a culture of respect, trust and collegiality, and where staff perform to exceptional standards, there is little need for leaders to struggle with the 'daily bread' of dilemmas that are the hallmark of educational leadership. Such utopias seldom exist and in reality educational leadership work is full of dilemmas of various kinds. These dilemmas usually display a fundamental characteristic of tension between achieving competing goals or aligning competing values that are strongly held.

To resolve such dilemmas, a leader needs to confront rather than avoid the dilemma; and to find a resolution that is productive for both the organisation and for the individual in terms of present and future relationships with the leader and with other colleagues. As a practitioner (where I learnt at first hand about the nature of such dilemmas and the absence of productive resolutions) and now as an academic with a strong commitment to developing leaders, I have gathered evidence that such dilemmas emerge in almost every aspect of leading and managing educational organisations. Study of dilemma resolution that creates productive relationships arises in numerous contexts and can be viewed from many perspectives.

The chapters in this book describe a variety of contexts in which educational leaders need to create productive relationships. In each context there is a body of theory to critically inform effective practice. In each chapter I have approached this body of theory to examine and explain the relevance of understanding and dealing with complex problems productively. Ultimately, any educational leader must direct their efforts towards achieving excellent learning outcomes for students. Teacher and leader learning are critical to achieving this. I believe that this book shows how effective leadership and management can focus on realising this goal through creating productive relationships between the professionals responsible for the quality of teaching and learning.

Chapter overview

In Chapter 1, 'Concepts of educational administration, management and leadership', there is an overview of this field and its fundamental purpose which is to provide understandings of the core concepts and purposes to inform and improve practice. In systems and organisations, the challenge of solving complex problems is the core work of administrators, managers and leaders, and it is likely to result in effective outcomes if the problem-solving process is productive rather than defensive.

In Chapter 2, 'The leadership of teaching and learning', the idea of what it means to be an effective leader of the core business of teaching and learning is explored with reference to a literature base that spans nearly 30 years. The tasks of educational leadership (variously named instructional or academic leadership) can be performed directly or indirectly to influence student learning outcomes. Direct educational leadership involves the leader personally in instructionally focused activity. In this chapter I have sifted the most valuable messages from the literature to provide clear direction on the activities that educational leaders should prioritise in order to make a difference. Indirect educational leadership involves many people in performing the direct tasks. Key educational leaders create and sustain conditions that affect the climate of learning and teaching in the organisation. Much of the literature is consistent in referring to a critical condition for effective leading of teaching and learning, which is centred on the development of productive relationships through conversation that is productive.

Chapter 3, 'Organisational learning in a learning organisation', lays the foundation for creating conditions that lead to productive relationships. The concept of learning about the sources of problems and adopting guiding values that are productive rather than defensive, is central to effective leadership and management. An organisation that commits to this type of learning is not choosing an easy option but an effective one, because it creates the opportunity for members to feel confident about and trust others in problem-solving efforts, and this in turn strengthens productive relationships. Productive relationships in organisations which are open to learning are characterised by the high value placed on the use of valid information, joint solution-finding and a relentless commitment to monitoring agreed solutions in order to effectively solve problems.

Chapter 4, 'Managing dilemmas through productive dialogue', sets out the expectations placed on the leader to engage in and model demanding learning about the nature of dilemmas and skills needed to resolve them. In a culture where leadership dilemmas are recognised and addressed through the use of productive dialogue there is a possibility of effective resolution of complex problems. It is also possible that this way of resolving dilemmas creates the sort of productive relationships that lead to future dilemmas being handled in effective ways.

In Chapter 5, 'Managing and developing professional performance', we see that it is in performance management contexts related to the appraisal and development planning of staff that leadership dilemmas arise and challenge the productive nature of relationships. In this context, relationships are often at their most difficult because of the inherent tension between accountability and development in appraisal activity. The tensions between achieving organisational goals and simultaneously achieving individual goals further test the leader's ability to build and utilise productive relationships. Without a foundation knowledge of the principles of organisational learning and the practice knowledge of how dilemmas should be managed, and the skills of productive dialogue, appraisal and development activity often becomes a technical exercise, without the necessary deepening of problem understanding and professional learning that would make these activities effective.

Chapter 6, 'Managing decision-making collaboratively' highlights the need for leaders to be able to make decisions about the sort of problems they are dealing with and the degree to which collaboration is used. It has links to understanding the particular challenges of complex problems that are introduced in Chapter 3 (about organisational learning) and Chapter 4 (about managing dilemmas) and the need to build trust in a culture of shared decision-making. If what people experience in the course of being included in making decisions is positive as well as realistic, then productive relationships can be fostered. In turn, these productive relationships provide the conditions for ongoing effectiveness in making decisions collaboratively.

In Chapter 7, 'Productive teamwork', the importance of teams in organisations is stressed in relation to these being the units for learning that lead to effective problem-solving which can only happen when team members are able to engage in dialogue that is productive rather than defensive. Both team leaders and team members need to be skilled in solving problems productively so that consequently they establish highly effective productive team working relationships.

Chapter 8, 'Strategic leadership and management', requires an alignment between plans for the organisation and the various individuals that contribute to the organisation's goals. A key aspect of strategic leadership is a focus on the human resources that enable plans to be implemented and this, in an educational organisation, raises the unavoidable question of how to secure the most effective teachers and create conditions to retain them. Sound strategic planning is based on understanding current problems and the organisation's capacity for innovation and then formulating academic focused goals. When dilemmas act as barriers to goal achievement it is the leader's responsibility to achieve a mutually productive relationship between the organisation and the individuals in it to achieve its educational purposes.

In short, productive relationships are powerful when they:

- provide an avenue for genuine collaboration;
- demonstrate and enable trust;
- are the arena in which complex problem-solving can occur;
- are utilised to resolve leadership dilemmas through productive dialogue; and
- become embedded in the culture of a learning organisation.

MANAGING EFFECTIVE RELATIONSHIPS IN EDUCATION	
THEMES	**CHAPTERS**
Understand the importance of productive relationships in decision-making in administration, management and leadership of educational organisations.	Chapter 1 Concepts of educational administration, leadership and management
Use productive relationships to influence teaching to improve student learning.	Chapter 2 The leadership of teaching and learning
Use productive relationships as the basis for solving complex problems in a culture of organisational learning. Build productive relationships through using productive conversations to resolve leadership dilemmas.	Chapter 3 Organisational learning in a learning organisation
	Chapter 4 Managing dilemmas through productive dialogue
Employ productive relationships to collaborate and build trust in order to solve problems of practice that impact on quality learning and teaching.	Chapter 5 Managing and developing professional performance
	Chapter 6 Managing decision-making collaboratively
Make productive relationships a foundation condition for effective teamwork and goal achievement.	Chapter 7 Productive teamwork
	Chapter 8 Strategic leadership and management

CHAPTER ONE

CONCEPTS OF EDUCATIONAL ADMINISTRATION, MANAGEMENT AND LEADERSHIP

Building productive relationships

In educational systems and organisations the core work associated with administration, management and leadership is the resolution of educational problems. When these problems are complex and contain tensions between collective organisational aspirations and interests and those of individuals, they present particularly challenging situations. The practitioners who perform administrative, management and leadership roles in these organisations can approach complex problem-solving through building productive relationships that provide a foundation for effective practice.

Naming the field of practice, study and research

If researchers and practitioners search for knowledge that supports the intent to perform the roles of educational administrators, educational managers or educational leaders effectively and productively, then an understanding of these concepts is essential. The terms educational administration, educational management and educational leadership have in common a focus on the core business of educational organisations, namely, teaching and learning. Leaders in educational organisations will be familiar with all three of the terms administration, management and leadership which define broad concepts in relation to the way in which education is organised in formal and informal ways. Yet, usage of the terminology in the literature and in the day-to-day parlance of the workplace, indicates that there are manifold meanings assigned to each concept separately, and there are often confusing or conflicting explanations of the links and relationships between these terms.

Together the terms have been used to *name* a particular field of knowledge about theory and practice within the discipline of education. This gives rise within the field to some confusion for those not familiar with the terminology because scholars use the terms variously in theorising about and examining the application of these concepts to educational organisations. Further confusion is inevitable because in practice the terms have often been used to denote functions, roles and tasks in ways that have little connection to the original and conceptual meaning(s) of the terms. Take, for example, the job title of 'administrator', which is often used in higher educational institutions to identify staff in clerical roles. This meaning is also common in many British-influenced contexts where for example, according to Dimmock (1999a), leadership is described as higher order tasks, management is described as routine maintenance and administration as lower order duties. Yet, in contrast, a completely different type of role is performed by those in 'public administration' which is the academic field from which educational administration has evolved as a separate entity.

Historically, the oldest term in our field is educational administration and it has a strong North American affiliation which is reflected in the naming of textbooks, book titles, scholastic journal titles (*Educational Administration Quarterly*), journal article titles and specialist qualifications (Master of Educational Administration). In the USA, degrees in educational administration span a broad spectrum of career choices which may or may not be related to engagement in instruction per se. For example, many academics with master's and doctoral degrees in educational administration choose non-instructional administrator career pathways in American universities and community colleges in roles related to such areas as financial management, admissions or student services.

Bush (2003) says the term educational administration is also much in evidence in Australia. On the other hand, in England for example, the term educational management is more prominent. Around the world, the term educational leadership rose to popularity in the mid-1990s for a number of reasons which will be discussed further on. One consequence of this deification of leadership is evidence of a flurry of name-changing to replace the terms administration and management with 'leadership'. One example of such a name change is the renaming of the journal of the British Educational Leadership, Management and Administration Society from *Educational Management and Administration* to *Educational Management, Administration & Leadership* in the early years of the millennium. Owens (2004) makes reference to the 'rhetoric of reform chic' (p. 275) which contends that schools need leadership, not mere management – suggesting that the terms are mutually exclusive. Yet, he goes on to say, 'Educational leaders must – as must all leaders – be able to manage' and while we can argue strongly that what schools need is excellent leadership, it is 'false to argue that, therefore, principals should be leaders not managers, because they need to be both' (p. 276). There is certainly evidence that the term administration has also been replaced with leadership.

In my reading of the literature that deals specifically with attempts to unravel the semantics and conceptual shifts associated with the concepts of administration, management and leadership, I have been deeply influenced by the philosophy of Hodgkinson (1991). His provocative thinking has provided me with a platform to develop my own understanding of and continuing reflection on the concepts based on my reading, research of practice and ongoing interaction with the praxis of educational administration, management and leadership.

Educational administration

Here I must make it clear that I am inferring that administration is a higher-order task – not using the connotation that administration means clerical work. First, there is leadership *in* administration. In fact, it has been suggested that one term can easily replace the other – and we find in current writing that this is often the case. Secondly, we cannot talk about administration without also talking about management. This is because management is subsumed *in* administration. Thus the field term 'administration' incorporates aspects of the other two terms: management and leadership.

Hodgkinson (1991) has suggested certain aspects of administration that differentiate it from management. Administration is the highest form of systemic activity and is associated with policy, values, strategy, top management, involves art and deliberation, and above all requires a philosophical position. Administration is a large concept, most often associated with executive or governance functions and is systemically the highest point in a hierarchal sense, although there has been an elision of administration and management in many descriptions of organisational work. It would appear that the North American system still maintains the supremacy of administration. For example, school superintendents see themselves as administrators rather than managers because they are associated with the large values-based decision-making that is the hallmark of administration (Owens, 2004). Confusingly, the term management is used in a British context to describe administration functions such as policy formulation and organisational transformation which also imply a focus on vision and values (Bush, 2003).

One of the key dimensions of educational administration has been a focus on values. A value is defined as, 'a conception, explicit or implicit, distinctive of an individual or characteristic of a group, of the desirable which influences the selection from available modes, means, and ends of action' (Hodgkinson, 1991, p. 102). He identifies what he calls the *metavalues* – the imperatives that 'pervade the organization but are most potent and close to the surface of consciousness in the administrative/managerial subsystem' (p. 104). These are identified as the values of maintenance (for example, preserving the existence of the organisation), growth (which can mean power over competitors for example), effectiveness (exemplified by the accomplishment of desired ends) and efficiency (which requires maximising use of resources). There are, of course, myriad other philosophical positions and beliefs from which values that are seen as desirable by administrators are derived (Begley, 1999; Haydon, 2007). The challenge that arises for administrators at this high level of system and organisational leadership is a matter of sometimes having to choose between these desirables and deal with the conflict among established desirables and other values in order to make decisions about what is right and good. These are moral conflicts and as Hodgkinson (1991) states, 'educational leadership is especially difficult, especially challenging and especially moral' (p. 63) because in educational contexts there is often a lack of goal specificity, ends and means are often unclear, and the raw material of education in contrast to other fields of administration is 'intractably mysterious, for it is human nature itself' (p. 62).

For administrative leaders in education there will always be problem complexity creating moral or ethical dilemmas that arise and challenge practitioners at central and local system levels. An understanding of the nature of these dilemmas and the role of productive relationship-building between stakeholders in resolving them is what this book is about.

Educational management

A synthesis of definitions drawn from both generic and educational management theorists defines management as the act of working with and through others to achieve the organisation's goals. The emphasis is on action and authority relationships with others, implying that managers need to be engaged in managing *people* (Razik and Swanson, 1995). Another view contrarily suggests that not only are management and leadership different; they are also mutually exclusive. According to Owens (2004, p. 275), 'This view correctly derives from the fact that one manages things, not people, and one leads people, not things. We manage finances, inventories, and programs for example, but we lead people'. So, at the very outset it is necessary to accept that there are competing definitions.

In my view, leadership is subsumed within management in the context of educational settings where the formal work demands management. Here, management differs from the lofty, philosophical and value-based practice of administration to be more action focused. And for management to be effective there must be leadership, in the sense of being able to influence change that impacts on practice and, ultimately, on the organisation's capacity to learn and improve.

The aspects of management that place it at a lower level than administration are, according to Hodgkinson (1991) 'subtended from and subsumed by the larger concept of administration' (p. 51). These aspects are execution of tasks, dealing in facts rather than values, professional specialism, tactics, middle management, activity and concern with detail. These aspects of management dovetail with administration aspects. In reality, neither set of functions can exist in isolation from the other. Because both sets of processes permeate the entire organisation they are joint administration/management aspects. A principal, for example, might find themselves engaged in administration in the morning and management in the afternoon if they were interested in drawing such distinctions between their activities. In higher education settings academic leaders such as deans and department heads experience the constant pull between attending to matters of policy and matters of people.

Linking administration and management

An illustration of the link between the concept of administration and the concept of management is provided in Figure 1.1 which is replicated from the work of Hodgkinson (1991). This conceptual framework shows the key activities of administration encompassing philosophy, planning and politics which are related to *policy making*, while the key activities of management are mobilising, managing and motivating and are related to the function of *policy implementation*.

Figure 1.1 illustrates how the monitoring phase feeds back in a systems theory sense to the philosophy phase to create a dynamic cycle of policy-making (administration) and policy implementation (management). This total process, Hodgkinson argues, 'can be conceived as the general field of leadership' (1991, p. 64). He draws attention to the central problem of administration when he says:

> The principle is always the same: a movement from ideas to things or events via the mediation of people. That is, the intellectual realm modifies the reality realm of the physical or natural world by human action. The central problem of administration, then, becomes the motivation of this action, and, more precisely, since administration is always of a collective, it is to reconcile the self-interest of the individual organization member or client with the collective interest of the organisation. (pp. 64, 65)

It is at the point of implementing policy and plans that managers most often encounter complex problems related to motivating action. Here the work involves reconciling individual self-interests and collective organisational interests which lie at the very heart of dilemmas that must be both recognised and managed by leaders to achieve effectiveness.

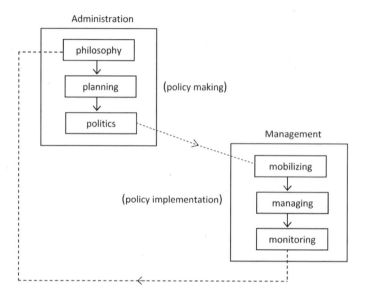

Figure 1.1 *Administration and management (source: C. Hodgkinson, 1991, p. 64,* Educational Leadership: The Moral Art, *State University of New York Press with the permission of SUNY Press)*

In the language of systems, Hodgkinson asserts that 'leadership *is* administration' (1991, p. 53). And leadership *is in* management too. If leadership is a concept that relates to influencing people, then, Hodgkinson's view of management as being concerned with *mobilising, managing* and *monitoring* of policy implementation surely requires the manager to act with and through other people. And, when the organisation functions to encompass both the administration and management dimensions of the processes delineated in Figure 1.1, there is a need for leadership to be embodied in singular or distributed forms, in formal and informal ways that can impact directly or indirectly on the core work of an educational organisation, namely, teaching and learning.

Across the developed world, moves to make schools and higher education institutions more autonomous through forms of decentralised site-based management (see Bush, 2003, for example) have highlighted the need for improving the quality of internal administration and management. This self-management (and in some cases self-governance) trend in many countries such as Australia, England and Wales, Hong Kong and New Zealand, has also contributed to a blurring of boundaries. Consequently, boundaries between the broad functions of educational administration and educational management are less defined, with administration functions often being performed at both a central national level and a local institutional level.

An example of the elision between educational administration and educational management can be seen in the following example of New Zealand. Here the sweeping reform of education administration in the late 1980s led to the establishment of self-management and self-governance for schools and higher education institutions.

The case of reforming education administration in New Zealand

In the early childhood, compulsory (schools) and tertiary sectors, the 1980s was a decade of considerable reform in this country (Parliament of New Zealand, 1988a, 1988b, 1989). Across the sectors the government agenda was to decentralise and empower the institutional unit with the ability to self-manage and, in the case of school and post-school education, to engage in self-governance. One consequence of what is popularly called the self-management reforms was a blurring and blending of the previously distinctive functions of administering and managing education because the disestablishment of central bureaucratic control devolved aspects of both policy-making and policy implementation to the local level. In the case of tertiary education institutions and schools, the establishment of councils and boards of trustees respectively vested the policy-making (administrative power) that had hitherto been more distant from the institution, within the institution itself in a partnership that was intended to give the governing bodies control over the management of the school or tertiary institution and the chief executive the power to carry out day to day management functions (Government of New Zealand, 1989). In both cases an expectation to chart the course of the organisation via strategic plans and charters was used as an accountability and developmental mechanism. This has not meant an abrogation of central administration by the Ministry of Education as it functions to provide the highest level of bureaucratic control and policy development for the system as a whole. Thus educational administration and management occur at both the system level and the local unit level, but with much greater emphasis on the ability of these educational organisations to determine the desirable values and vision for their future while they manage the complex problems in day-to-day practice. This is ultimately the field in which educational leadership occurs.

Educational leadership

Because the concept of educational administration is concerned with the large and all-pervading executive and governance level matters of vision, values, strategy and goals, it is not difficult to connect these to conceptions of leadership when it is defined as power to determine and influence the aims and purpose of education (Bush, 2003).

Undoubtedly, the notion of leadership implies some sort of influence. Yukl (2002), writing about leadership in organisations, states that, 'Most definitions of leadership reflect the assumption that it involves a social influence process whereby intentional influence is exerted by one person [or group] over other people [or groups] to structure the activities and relationships in a group or organisation' (p. 3). The view that leaders influence others' actions to achieve desirable ends is also linked to the initiation of change (Cuban, 1988; Gronn, 2003; Hunt; 2004).

There are many examples of distinctions drawn between leadership and management. Bush (2003) suggests that leadership is linked to values or purpose, while management relates to implementation and technical issues. Owens (2004) alludes to managers who manage 'things' and leaders who lead 'people'. Spillane and Diamond (2007) say that management practice centres on maintenance, while leadership practice typically focuses on initiating change.

In contrast, a number of writers argue for a less firm distinction on the grounds that there is an intimate connection between leadership and management, and considerable overlap in respect of motivating people to work towards a common purpose (Fidler and Atton, 2004). Both leadership and management are necessary (Bolman and Deal, 2008; Owens, 2004). Leadership itself is viewed as one of the tasks of managers (Hunt, 2004). While leadership and management tasks may be performed by different people, they may also be vested in one person where, in many situations, leadership and management activities occur in tandem. For example, 'The same leader can pursue both management and leadership in the same organizational routine' (Spillane and Diamond, 2007, p. 154).

I have stated elsewhere (Cardno and Fitzgerald, 2005) that I have a view of 'management that encompasses the notion of leadership within it rather than a separation where leadership is often elevated and management denigrated to a level of mere managerialism' (p. 317). Gronn (2003) reminds us that the work of managers in educational organisations is what they are contracted to do. He says, 'Leadership, on the other hand, while it may be part of what managers do, is by no means the whole of it. Nor do managers have a monopoly on leadership … which is open to any organisation member' (p. 6).

So, it could be said that leadership overlaps with two similar terms: administration (when it means higher-order thought and action related to whole systems and organisations) and management (when this relates to working with and through other people to achieve the organisation's goals). Ultimately, the work of an educational leader will involve leading and managing, and doing this with a focus on the key task of the organisation, which is learning and teaching.

It is important to note that the context for discussing leadership here is an educational context related to the organisation of educational institutions across a system that encompasses several sectors: early childhood education, schools (primary and secondary) and higher education institutions. First, we need to narrow our conception of the leadership concept to the context of the organisation because the body of knowledge about leadership is enormous, and even in relation to the context of educational organisations it is complex and confounded with confusion. While, as Hodgkinson (1991, p. 50) says, 'The term leadership is elusive, ambiguous, much abused', and may even be discounted as 'a mere incantation for the bewitchment of the led' (p. 53), it is nevertheless the expectation that both leadership and management occur in educational settings. In reality we will need to live with these terms that can be used synonymously, used to express different sides of the same coin, and used to indicate the scope of activity that influences and implements change in educational organisations.

In the process of leading and managing in educational organisations it is inevitable that complex and conflicted situations will arise where multiple stakeholders, multiple values and multiple goals may create tensions that become challenging. The leader's role is to reconcile conflicting demands and desires to achieve what is best for the organisation and for the individuals in it; and to do so in ways that reflect allegiance to the building of respect, trust and true partnership in the endeavours focused on the achievements of learners. Hence, it is the people that are managed and led, and all who contribute to management and leadership who are the subjects of the ideal of achieving productive relationships. I believe that building and then utilising productive relationships as the basis for effectively resolving complex problems of educational leadership and management is the most powerful means we have at our disposal to make a difference.

CHAPTER TWO

THE LEADERSHIP OF TEACHING AND LEARNING

Building productive relationships

When the work of educational leaders comes closer to teaching and learning, it needs a narrower focus. The main work of an educational leader is with teachers. In their engagements with teachers the leader needs to build productive relationships which allow critical problems of practice to be addressed. Through solving such problems effectively the educational leader can influence the organisational conditions which affect learning outcomes for students. Our interactions with others and the degree to which we can be effective depend on the ability of the organisation to learn and to solve complex problems. Such conditions can allow the parties in a workplace relationship to be productive and to resolve issues in ways that impact positively on students' and adults' learning experiences.

Educational leadership

This chapter is about the *leadership of teaching and learning.* This is often called *instructional leadership* in the North American literature which still largely dominates the study of this phenomenon in schools. In higher education, it is most often referred to as *academic leadership* and extends to the ability to influence not only learning and teaching, but also research.

The core work of educational leaders must lie in influencing teaching and learning, and doing so in ways that positively affect the educational achievement of students. Donmoyer and Wagstaff (1990) state that 'An instructional leader is someone who has a significant impact, for better or worse, on student opportunities to learn in the classroom' (p. 20). Several meta-analyses of quantitative research studies have established that leadership does have an indirect and at best a moderate effect on student learning (see for example Lashway, 2006; Waters et al., 2004). However, research about this connection is very thin on the ground. Instead, there is a heavy reliance in the literature on producing sets of dimensions in which leadership activity occurs, and descriptions of the tasks that educational leaders should engage in as they go about the daily business of being instructional leaders, curriculum leaders, professional leaders, academic leaders and pedagogical leaders – in other words, leaders of teaching and learning.

This vast array of terms shows how concepts about leading teaching and learning have been conceptualised in many different settings and countries. Reviewing several decades of research in the field of educational leadership, it is salutary to note that clear linkages between leadership and learning outcomes for students are not empirically established to any great extent. The relationship remains untested except in a few studies (Robinson, 2008). Further recent studies that synthesise literature related to the school sector (see, for example, Goldring et al., 2009; Robinson et al., 2009; Seashore Louis et al., 2010) are beginning to address this issue and point to dimensions of leadership that might indirectly influence student outcomes more effectively.

The term educational leadership is used, very broadly, to describe the field of study about leadership in educational institutions. It includes all of the other terms and indicates a focus for the work of leaders in educational settings. It is a concept associated with both leadership and management:

- Leadership – because at the heart of educational leadership lie educational purposes and educational goals; the ends to be achieved in relation to learning outcomes for students.
- Management – because the management practices of leaders provide the means by which educational goals are met.

Every task related to leadership and management should be conceived as interrelated activity that moves the organisation and the individuals in it towards goal achievement, which improves teaching and, ultimately, improves student learning outcomes. From their deep examination of the literature on leadership, Seashore Louis et al. (2010) synthesise a definition as follows: 'Our general definition of leadership highlights these points: it is about direction and influence. Stability is the goal of what is often called management. Improvement is the goal of leadership. But both are very important' (p. 10). As Starratt (2003) states, 'I believe that the core work of school leaders must be involved with teachers in seeking to promote quality learning for all children, and that management tasks serve that core work' (p. 11). What this means is that principals and teachers work together in productive ways to improve teaching and learning.

Although the language in much of the core literature is specific to the schools sector, it does not mean that the ideas are not applicable to higher education and early childhood education settings. In the tertiary sector research, the term 'academic leadership' is often identified in an attempt to include academic work (teaching and research) within the scope of leadership. Ramsden (1998), however, applies the term to all levels of an organisation, from strategy-making to teaching. In early childhood education, Ebbeck and Waniganayake (2003) assert that currently, 'there is no agreed definition of leadership in the early childhood field, nor do we have a publicly acknowledged list of our leaders and of what we expect of our leaders' (p. 17). Yet, both Ebbeck and Waniganayake (2003) and Rodd (2006) include teaching expertise and developing/mentoring teachers among the wide array of skills and attributes that they draw from generic business management theory as relevant to leadership in this sector. In the small literature on educational leadership in early childhood settings there is little evidence of the emergence of a concept of leadership that has a narrow and specific focus on teaching and learning apart from the broader all-encompassing functions of leadership and management.

Effective educational leaders know what to focus on in order to influence the quality of learning and teaching. Messages from the literature and research on educational leadership are critically important in directing leadership focus so that the greatest impact can be achieved. Hence, knowledge of research studies helps to point leaders in the right direction when they have to make choices about their priorities for action.

Narrow and broad conceptions of educational leadership

When educational leadership is conceptualised narrowly, it means that the school or institutional leader has a role in which their leadership of teaching and learning is the sole or primary function. This narrow view of educational leadership has an historical element related to principalship (or being headteacher of a school), a role in which the school leader performed a 'leading teacher' function. Thus their main work was in, or very close to, the classroom. In both the UK and New Zealand, headteachers/principals of middle- to large-sized organisations no longer have the time to be directly engaged in influencing teaching at the chalkface, because they have assumed considerable organisational and management responsibilities. It could be argued that the concept of instructional leadership itself, with its close focus on teachers and teaching, has outlived its usefulness. Leithwood

(1994), cited in Harris (2005, p. 83) states that, 'instructional leadership images are no longer adequate because they are heavily classroom focused', implying that wider school development issues may be set aside in favour of the tighter focus.

The intensification of the principal's role has led to them being beset by many new management demands, with the consequence that the direct enactment of instructional leadership in its fullest sense was not feasible. Since then, a broader view of the concept of school-based instructional leadership has been argued for. For example, Donmoyer and Wagstaff (1990) expressed the belief that the principal can be both a school manager and an instructional leader because the organisational management aspects of the principal's role impact indirectly on the quality of instruction in classrooms. Nearly two decades later, instructional leadership appears to be alive and well as a concept that is central to, but not the only concern of, effective school leadership. Hoy and Hoy (2009) state that:

> A critical role for all principals is that of instructional leader. We are not suggesting that principals alone are responsible for leadership of instruction. Clearly that is not the case. Leadership in instructional matters should emerge freely from both principals and teachers. After all, teachers deliver the instruction in the classroom; they have expertise in curriculum and teaching, and they have mastered a substantive body of knowledge. Principals, however, are responsible for developing school climates that support the very best instructional practices. (p. 2)

The key message here is that a broader conceptualisation of educational leadership implies that the principal is not the sole instructional leader and that the focus of leadership activity can be broader than the classroom. This view of educational leadership includes a focus on developing the climate and conditions and exerting influence indirectly to enhance the quality of teaching and learning.

Direct and indirect forms of educational leadership

Leadership can take both direct and indirect forms. Hunt (2004) reminds us that there is research evidence that accurately describes leadership as having 'a direct impact for good or ill' (p. 28). The direct form of leadership involves interaction and communication with those led, on a face-to-face basis. In indirect forms of leadership, distance is imposed between the decision-making at a higher level and implementation at the core level because of multi-level leadership structures, or a strategic orientation to the leadership. In these situations the leadership at higher level has indirect effects that cascade down the hierarchy.

We can broadly categorise the expectations of instructional leaders to identify those tasks that directly influence what happens in classrooms, as well as those that influence teaching and consequently influence learning from a greater distance – by indirectly shaping the environment in which the curriculum is delivered. Direct instructional leadership 'assumes that the critical focus for attention by leaders is the behaviours of teachers as they engage in activities directly affecting the growth of students' (Leithwood et al., 1999, p. 8) and almost all the research studies in the 1990s were conducted in primary school settings. Current research is strongly questioning the possibility of this direct form of educational leadership being enacted in secondary school settings. Seashore Louis et al. (2010) have alluded to two distinct but complementary sets of actions that principals take to influence instruction. These are (1) instructional actions involving direct engagement with individual teachers and (2) actions that are indirect and build instructional climate to support professional learning. Principals in large secondary schools are unlikely to be able to perform instructional actions themselves; instead, this sort of direct educational leadership role would be performed by the heads of department. The alternative to ineffective direct instructional leadership is its indirect form. Here, direct instructional leadership tasks are delegated to other senior managers or distributed across a different level of management. Now, the principal is able to focus on what Starratt (2003) refers to as the 'whole school's learning agenda as an integrated unity' (p. 13) with a wide focus and concentration on the 'big picture' issues and long-term vision.

The focus of educational leadership activity

In the context of schools the terms educational leadership and instructional leadership are often used interchangeably because the focus is instruction. Whether the form of educational leadership is direct or indirect it needs to encompass a number of tasks or activities. The leader can perform these directly or they can be distributed to others but they need to be priorities that are effectively managed. There have been clear messages conveyed in a vast body of research on this subject spanning more than three decades. This research has influenced practice in several ways. First, it is utilised in describing roles and expectations of educational leaders; secondly, it provides frameworks for the assessment and development of leadership in educational settings; and thirdly, it is of considerable critical guidance to leaders themselves in relation to their own understanding of theory and its application to practice.

Weber's (1987) seminal synthesis of the literature results in his suggesting a composite model that integrates the most significant ideas about instructional leadership activity derived from research and practice (see Figure 2.1).

He presents this in the form of six major functions of instructional leadership that are interrelated. The functions are (1) setting school academic goals; (2) maximising effects of instructional organisation; (3) hiring, supervising and evaluating teachers; (4) protecting instructional time and programmes; (5) setting standards for achievement and setting the tone for learning climate; and (6) monitoring achievement levels and evaluating programmes.

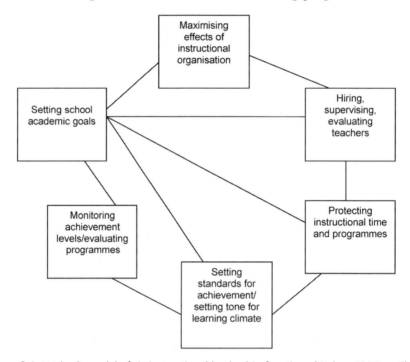

Figure 2.1 *Weber's model of six instructional leadership functions (Weber, 1987, p. 6)*

While he draws the conclusion that the principal is undoubtedly expected to be the instructional leader, this model offers the option for the principal to exert influence in a more indirect or tangential way. The principal is guided towards a close involvement with both academic ends and means by performing the six leadership functions which 'are sometimes shared and sometimes not shared, either *de facto* or intentionally' (Weber, 1987, p. 3). The most important of all the functions, according to Weber, is the setting of instructional goals because it potentially involves all the other areas of concern.

It is illuminating to then read the findings of a Best Evidence Synthesis (BES) of school leadership literature conducted in New Zealand (Robinson et al., 2009). This alludes to five leadership dimensions derived from direct evidence in the synthesis of selected literature, to be taken into account as having an impact on student outcomes. These are: (1) establishing goals and expectations; (2) strategic resourcing (including staff recruitment); (3) planning, co-ordinating and evaluating teaching and the curriculum (through direct involvement including classroom visits and giving teachers feedback); (4) promoting and participating in teacher learning and development; and (5) ensuring an orderly and supportive environment. This BES also used indirect evidence from studies of interventions which had an impact on student outcomes. Inferences were drawn about the role of leadership in creating these conditions, and this resulted in a further three dimensions being proposed. These were (6) creating educationally powerful connections (between individuals, organisations and cultures) that focused specifically on student learning; (7) engaging in constructive problem-talk (involving the naming and addressing of problems and understanding of how they are sustained); and (8) selecting, developing and using smart tools (noting that tools are smart if they 'promote teacher learning about how to promote student learning' (p. 44).

The seminal and current literature confirms the importance of specific dimensions that indicate the foci of activity in the effective leadership of instruction. The set of dimensions proposed by Robinson et al. (2009) has much in common with the six broad factors proposed by Weber (1987) and the dimensions appear to confirm that the focus on classrooms is still central but that the creation of organisational *conditions* or *climate* to support teaching and learning is no less important. Overarching both these syntheses of the literature is the view that the leadership of instruction requires leaders to work with people to motivate them towards achieving goals. Weber (1987) alludes to the leadership process requiring trust and interpersonal effectiveness in relations with staff and students. Twenty years on, Robinson et al. (2009) also refer to the critical role that is played by relational trust in the achievement of better learning outcomes. The theme of relational connectedness between principal, staff and school community is also evident in accounts of effective principalship (Notman and Henry, 2009; West-Burnham, 2009). This issue of trust in the course of building positive relationships is echoed in the cross-sector literature on higher education (Ramsden, 1998) and early childhood education (Rodd, 2006). It has particular relevance in relation to the way educational leaders are challenged by complex problems in which collegial relationships and organisational goals may often be in tension (Cardno, 2007).

The most compelling contributions on the instructional leadership tasks and activities that should be prioritised in order to positively affect student learning, come from a number of large research studies which synthesise quantitative results of numerous studies reviewed. Lashway (2006) has summarised results of three major research projects (Hallinger and Heck, 1998; Leithwood and Riehl, 2005; Waters et al., 2004) in terms of the core leadership behaviours identified. These are associated with four major roles which are:

- setting direction (the leader provides focus; sets goals collaboratively and monitors achievement of high expectations);
- developing people (the leader evaluates performance and builds people capability, including their own);
- leading change (leaders pioneer change and monitor impact on student learning); and
- establishing managerial order (leaders ensure an orderly environment; consistency in rules and structure and protect instructional time).

When educational or academic leaders choose to focus on the key activities that constitute educational leadership they can do this directly or indirectly. Table 2.1 summarises the possibilities for and the actual form of such activity that is focused on instruction.

The direct or indirect activities of educational leadership are enacted upon a foundation of knowledge about education in general, and teaching and learning in particular. Leaders must be knowledgeable about theory and practice relating to teaching content, assessment and achievement at specific or general levels according to how close or how distant they are to actual instruction.

Leaders' pedagogical/andragogical knowledge

Refocusing leaders on the pedagogical domain is a theme that can be traced in literature that refers to pedagogical leaders (see, for example, MacNeill and Cavenagh, 2006; White, 2008). The focus on pedagogical knowledge – of the educational leaders themselves and of teachers and teaching teams – is also evident in the expectation that principals of successful schools 'are knowledgeable about effective pedagogy and about what works for the individual needs of different students in their particular contexts. They are recognised in their schools for their professional knowledge and strengths as pedagogical leaders' (New Zealand Ministry of Education, 2008). According to Robinson (2007), principals as pedagogical leaders participate in and promote professional learning, work with other pedagogical leaders to solve pedagogical problems, obtain the resources needed and plan and monitor the quality of teaching. As well as continuing to develop their own pedagogical skills, educational leaders need to know 'what "good pedagogy" actually looks like' and assist 'their learning communities to develop a clear conceptual understanding of what is actually meant by the term pedagogy' (White, 2008, p. 18) so that the goals, strategies and processes for teaching can be established collectively and the learning outcomes rigorously evaluated.

In discussion of the concept of pedagogical leadership, it is important to clarify that the focus is not entirely on principals or leaders alone, but on leadership capability that makes pedagogical leadership possible. In

Table 2.1 Possibilities for and forms of direct and indirect instructional leadership

Direct instructional leadership	Indirect instructional leadership
Possible in primary schools, small secondary schools, early childhood education settings and small units in higher education settings	Possible in all cases as indirect activity complements direct activity. This indirect form is particularly applicable to larger primary schools, most secondary schools and higher education institutions
Performed by principals and head-teachers in school and early childhood education settings and by programme/curriculum leaders in higher education	Performed by principals and headteachers in school and early childhood settings and by deans and department heads in higher education
For example, *direct instructional leadership* takes the form of: – teaching and modelling teaching for others – personally engaging with individual teachers on a regular basis involving coaching situations – observing and providing feedback about classroom teaching – personally conducting perform-ance appraisals of staff, assisting with the setting of developmental goals and arranging development for individuals – personally arranging/participating in professional development events for the whole staff – personally ensuring that teaching time is protected – personally arranging teaching schedules to maximise effects of instructional organisation – personally setting standards for student assessment and achievement – personally monitoring student learning outcomes	For example, *indirect instructional leadership* takes the form of: – leading other educational leaders in the organisation – leading strategic activity related to setting direction and goals for the whole unit, such as alignment of academic goals from institution-wide to classroom level – leading strategic activity related to decisions and resources that affect the learning climate, tone and environment, such as the scheduling of teacher time and protection of instructional time – leading strategic activity related to recruiting high quality staff and indirectly monitoring their performance – leading change that impacts on student learning, such as teaching and learning improvements – creating conditions that make dialogue about change and improvement possible – personally appraising the performance of key educational leaders and overseeing their delegated appraisal of other leaders who in turn appraise teachers – delegating to other leaders the direct tasks of instructional leadership – overseeing the regular evaluation of programmes and student learning outcomes – establishing and monitoring systems and processes that create order and effective management to support teaching and learning

advancing the importance of the pedagogic capability of leaders to utilise content knowledge effectively in pursuing the improvement of student learning outcomes, Robinson (2010) states that 'the leadership content knowledge required to improve learning and teaching is so great that it cannot be located in the head of any individual leader, nor even in the combined cognitive resources of a leadership team' (p. 3). One important view of what leadership content knowledge actually comprises is suggested by Stein and Nelson (2003), who define this as 'the kind of knowledge that will equip administrators to be strong instructional leaders' (p. 424). They depict this knowledge as embedded in several layers of school hierarchy, as do Robinson et al. (2009). In signifying the critical need for pedagogical leadership, the emphasis is on developing capability for provision of such leadership from multiple leaders at a variety of levels in the organisation and not assuming in the case of schools, for example, that the principal or any other single person can wear this mantle alone. The principle that leaders of learning need a particular kind of knowledge in order to effectively influence student outcomes (Gronn, 2009) can also be applied to those who lead learning in higher education institutions.

The term *andragogy* is more pertinent when discussing adult teaching and learning (Knowles, 1980). The principles of andragogy (the art or science of helping adults learn) are these:

- It is important to let learners know why something is important to learn.
- Learners are shown how to direct themselves through information.
- Learning content/topics should be related to the learners' experiences.
- The educational focus is on facilitating the acquisition of and critical thinking about the content and its application to practice.

Furthermore, as Pew (2007) asserts, adult learners will not learn until they are ready and motivated to learn and 'this requires helping overcome inhibitions, behaviours, and beliefs about learning' (p. 17).

In relation to educational leadership, this definition of andragogy has two significant implications. First, educational leaders in higher education should be well versed in what constitutes effective teaching and learning in order to lead the academic programmes. As academic leaders, they need to pay attention to the conditions that they can directly influence in order to indirectly influence successful learning outcomes for students (Gardiner, 2002). The vast body of knowledge that now exists in relation to strong distributed instructional leadership in school settings could well be extrapolated to higher education contexts. Secondly, educational leaders in all sectors are likely to benefit from knowing what works and what counts in relation to adult learning, because their influence on changing teacher practice is at the heart of educational leadership. Hence, it is essential to have knowledge of the principles and practices that they should use with their own teachers in their professional learning and development.

Academic leadership in higher education settings

Unlike the research conducted in the school context, there is a very limited literature that discusses the concept of academic leadership in higher education in relation to improving student learning outcomes per se. However, contemporary concerns about a knowledgeable workforce and the costs of higher education have turned the spotlight on this sector. Governments in several countries, including Australia and New Zealand, are demanding greater accountability and transparency from institutions of higher education. Consequently, there is interest in research that connects leadership and student learning in seeking to improve success rates for students.

The term *academic leadership* appears mostly in relation to the leadership of curriculum and learning in the tertiary sector. A wide-net approach, that accords the designation of academic leader to all who lead (at many levels) in an academic institution is similar to the concept of academic leadership captured in recent Australian research (Scott et al., 2008). In this study, the specific aim to clarify what leadership means in a higher education academic context confirms the assumption that a very eclectic view is generally taken of the practice of academic leadership. The authors conclude that academic leadership occurs at a number of levels and in both direct and indirect forms. It has different meanings for the different roles performed, yet common ground has been identified by these same authors, who affirm that: 'The study has identified a number of areas of focus in academic leadership that cut across the majority of leadership positions studied. These include: policy formation, managing relationships, working with challenging staff, involvement in various aspects of planning and attending meetings' (Scott et al., 2008, p. xvi). Somewhat paradoxically, these authors also couch the meaning of academic leadership in very specific terms when they refer to an academic leader as 'a learning and teaching leader' (p. 73).

Marshall et al. (2000) assert that their attempts to clarify the meaning of academic leadership in one institution revealed a lack of consensus that is also evident in the literature. A clear outline of the concept of academic leadership comes from the work of Ramsden (1998) who asserts that 'academic leadership is both identical to leadership in other organisations, and idiosyncratic to university environments' (p. 123). It can be understood with a broad framework of generic management ideas yet it has some special characteristics related to the nature of academic business. One of the researched requirements of effective academic leaders is that they have the appropriate credentials and academic experience to build relationships in which other academics value their judgement in matters academic. A key role of academic leadership is working with and through staff to achieve the educational objectives of the unit. As Ramsden (1998) states, 'First and foremost, academic leadership must provide the means, assistance and resources which enable academic and support staff to perform well' (p. 8).

A more focused view of academic leadership that impacts directly on student learning is provided in the work of Gardiner (2002) who asserts that leaders in higher education need to develop management and leadership skills in order to ensure high-quality learning experiences for each student. His thesis is that the substantial body of research about adult student learning and development remains largely unused in American colleges and universities, and this prevents academic leaders from being able to provide the conditions that are essential for effective student learning and success. He challenges academic leaders to translate mission statements into practice through clearly articulated goals and objectives that describe intended outcomes for each programme. He also suggests areas that an academic leader should actively engage in which assume an understanding of andragogy. These tasks are:

- providing a high-quality programme of assessment;
- providing a balanced curriculum;
- providing excellent academic advising for students;
- ensuring active involvement of students in all their study components;
- creating an engaged and supportive campus environment;
- providing support and development for staff; and
- maintaining and increasing momentum for improved student learning.

In this conception of academic leadership there is no doubt that leadership activity is directly focused on student learning and the creation of conditions to support those in the front line of curriculum delivery.

The practice of academic leadership is not without its challenges, and much of the research that is about academic leadership *in* rather than *of* higher education institutions deals with issues related to middle level management carried out by department heads and curriculum or programme managers. Smith (2005) alludes to the different experiences of staff in a research-driven setting as opposed to those in teaching-driven institutions and conjectures that this leads to differing forms of academic leadership. In the former research-driven environment, department headship is commonly a temporary (fixed-term) appointment and these academic leaders know they will need to return to their research role or, while incumbent, need to ensure that their own research is not neglected (Bryman, 2007; Smith, 2005). In teaching-driven environments, the challenge is to balance the teaching and management roles. Even without the further complication of research, the role is complex and demanding and job satisfaction if often contingent upon intrinsic rather than extrinsic rewards (Murphy, 2003).

A common trend discernible in the literature relates to the importance of ensuring leadership succession – especially for department chairs/heads (see, for example, Wheeler, 2002). A study of academic leadership in Australian universities points to a 'leadership succession crisis' (Scott et al., 2008) and suggests that providing tailored and adequate development to support academic leaders in their specific roles (based on capability frameworks) is one way of overcoming this problem. Other research suggests that a gap in academic leadership role clarity and development could be overcome through more effective assessment of the performance of academic leadership roles (Heck et al., 2000). In this study, the instrument developed to measure academic administrator performance effectiveness at the level of deans indicates the aspects that are considered to be important in the practice of academic leadership. These are: (1) vision and goal setting; (2) management of the unit; (3) interpersonal relationships; (4) communication skills; (5) research/professional/campus endeavours; (6) quality of education in the unit; and (7) support for institutional diversity.

Like the concept of instructional leadership in school settings, academic leadership can also be conceived broadly or narrowly, directly or indirectly. It involves both leadership and management. At its heart is the assumption that leading and managing are concerned with teaching and learning and the trusting relationships established between academic peers are a vital ingredient of effectiveness.

Levels and layers of educational leadership

We know that educational leadership occurs at several levels in and beyond an organisation. Hence, in talking about educational leadership it is important to recognise the way the term is used. On the one hand, the term has a wide and general application at all levels of education where decisions about education are made at an organisational level. On the other hand, its usage may be highly context-specific and its focus narrowed to the classroom.

National and district level leadership (beyond the organisation)

In some large education systems there are many levels of leadership – especially in relation to the administration and management of schooling. In the USA, for example, the state and the district play significant roles in what happens at the school level. In this system, principals lead and manage schools but are subject to management themselves as they are accountable to supervisors at the district level. In England and Wales, the local education authority provides a tier of management and leadership between a national Department of Education and schools. In Australia, federal and state government agencies are layers of leadership that exist above that of school-level leadership even when schools may have a considerable degree of self-management devolved to them. In New Zealand, where schools are self-governed and operate with a high degree of self-management, they are subject to central Ministry of Education policy that guides implementation of a national curriculum and provides funding for staffing and operations.

In the case of early childhood institutions, their overall administration and management varies in terms of state control or privatisation. The top management of these institutions would have little to do with day-to-day teaching and learning matters, although in many systems the arrangements involve a level of management (usually supervisory) between the unit and the national or district system.

At this beyond-the-organisation level of educational leadership, the meaning of educational leadership is closely akin to what Hodgkinson (1991) describes as educational administration – the highest form of systemic activity associated with policy, values, strategy and top management. Most of the research on educational leadership *in* educational organisations focuses on what goes on at the unit, school or building level. The impact of decisions made above this level is significant, but it is the actions of the educational leaders at the front, and in front of the students, who are ultimately accountable for achieving the educational goals of their units.

Senior level leadership (of and within the organisation)

Most higher education organisations around the world are self-managed and have an executive level of organisational leadership that is considerably removed from the units that are involved in the practice of delivering learning programmes. Institutional- and faculty-level leadership are consistent with this high level of leadership – but cannot be compared to the concept of senior level leadership in schools. Bryman (2007) alludes to the fact that there are separate literatures that deal with the concept of leadership *of* universities as opposed to leadership *in* universities. In terms of educational leadership construed to mean academic leadership, the unit of study has generally been higher education schools (deans) and departments (chairs and heads).

In terms of schools, senior level (sometimes called executive level) leadership and management is the preserve of principals, assistant, associate, deputy, vice principals and others with a significantly senior role in the hierarchy. The principal has been at the centre of most of the research on school leadership although recent studies highlight the need for educational/instructional leadership to be distributed or disbursed to a much greater extent. There appears to be a greater acknowledgement of the expansion of the principal's role and the implications of this for effective educational leadership. A North American study has highlighted some very significant issues for both policy and practice in this area. Seashore Louis et al. (2010, pp. 102–3) have synthesised the implications from the findings of their study that investigated the links between effective leadership and student learning. They propose that:

1. In order for principals to devote more time and attention to the improvement of instruction, their jobs will need to be substantially redesigned.
2. Distribution of leadership to include teachers, parents, and district staff is needed in order to improve student achievement.
3. District-level and state policy-makers must assume the responsibility for nurturing principals' dispositions toward the distribution of leadership.
4. Policy-makers and practitioners should avoid promoting conceptions of instructional leadership which adopt an exclusive or narrow focus on classroom instruction.
5. Significant additional support should be provided for middle and high school principals to foster the kind of instructional leadership that is 'workable' in their larger and more complex settings.
6. Educators and policy-makers should avoid 'one size fits all' leadership development programmes.

These views are mirrored in other school-leadership studies that focus on educational leadership at a senior level in school settings (see for example Robinson et al., 2009). They also have some transferability to higher education settings where, because the units are usually very large, the department is often of a similar size to a school building. However, in general terms, although deans are often in a senior leadership band in organisational structures, department or unit heads in higher education fall into a level of middle rather than senior management. A further distinguishing feature across sectors is that those with senior leadership designations have minimal engagement in general with teaching while middle level managers most often teach and manage (and may also research in higher education settings).

Middle-level leadership – structural distribution

Many teachers in educational organisations assume responsibilities beyond teaching but are not necessarily middle-level instructional or academic leaders in terms of structure and hierarchy. In higher education, this role is usually the preserve of academics who lead departments and also teach, and this is also usually the case in secondary schools. The concept of mid-level leadership in primary schools has also attracted attention in relation to the distribution of curriculum leadership (Cardno, 2006). Common threads running through the literature relate to expansion of the middle manager's role and its growing complexity and demands; the challenge of balancing time to teach with time to manage, heightened demands for accountability, and a current focus on the need for training specific to the role (Bennett et al., 2007; Filan and Seagren, 2003; Hammersley-Fletcher and Kirkham, 2007).

As the roles and demands of senior leadership expand, it is assumed that they can use organisational structure to distribute the load to lower levels within the hierarchy. This meaning of distributing leadership is related to what Gronn (2003) terms the multiple form of distributed leadership where structural arrangements provide many leaders at a range of levels so that leadership responsibilities can cascade from the top to the bottom and across the organisation. However, the very notion of distributing leadership is fraught with multiple and often contradictory meanings. What is often actually distributed is not leadership at all but a raft of tasks and accountabilities related to management functions. In these cases, delegated management is a more accurate description.

However, when the concept of distributing leadership is associated with the concepts of instructional and academic leadership, then in actuality both management (maintenance tasks) and leadership (change management) are being shared or shifted as the case may be. In the literature that clearly demonstrates a renewed interest in the potential of instructional leadership to improve student learning, the idea of distributed forms of leadership is given prominence and promoted as essential to the achievement of effectiveness (Pont et al., 2008; Robinson, 2008; Seashore Louis et al., 2010). By signalling the importance of spreading, sharing, disbursing and distributing the tasks that constitute educational leadership, attention is focused on the means by which change is achieved for the whole organisation and for teams within it. Ultimately, it is by working with and through other colleagues that leaders achieve goals and attend to the problems that beset goal achievement. In these work-related interpersonal relationships, trust-building is crucial to the effective enactment of educational leadership tasks. Because the school principal has been the central focus of much of the research base about leadership in educational settings, there is a paucity of literature related to how mid-level leaders can effectively enact a more direct form of instructional leadership in the front line when it comes to relationship-building or -breaking.

Assessing and developing educational leaders

The often unstated goal of many of the studies that have been conducted about school leadership is to point the way towards the assessment of principal effectiveness. The starting point to achieve this is to know what to assess. Goldring et al. (2009) highlight one issue in particular. They state that, 'Because of the complexity of the principal's role, the main difficulty in the field of school principal leadership assessment is identifying the leadership dimensions that should be assessed' (p. 2). Further challenges are related to the use of appropriate methods and the utilisation of results of evaluation tools. Around the world, this issue continues to challenge policy-makers and researchers commissioned to find answers to address concerns about the behaviours leaders should engage in, how the impact of leadership practice on student learning can be measured, and how leaders can be developed to become more effective (Goldring et al., 2009; Robinson, 2010).

In order for school principals to be effective in the many dimensions of educational leadership indicated in the vast literature of this field, they have to be able to perform particular tasks in specific ways to demonstrate capability. In the case of New Zealand, a synthesis of research literature (Robinson et al., 2009) has pointed to four specific knowledge, skills and dispositions as capability sets that will enable school leaders to more effectively focus on the leadership of teaching and learning. The nature of these capabilities is that they are complex and overlapping and demonstrating capability will require a 'seamless integration of knowledge, skills and dispositions' (p. 174). These capabilities are:

1. Ensure administrative decisions are informed by knowledge about effective pedagogy.
2. Analyse and solve complex problems.
3. Build relational trust.
4. Engage in open-to-learning conversations.

On their own, principals in any but the very smallest of schools, will be unable to practice the sort of direct instructional or pedagogical leadership that will bring the above knowledge, skills and dispositions into play in daily activity. Consequently it is vital that the thinking about how these competencies are enacted is directed to a broader stage. This extension of leadership activity beyond the principal to school-wide arenas is patently evident in the recent international research recommendations for policy and practice (Robinson et al., 2009; Seashore Louis et al., 2010; Southworth, 2004). This is a starting point for thinking about how leadership can be more broadly configured in relation to learning. Gronn (2009) postulates that while researchers now seem persuaded as to the shortcomings of 'leadership conceived as individually focused action, and have begun substituting a distributed or shared approach, they may have adopted a template which does not accurately accord with the realities of practice' (p. 83). He proposes that if effectiveness (and the assessment of this) is going to be construed as a school-wide rather than individual construct, then a spread of leadership that is knowledge-based might in fact be of a form that is more complementary rather than differentiated – a hybrid form of leadership that has yet to be mapped. However, at this stage of assembling evidence about educational leadership it is imperative that mid-level managers and leaders are included as key actors in the practice of education leadership. The focus of research needs to shift to this level of the organisation in a way that connects it to the leadership of the unit or school head.

The dimensions of mid-level leadership action that impact on student outcomes have yet to be confirmed or assessed or developed in relation to the context of schools. In higher education contexts, however, a study of academic leadership capabilities for Australian higher education (Scott et al., 2008) has contributed valuable insights about key competencies and capabilities that are important in effective learning and teaching leadership. As a large proportion of participants in this study were academic leaders in head of department and programme leadership roles, it is assumed that the results are pertinent in relation to mid-level academic leaders in these roles in higher education contexts.

Key competencies deemed to be important were self-organisation skills, university operations and learning and teaching. Three broad sets of capabilities were identified as follows:

- cognitive capabilities (flexibility and responsiveness, strategy, diagnosis);
- interpersonal capabilities (empathising, influencing); and
- personal capabilities (commitment, decisiveness, self-regulation).

This study recommends that the importance of learning and teaching in the role needs to be highlighted to attract a new generation of leaders to this critical role and that further studies need to identify the characteristics of learning and teaching leadership that lead to significant improvements in student learning outcomes. In all education contexts, early childhood, schools and higher education, interest now needs to be firmly focused on what it will mean for leadership at the middle level of the organisation to be assessed and developed, and the challenges inherent in this agenda.

The importance of relationship-building

Anyone who leads teaching and learning at any level in an educational organisation will need to engage interpersonally with others. When the form of this leadership is direct, as is often the case in small primary schools and early childhood education settings, the leader's daily interactions with teachers are the focus. As leadership becomes more indirect (in larger units), those interactions also take place between the middle-level direct educational leaders (teaching team leaders) and those responsible for their performance (senior leaders). It is these senior-level leaders who can thus indirectly influence the quality of teaching and learning. These interactions are characterised by informal and formal communication about practice – in other words, talking to teachers and middle-level leaders. The importance of 'teacher talk' is confirmed in several research arenas.

In a study of educational leadership in small primary schools in Britain, Southworth (2004) found 'that at the very heart of educational leadership lies the ability to engage with teachers and to create opportunities for professional discourse' (p. 108). A North American study (Blase and Blase, 2000) confirms that teachers judged the instructional leadership of principals positively when this provided them with opportunities for talking with the leader in the form of conferencing around teaching practices. This concept of conferencing is a part of instructional supervision common in teacher appraisal practice, involving observation of and feedback about practice. Offering such opportunities for teachers to engage in dialogue about pedagogy, professional discourse, and general conversation about their work is undoubtedly viewed as positive leadership behaviour and many hundreds of both planned and impromptu interactions that formal leaders have with teachers provide such opportunities. In most cases, such communication is premised by collaboration and mutual commitment to achieving agreed goals. There are cases, however, that arise when problems of practice are detected and it is neither easy nor pleasant to engage in a conversation that might contain potential for conflict or unpleasantness.

When it is necessary for leaders and teachers to engage in conversations that are difficult, then the relationship between the parties is tested and may be part of the difficulty involved in attempting to resolve a problem of practice. An educational leader does not have a choice when it comes to dealing with such problems because they are accountable for resolving them. When an educational leadership problem poses a threat to maintaining a sound or positive collegial relationship, yet also has an imperative to be dealt with because of a negative impact on student learning, then it may well be a leadership dilemma (Cardno, 2007). In such circumstances leaders who have built trusting relationships with colleagues are likely to be more productive in bringing about desired change.

Both senior-level and middle-level leaders in educational organisations are key players in leading teaching and learning in ways that impact positively on student learning experiences and outcomes. The substantial research base that now exists in relation to examining what works in efforts to improve teaching and learning clearly illuminates leadership activities that should be prioritised because they have the greatest likelihood to effect change. The common strand that runs through the literature, whether it refers to higher education, school or early childhood sectors, is the management of relationships between professionals who are accountable for student learning. The findings of an Australian study on academic leadership in higher education confirm that leaders themselves consider the following capabilities to be important. First, the cognitive capability of being able to diagnose the underlying causes of problems and taking appropriate action to address these. Secondly, the personal capability of being able to admit to and learn from errors. Thirdly, the interpersonal capability of empathising and working productively with others (Scott et al., 2008). These are the sorts of capabilities that involve effective professional relationship-building which is a core condition for educational leadership effectiveness. Ultimately, those with leadership accountability are expected to take the lead and create organisational conditions that build and constantly test these professional relationships.

CHAPTER THREE

ORGANISATIONAL LEARNING IN A LEARNING ORGANISATION

Building productive relationships

Effective educational leaders create conditions that make it possible to improve teaching and learning. Organisational learning contributes to the positive and long lasting resolution of problems of practice. Organisations depend on individuals who learn, because people bring the ability to learn to the organisation. People can model this learning in everyday problem-solving or they can block learning when the organisation has to solve complex problems. An organisation that commits to learning which enables productive behaviour is able to build productive relationships.

By engaging in conversation, discussion and dialogue – essential features of people working together – we meet barriers to achieving what should be common purposes. In this chapter I suggest that an organisation will be more able to achieve its desired purpose if its members forge productive relationships strong enough to sustain the challenges of learning as individuals, in teams and as an organisation.

The idea that an organisation can learn in order to survive, change and improve has swept pervasively through the worldwide arena of leadership and management theory and practice over the past three decades. This idea has influenced the way we think about an organisation and its potential for learning. Senge (1990, 2006) launched the ideal of the 'learning organisation' as an aim for all organisations to aspire to. His work builds on the seminal work of Argyris and Schön (1978, 1996) who provided a research base for the theory and practice of a process for 'organisational learning'. An organisation that embarks on the journey of becoming a learning organisation must ultimately understand and apply knowledge and skills that enable organisational learning to occur.

There are two terms that represent different streams, *organisational learning* and *the learning organisation*, which have often been confused or in fact, used interchangeably (for example see Boreham and Morgan, 2004). Sun and Scott (2003) propose precise definitions to distinguish between these two streams. In their view, regarding organisational learning: 'This is the learning process used in the organisation. It deals with the question of how *individuals* in the organisation learn' (p. 204). With regard to the term learning organisation, they say, 'This is where learning takes place that moves *an organisation* towards a desired state' (author's emphases). Both streams that deal with the learning in and of an organisation are examined in some detail further on.

In the literature about organisational learning in schools (see for example Leithwood et al., 1998) the terms learning organisation and organisational learning appear to be used synonymously to mean a process by which actions are improved through better understanding of the common purposes that people are pursuing. Thus organisational learning is presented as a non-problematic way of developing shared knowledge and common goals as a response to internal and external pressures for change and improvement. This collective search for solutions is one meaning given to the concept of organisational learning. However, in this chapter I adopt a far more specific view drawn from well-established literature that points not only to aspirations for people in organisations learning together, but also to the reasons that *stop* them from learning at critical points of the process. This literature suggests that in order to be effective it is necessary to examine the norms that guide the processes for an organisation to learn.

Fundamentally, both the theory sets of the learning organisation and organisational learning are normative theories; that is, they are about the improvement of practice through processes that are intervention oriented based on the assumption that there is a 'right' and 'wrong' way of doing things with either learning or non-learning consequences. This raises questions about the role that leaders and managers should play in relation to enabling an organisation to learn. Are they then expected to undertake the interventions to promote learning themselves? Are they to contract consultants who intervene? And what would compel them to do this? These and other questions lend themselves to a consideration of the role of learning leaders.

Learning leaders

Gronn (1997) argues that despite the numerous case examples provided by Argyris (1985) to prove learning dysfunction in organisations, this author does not clearly indicate the role he sees leaders playing as learning facilitators. Yet, Argyris and Schön (1996) suggest that leaders can foster a learning culture by 'envisioning it and communicating the vision' (p. 185) for a process of learning to become part of the culture. Senge (1990) talks about a new view of leadership; one that transcends a traditional view in which others look to great leaders for vision and the power to instigate change. According to Senge, the new leader is concerned about building capacity for learning within the organisation. They expand the capabilities of others to understand and resolve complex problems.

Organisational leaders need to be effective decision-makers and problem-solvers – a major responsibility of all administrators according to Hoy and Miskel (2008) in order to ensure that the organisation not only meets its goals but also moves towards its desired future. In striving to achieve this, leaders who understand the demands of organisational learning, and how this contributes to a learning organisation, can act in ways that impact productively on the culture of the organisation and create possibilities for both interpersonal effectiveness and organisational effectiveness. This is important because when culture is viewed as a deep, complex anthropological model that explains the hidden and complex aspects of organisational life, it is a concept that can help us understand the way individuals and organisations behave.

Schein (2010) defines the culture of a group as 'a pattern of shared basic assumptions that the group learned as it solved its problems of external adaptation and internal integration, that has worked well enough to be considered valid and, therefore, to be taught to new members as the correct way to perceive, think, and feel in relation to those problems' (p. 18). From this perspective, becoming familiar with the patterns of problem-solving embedded in the culture of an organisation is an aspect related to both existing members and the socialisation of new members as rules and routines are employed by all. If an organisation had developed ineffective ways of making decisions and solving its problems, these are perpetuated because they are passed on to others as the right and only way to think and act and such norms usually remain unquestioned. If, on the other hand, the organisation had developed effective organisational learning processes, then the culture would reflect values that welcome examination of the norms themselves and openness to change that is conducive to the 'organization's capacity for conscious transformation of its own theory of action, and to individuals' ability to appreciate and transform the learning systems in which they live' (Argyris and Schön, 1978, p. 331). Schein (2010) links organisational culture to the learning organisation and argues that in a world of turbulent change organ-isations have to learn even faster. Hence they need 'learning leaders' (p. 367) who can create learning cultures.

From an organisational culture perspective, the leader has to model learn-ing, support learning, encourage learning and facilitate learning so that the *rightness* of learning permeates the approach taken by all members of the organisation as they go about solving their problems. This is a value position and assumes that learning is accorded a high value by all members of the organisation. The idea that members must hold a shared assumption that learning is a good thing comes from Schein (2010) who suggests that a 'learning gene' must be part of the DNA of a learning culture. He says that 'learning to learn is itself a skill to be mastered' (p. 366). In a learning cul-ture leaders seek feedback and are willing to ask for and accept help. They are also willing to try new ways of doing things, hence, reflection and exper-imentation should be strongly held values and leaders must make both time and resources available for members to engage in these practices to solve complex problems.

Complex problem-solving

Organisations learn when they are able to respond to their environment in ways that make it possible to discover the sources of problems (Senge, 2006). As Robinson (1995) states, 'organisational problems are discrepancies between current and desired states of affairs, with the discrepancy arising either from dissatisfaction with a current practice or a desire to institute a practice where none currently exists' (p. 71). Attempts to solve problems are usually based on previous efforts which have become embedded in the memory of the organisation in the form of organisational routines. When rou-tine solutions do not produce satisfactory results it becomes important for an organisation to search for the sources of complex problems. Senge (2006) cautions against the tendency to deal with symptomatic (or surface) solutions because this may merely 'shift the burden' rather than address the underlying causes of a problem and result in the problem remaining unaddressed and, in the long term, resurfacing. An example of such a problem in a school, that recurs with regular frequency, is the request from a parent to have their child moved to a different classroom. In spite of schools espousing policy and pro-cedure that prohibits the moving of a child from an assigned classroom and teacher to a new one, there are many instances of leaders backing down when the pressure is intense. In such circumstances, the opportunity to learn about the sources of such a problem is not embraced for a number of par-ties: leader, teacher, parent and child. While the immediate issue is seemingly quickly solved with the relocation of the child, a whole new raft of issues may well emerge, triggered by the move and the norms that led to it. This is indeed a classically complex problem and finding quick solutions is not always the best answer.

There are many types and shades of problem complexity that pose challenges for leaders who set out to resolve such problems and feel accountable to achieve long-term resolution in order to reduce negative consequences for the organisation. For example, Leithwood et al. (2004) refer to the demands of novel and unstructured problems where problem-relevant knowledge may be lacking. Another challenge of problem complexity relates to the emotions that are engaged when dilemma situations are encountered (Murphy, 2007). A particularly challenging problem is a dilemma that involves tensions between achieving the goals of the organisation, on the one hand, and maintaining positive relationships with colleagues, on the other hand. When leaders encounter problems of this nature, it is likely that it is a complex and recurring problem which needs to be understood and addressed as a 'leadership dilemma' (Cardno, 2007). The need to approach such problems in productive ways requires a fundamental understanding of the concept of organisational learning which underpins the learning capability of individuals and the organisation to solve complex problems.

Learning case for reflection: a complex problem

A department head in a higher education institution may encounter this sort of problem complexity in relation to making changes to a programme that has been offered for several years but now seems to be floundering. The recently appointed Head of Department (HOD) has replaced her predecessor with a clear mandate for change. The organisational concern is about streamlining programme offerings and withdrawing programmes that are no longer financially viable. Yet, the executive leadership group is also aware that the suite of programmes is of considerable value to the community and is supported by the governing body. In addition there is huge campus support for the staff whose jobs would be threatened by programme closure. The new department head has also been made aware of two particularly challenging staff members who are also a concern because of their poor performance. There has already been an agitated response to future plans for the programme from current and potential students. The previous department head left under a cloud but the majority of staff were supportive of his decision to fight to retain the programme. In his efforts to solve the problem he appointed a new senior lecturer and bolstered the budget at the expense of other programmes. The problem persists and has been inherited by his successor.

(Continues)

(Continued)

The newly appointed HOD finds this problem legacy is consuming all her time and energy and is emotionally draining as well. Her only ally, seemingly, is the recently appointed senior lecturer who is viewed by the rest of the staff as a financial and collegial burden.

1 What could be a starting point for getting to the problem sources that create complexity in this case?

2 What would you do if you were the HOD?

3 What would you do if you were the new senior lecturer?

4 What might make learning from mistakes possible?

Organisational learning

In an organisational learning approach, effectiveness is viewed normatively as the ability to find out what is wrong when problems persist, and to learn from mistakes in order that long-term, recurring problems can be solved. It is also necessary to learn about what might be limiting or constraining the discovery of errors. For the learning to move beyond the individual level and become organisational, the results have to be held in the memories embedded in the organisation's environment. When an organisation learns, it is able to change its theory-in-use – a particular organisational behaviour based on the values, beliefs and assumptions that guide action.

The intellectual roots of the normative theory of organisational learning in relation to the improvement of practice through a process of inquiry can undoubtedly be traced to the seminal work of Chris Argyris and Donald Schön (1974, 1978). Their contribution to the field of study is significant in our understanding of the nature of complex organisational problems and why the best efforts to resolve them may be *unsuccessful*. According to Argyris and Schön (1978), organisational learning involves the detection and correction of error. They distinguish between two types of organisational learning in this way. When error is detected and corrected in such a way that allows the organisation to continue with its present policies or objectives it is a process of *single-loop* learning. In other words, the learning is limited to an adjustment of action – just as a thermostat responds to temperature information and corrects heating or cooling requirements. When the error detection and correction involves modification of an organisation's underlying norms, policies and objectives

– then *double-loop* learning occurs. These types of learning occur at both the individual and organisational levels.

Theory of action approach

In order to understand the demands of double-loop learning (which is needed for organisational inquiry to occur) Argyris and Schön (1974, 1978) adopted what they call a 'theory of action' perspective or approach – to enable collaborative inquiry among people in organisations. What these authors have considered is that organisations may have theories of action in the same way that individuals have theories of action that inform their actions. Theories of action determine human behaviour because these are the fundamental beliefs we hold and actions we take in setting out to effectively solve a problem. They are described by Dick and Dalmau (1999) as 'mechanisms by which we link our thoughts with our actions' (p. 10). They are also defined as 'bundles of beliefs and values which guide our behaviour' (Cardno, 1998a, p. 2). Argyris (1977) explains that theories of action have several elements: values that govern our action, action strategies we choose to implement, consequences for ourselves and for others, consequences for learning and, finally, the degree of effectiveness.

These theories take two forms. First, an espoused form, which we state and which is what is usually provided when asked how one would behave under certain circumstances. Argyris and Schön (1978) call this espoused form the 'theory of action to which he gives allegiance and which, upon request, he communicates to others. However, the theory that actually governs his actions is his theory-in-use' (p. 11). Secondly, this theory-in-use form of one's theory of action is demonstrated in actual practice. A person's theory-in-use may or may not be compatible with what they espouse and the person may or may not be aware of the incompatibility between these two forms of their theory of action. A simple example of this, in organisational terms, is that a school's *espoused theories* could be indicated in promotional material distributed to prospective parents, on a website, in a prospectus, in organisational charts and in policy statements. The actions taken by individuals on behalf of the school would demonstrate *theory-in-use* and, if these actions were not compatible with public espousals, there could be negative consequences that the school should correct – thus requiring processes for organisational learning to be utilised.

This is no easy task. While many researchers and practitioners in the field of educational administration, management and leadership are inspired by the concept of organisational learning, they may have little realisation of the learning challenges that are presented in a theory of action approach where the learning resources are provided in the shape of knowledge about defensive and productive theories of action, and the type of learning associated with these.

Defensiveness

The continuing existence of an organisation depends among other things on its ability to solve problems that act as barriers to achieving the organisation's goals. However, organisational learning is constrained by a pervasive condition of defensiveness. According to Argyris (1985) this condition persists because defensiveness is not recognised as counterproductive to learning. He says, 'defensive routines are rewarded by most organizational cultures because the routines indicate a sense of caring and concern for people' (1990, p. 29).

Problems caused by defensive routines compound in organisations because leaders find themselves in a double-bind. They are expected to know what is going on; it is not acceptable for them not to know what is causing problems. Yet, in order to find out what is blocking the resolution of a difficult issue they must expose their façade of confidence, admit to uncertainty and consider how they might be personally implicated in order to be open to the views of others. Capable leaders are usually very skilful in using defensive strategies to maintain an aura of capability and not reveal the thinking behind decisions. Inevitably, even the most capable individuals become the carriers of defensive routines, and organisations become their hosts.

Argyris (1990, 1992) asserts that most organisations not only have great difficulty in addressing this organisational learning paradox, but are not even aware that it exists. This is because they mistakenly assume that learning is limited to correcting errors in the *external* environment and they fail to focus inward; to identify ways in which people inadvertently contribute to the organisation's problems. This implies that the interpersonal relationships among individuals and their learning associated with resolving interpersonal problems effectively are part of an organisational problem.

In organisational learning there is a constant and complex interaction between the learning of individuals and the learning of the organisation. For this reason Argyris and Schön (1996) state, 'We take individual practitioners as centrally important to organizational learning, because it is their thinking and action that influence the acquisition of capability for productive learning at the organisational level' (p. xxii). The focus of these authors is on organisational *inquiry* – which 'occurs when individuals in the organisation inquire, in interaction with one another, in an effort to produce productive organizational learning outcomes' (p. xxii).

Defensive and productive theories of action

If individuals are to move to double-loop learning, they need to become aware of the way in which they are inclined to defensive rather than productive ways of reasoning. This is attributed by Argyris and Schön (1974) to a master programme that guides a theory of action for defensive reasoning and behaviour which they have named Model 1. In this model of a theory-in-use, although one may espouse a non-defensive stance, the overriding concern is to block information which we personally feel will create unpleasantness or lessen our control of a situation.

An alternative theory-in-use is Model 2. While this model is often espoused as a theory of action, research shows that it is not easily put into action. When action is framed by Model 2, the concern is with generating information in an effort to increase the possibility of critical reflection-in-action. Table 3.1 summarises the guiding values and strategies that are associated with a defensive theory-in-use (Model 1) and a productive theory-in-use (Model 2) as we attempt to solve problems.

When organisational members develop productive relationships between individuals and in teams, they are increasing the possibility that they will develop shared assumptions about learning. If that learning can extend to reflective inquiry about why a particular problem remains unsatisfactorily solved, it opens up the possibility of organisational members engaging in deep learning. Deep learning takes one to the sources of problems, looks beyond the surface features and considers ways in which information and conflict can be surfaced rather than suppressed. It requires an understanding of why a dominant model of behaviour (Model 1) inhibits the possibility of learning when this is most needed and how a different set of values and strategies (Model 2) offers possibilities for learning that matters. Being able to examine and alter defensive values to productive values involves a particular type of learning called double-loop learning.

Table 3.1 Guiding values and strategies in defensive and productive reasoning

Model 1 theory-in-use	Model 2 theory-in-use
Defensive reasoning Blocking information which we personally feel will create unpleasantness or lessen our control of a situation	*Productive reasoning* Generating information in an effort to increase the possibility of critical reflection-in-action
Guiding values Win, don't lose Avoid unpleasantness Maintain control	*Guiding values* Seek and give valid information Share control and solutions Monitor solutions jointly
Action strategies Not checking assumptions Giving indirect or mixed messages Not explaining reasoning Using questioning to control	*Action strategies* Checking assumptions Being forthright Disclosing reasoning Asking questions as genuine inquiry

Double-loop learning challenges

The challenge in double-loop learning lies in discovering and modifying practices that act as barriers to the resolution of complex problems, especially in situations where there is conflict. We use particular strategies, guided by particular beliefs, to achieve our goals. For example, we tend to draw on what we consider to be an effective strategy when we have to give someone negative feedback, or when we are faced with a very defensive person in a conflict situation.

An example of single-loop learning is the ability to learn a new strategy for suppressing defensiveness in an effort to be effective. In a single-loop learning mode, beliefs about what is effective practice are governed by values of winning and avoiding unpleasantness. Whenever a new strategy is adopted, it is guided by these same values. If one strategy fails, if a problem or an error is detected, or if we become aware of a mismatch between an intent and a predetermined outcome, a single-loop learner will change the action or strategy. However, the value base that guides a range of actions is not questioned in single-loop learning (see Figure 3.1).

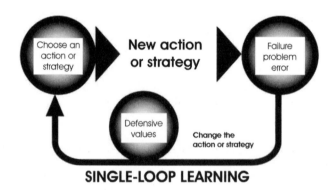

SINGLE-LOOP LEARNING

Figure 3.1 *Single-loop learning*

In a double-loop learning approach, a new learning loop is evident. This requires us to re-examine the foundation values in which beliefs about effectiveness are grounded. Double-loop learning would occur when we change the governing values of our theory-in-use. For example, we become concerned with the surfacing and resolution of defensiveness (the sources of threat and embarrassment) rather than its suppression. If one is prepared to engage in double-loop learning, then one is prepared to operate on a changed set of values (see Figure 3.2). These governing values will include the search for valid information as a paramount value that sustains genuine commitment to seeking and monitoring solutions jointly so that they are long-lasting.

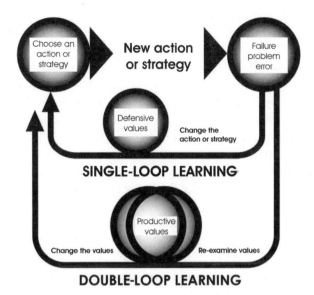

Figure 3.2 *Double-loop learning*

In summary, single-loop learning occurs within the constraints of defensive values, permitting alternative actions but not alternative thinking. It is the commitment to an open-to-learning approach that sets double-loop learners apart.

When leaders become aware of the possibilities suggested in an organisational learning approach, they may be compelled to reflect critically on their past and present problem-solving efforts and consider how they, as learning leaders, can influence the way the organisation learns. This may happen in several ways. For example:

- leaders may increase their own knowledge and skills associated with organisational learning;
- leaders may pave the way for senior and middle managers to learn about the importance of developing a learning culture in the organisation and then build their organisational learning capacity;
- leaders may use consultants to assist them and other leaders in the organisation to examine why their problem-solving efforts are ineffective; or
- leaders may be required by external agencies to address inadequacies in problem-solving efforts.

While the idea of organisation learning is highly appealing as a means of strengthening organisational effectiveness, enacting it presents considerable challenges because of the implication that it requires an intervention to bring it about.

Organisational learning interventions

When these theories of organisational learning are shared with leaders as ways of thinking and acting that they could learn and practise, it is possible for both the promoters and the leaders to make assumptions about who will provide learning opportunities. Leaders *are* expected to lead the learning of adults in the organisation, because this is the cornerstone of building productive relationships. But, the big question remains. Is it the leader who teaches others in the organisation about the possibilities opened up when organisational learning occurs, or should leaders be contracting experts to do this? For example, do leaders take the initiative in instigating action research projects, when confronted with a large problem? How will managers be introduced to the theory and skills needed to engage in organisational learning through a theory-of-action approach? What exactly might trigger the need for organisational learning interventions? Sun and Scott (2003) comment that in the work of Argyris and Schön, 'the triggers that support the learning process are not addressed' (p. 205).

In their research into organisation learning in Canadian schools (Leithwood et al., 1998), a very broad framework of ideas was used to constitute an explanation of organisational learning (OL). Nevertheless, a useful finding is presented in terms of what might prompt a need for the process (which included discussions, staff meetings, workshops, observations of teaching, personal reading, and so on). This research reports that, 'OL can be stimulated by relatively everyday events: ongoing attempts at incremental improvement and the like' (p. 71).

It is possible that the trigger for a leader to take an interest in the possibilities of organisational learning from a theory-of-action perspective, is knowledge about the concept itself. Without this knowledge and the acquisition of associated skills, it is impossible to conceive of the need being recognised or acted on. However, armed with knowledge about the potential of organisational learning for solving complex, long-term problems, leaders encountering failure, critical events, challenges or crises, may be forced to consider ways in which they or others can intervene to bring about learning and change that begins to permeate the organisation and creates the ideal – a learning culture.

There are difficult issues from the intervenor's perspective as well. An intervention is intended to bring about change in individuals and organisations in the context of an agreed problem. Argyris and Schön repeatedly remind readers of the normative nature of their particular theory of action approach to organisational learning, and that it is intervention oriented. So it pays to keep this in mind and consider the role that would be played by a consultant using this approach to assist an organisation to solve its problems. Getting to the heart of the problems that organisations can learn from is no easy matter. The intervenor (consultant) or interventionist-researcher may find themselves challenged by the conditions in which they have to work. There is very little research about the use of organisational learning resources in schools, although the term has been used loosely in some studies about school development (see for example, Voogt et al., 1998). This raises the question: who will be the interventionists (consultants, researchers or practitioners) with sufficient expertise themselves to assist organisations, teams and individuals with this particular kind of learning in educational settings?

Educational leadership is a distinctive form of leadership, and what creates the distinction is its leadership of learning (Gronn, 2009). When leaders are challenged by an inability to solve a complex educational problem in order to bring about improvement in a learning situation, they may turn to others inside or beyond the organisation to seek advice or active intervention. If they are knowledgeable about the theory of action approach to organisational learning they may be in a stronger position to change the practice of others, as the following quotation aptly indicates:

> Theories of action are powerful both because they explain teachers' actions and because they shape how change messages are interpreted. By engaging teachers' theories of action, leaders help teachers make their beliefs explicit and help them evaluate those beliefs in relation to the proposed alternative theory. Successful theory engagement requires a deep understanding of the factors that sustain current practice and, therefore, of the challenges involved in changing it. (Robinson et al., 2009, p. 44)

Learning case for reflection: theories of action

Miriama is an experienced middle-level leader in a large primary school. In her group of six teachers who teach across two year levels she is the team leader. She is strongly committed to introducing the new writing curriculum scheme which the principal has decided to implement across the school. All staff participated in an afternoon of professional development to become familiar with the new programme at the end of last term and the expectation is that this term all teachers and students will be working with the new aims and methods for teaching and learning writing. Sally, one of Miriama's team, is not meeting this expectation. The principal has discovered this and has asked for an explanation. For Miriama this is not a new situation with Sally. A similar concern arose a year ago in relation to changes to the maths curriculum and Sally's intransigence over making changes to her teaching practice. She made some superficial adjustments but Miriama is aware that these were a token effort to change and that Sally (who is very experienced, very highly thought of by the parents and a popular teacher with the students) has gone her merry way ever since.

(Continues)

(Continued)

Miriama and Sally had a conversation that went like this:

Are you having difficulties using the new writing resources, Sally?

Not at all Miriama. They seem fine.

So why are you not using these? Even the principal has noticed that yours is the only room that hasn't handed in exemplars.

My kids are doing great writing projects. I don't know what all the fuss is about.

1 What learning is occurring in this interaction?

2 How could knowledge about a theory of action approach be used in this situation?

3 Is it likely that Miriama will revert to leaving Sally alone again to go her own way?

4 How would you use this as an opportunity to learn?

One of the similarities between the process-oriented organisational learning notion (Argyris and Schön, 1978, 1996) and the ideal-oriented learning organisation notion (Senge, 1990, 2006) is that both fall into the normative theory camp with a focus on the improvement of, rather than the description of, organisations and an imperative to intervene in order to improve learning. And, while both streams use the intervention of consultants to help organisations discover the barriers to learning, there are also differences – an obvious one being that the theories of organisational learning are encapsulated *within* the idea of the learning organisation.

The learning organisation

Senge (1990) says that learning organisations are possible because, deep down, we are all learners. He suggests that learning organisations are places where 'people are continually learning how to learn together' (p. 1).

Many of the ideas about why and how an organisation should learn have been popularised in Senge's (1990) book. He has stated that learning must go beyond adaptive (or survival) learning to include generative learning which is needed to create effective results.

Senge proposed that what would distinguish 'learning organisations' from other more traditional authoritarian and controlling organisations, would be the mastery of some basic disciplines that would influence the way the organisation responded to its external and internal challenges. Hence, the five disciplines that Senge presents. These disciplines are (1) personal mastery, (2) mental models, (3) building shared vision, (4) team learning and (5) systems thinking – which is the fifth and binding discipline that draws together the synergy of all the other disciplines.

Personal mastery

This discipline is about the organisation learning how to make a commitment to the personal learning of its members and in turn utilising that capacity for learning to benefit the organisation. Senge says that personal mastery is the discipline of continually clarifying and deepening our personal vision, focusing our energies, developing patience and seeing reality objectively. A leader's role in fostering personal mastery within an organisation involves being able to model a clear focus and vision and openness to the visions of others. In addition, this discipline has implications for the planning of professional development programmes that include aspects of personal development and growth within a holistic model of professional development (Cardno, 2005).

Mental models

The discipline of mental models starts with the ability to understand and share the deeply ingrained assumptions that influence our world views and the way in which we take action. People are not always consciously aware of their mental models and thus, in this discipline, learning begins with surfacing and sharing personal pictures of the world. Mental models explain why two people may see the same event very differently. Mental models are most often tacit, exist below one's level of awareness and usually remain unexamined and untested. A leader who is knowledgable about the discipline of mental models would create opportunities for others to learn how to hold conversations that were non-defensive and open to learning. In summary, the very concept that Argyris and Schön (1978, 1996) have termed 'organisational learning' has at its core the theory and practice that is needed for the discipline of mental models (as proposed by the theorists of the 'learning organisation') to be learnt by organisations.

Shared vision

In this discipline the aim is to foster a commitment towards a common purpose. It contains the set of tools and techniques for bringing together and aligning the disparate views and aspirations of a group of people. What is held in common should be a commitment to the organisation, yet while many organisations are capable of 'pulling together' in a crisis, once this is past the individuals may feel adrift. A shared vision is more than one person's vision imposed on the organisation. Senge (1990) states that, 'In a learning organization, leaders may start by pursuing their own vision, but as they learn to listen carefully to others' visions they begin to see that their own personal vision is part of something larger. This does not diminish any leader's sense of responsibility for the vision – if anything it deepens it' (p. 352). These leaders become stewards of a collective vision.

Team learning

The discipline of team learning is viewed by Senge (1990, 2006) as one of the most critical disciplines for organisations to master because teams are becoming the key learning unit in organisations. He states that, 'Individual learning, at some level is irrelevant for organizational learning. Individuals learn all the time and yet there is no organizational learning. But if teams learn, they become a microcosm for learning throughout the organisation' (Senge, 1990, p. 236).

The tools for team learning are those related to enabling engagement in productive dialogue and discussion as well as those that uncover and deal with forces that oppose the achievement of productive dialogue. Here, Senge refers to the defensive routines (Argyris, 1985) that thwart learning. Teams that know the difference between discussion and dialogue and can bring to bear knowledge and skills related to their mental models in the practice of productive dialogue are likely to be learning teams. Just as organisations develop defensive routines (practised ways or games that cover up the games organisations play to remain in control) so teams also develop routines that inhibit learning. Making such routines discussable is the major challenge in team learning. Leaders need to make it possible for teams to practise as this is the only way to develop the skills of dialogue. Since many of these skills cannot be developed without intervention by external consultants, this has implications for the arrangements made for the professional development of teams and the facilitation of team dialogue by experts.

Systems thinking

The discipline of systems thinking provides a way of seeing problems as connected components of a larger structure; as parts of a whole. Examples of systems are biological organisms, the atmosphere, industries, teams and organisations, to name a few. The elements of a system 'hang together' – drawn from the Greek verb *sunistanai* – meaning *to cause to stand together* (Senge et al., 2000). Hoy and Miskel (2008) assert that organisational life is complex because it involves an intricate network of social relationships within a system that should be considered holistically rather than in terms of its parts. So systems thinking is a discipline for seeing wholes.

The systems approach to problems looks beyond individual mistakes or failure to achieve a goal and focuses on examining the underlying structures that shape the actions of individuals and create consequences that are not desirable. The structure of an organisation is fundamental to the system. For Senge (1990, 2006) structural explanations for problems are extremely important as opposed to 'event' thinking. Generative learning requires a conceptual framework of systemic thinking, requiring the discovery of structural causes of problems. This does not mean that small, well-focused actions cannot produce significant and enduring improvement. This can happen when the change is in exactly the right place to produce 'leverage'. This is an important concept in systems thinking and Senge illustrates it with reference to the trim tab example. A trim tab is a small rudder on a ship's rudder. It is only a fraction of the size of the rudder and this system is engineered through the principle of leverage because its function is to make it easier to turn the rudder and, in turn, the ship. Yet its functioning is totally non-obvious – especially to those unfamiliar with the laws of hydrodynamics. It is similar to high-leverage changes in human systems which remain non-obvious until we understand the forces at play. It is forces at play within the organisation that are of the greatest concern, and systems thinking allows a leader to discover how they may be implicated in problems. However, for Senge and supporters of the 'learning organisation' concept, there are many forms of system thinking and many tools and techniques that have been developed to help organisations think systemically. In addition to this (the fifth) discipline, a learning organisation will need to master the other four disciplines: personal mastery, mental models, shared vision and team learning. So, the new work of leaders according to Senge (2006) will involve them in being designers, teachers and stewards.

The leader's role in a learning organisation

Senge proposes that as designers, leaders will be concerned about creating iterative design and learning infrastructures that will foster openness, experimentation and feedback systems. They will be teachers who recognise and grow the capability of their people and their capacity to learn. They will steward a vision that is shared and see themselves serving a larger purpose. Ultimately, a leader with an insight into what it takes to build a learning organisation will be concerned fundamentally about their own capacity to learn – as an individual, as a team member and as leader of the organisation. Such learning will ultimately be premised on the ability of the leader to engage with metaknowledge – knowledge about how they and others learn and use knowledge (Cardno and Fitzgerald, 2005). This has implications for the development of leaders and, in turn, the leadership of the professional development of other leaders in the organisation.

On the one hand, most portrayals of leadership tend to relate to a single leader – and in relation to schools this has mostly been the principal. On the other hand, the contemporary literature about educational leadership portrays leadership in organisational configurations that go beyond leadership vested in only the individual (Gronn, 2009). The importance of multilayered and shared leadership is captured in many depictions of the spreading of educational leadership across many positions. Mid-level leadership in particular is attracting considerable attention in the literature (Seashore Louis, et al., 2010). Certainly in secondary school and higher education settings, the distributing of leadership tasks from senior to middle level is a growing trend evidenced in the research base. Building the capabilities of these leaders to resolve complex problems and build trusting relationships with others is essential. A feature that connects the notions of the learning organisation with organisational learning is the importance of inspiring trust between individuals and in teams. Trust is in fact an implicit feature of organisational capability to learn.

Trust – a resource for organisations that learn

Complex problem-solving and engagement in productive interpersonal relationships are key capabilities for leaders who enable organisations that learn. These capabilities assume that educational leaders are able to participate in learning conversations. Such conversations both require and build relational trust between professional colleagues. When these conversations allow beliefs and assumptions to be openly and safely confronted, this contributes to trust building. This, in turn, is a further condition for the leader to establish in order to indirectly influence change in teacher practices which could, consequently, lead to better learning outcomes for students. When solutions to problems are imposed on people and when they are confronted with changes that they have had little input into, a low trust atmosphere is often created. Argyris (1990) reminds us that when problems are avoided and procedures are tightened up as a way of solving a problem, there is often a lack of trust behind the creation of more compliance measures. He says:

> Low trust has no ending; it can always become lower. The irony is that to deal with the issue by covering it up activates the downward spiral.
> High trust also has no ending. It feeds on itself and increases and expands.

In order for this expansion to occur, however, the issue of trust has to be dealt with openly and competently. Most individuals bypass it. (Argyris, 1990, p. 111)

In a similar vein, Bryk and Schneider (2003) assert that trust is demonstrated through the words and actions that express the co-operative and inter-dependent obligations of all the stakeholders in a school (students, staff and parents). Trust, they say, grows 'through exchanges in which actions validate these expectations' (p. 43). Without honesty and interpersonal respect trust may diminish. Leaders who make it a priority to establish conditions that are conducive to organisational learning should be aware of the way in which trust, or the lack of it between colleagues, affects possibilities for individual, team and organisational learning.

Because trust and distrust are attitudes that affect the way we think and feel, and thus determine the way we act, our behaviour when we encounter particularly challenging problems is conditioned by the level of collegial trust that is built between people. This, in turn, determines the extent to which defensiveness will be present. When leadership dilemmas are encountered, with their inherent tensions between achieving the goals of the organisation and preserving a positive working relationship with an individual (Cardno, 2007), trust has a pervading impact on how leaders and teachers act. It also affects ability to be open-to-learning in the course of that action. Trust can be a very fragile thing and may often be placed at risk when our ongoing relationships are defensive rather than productive. High trust enables learning and risk-taking to occur at both the individual and the organisational level.

The issue of risk is ubiquitous in relation to trust as many writers assert (see, for example, Bottery, 2004; Robinson, 2007) and is related to the extent that one is willing to make oneself vulnerable to another. As Tschannen-Moren (2004) states, trust becomes critical in the workplace when 'parties are dependent on one another for something they care about or need' (p. 17). In her terms, 'Trust is one's willingness to be vulnerable to another based on the confidence that the other is benevolent, honest, open, reliable, and competent' (p. 17). In conflicted situations, risk is entailed when we are uncertain about how someone might act – and taking the risk to be vulnerable by opening up one's thoughts and feeling to the scrutiny of others – can, in turn, actually develop trust between colleagues. Thus productive relationships can both develop out of trusting interactions and be used to create them.

Each of the facets of trust in a definition of trust provided by Tschannen-Moran (2004) (benevolence, honesty, openness, reliability, and competence) is examined briefly in relation to how they play out in a context of organisational learning where teachers and leaders are highly interdependent and attempt to engage in conversations about problems of practice.

Benevolence

This involves showing that one cares about the well-being of others. It is also about demonstrating care about the relationship itself. The risk related to this aspect of trust in our conversations is that the relationship is very seldom discussed (Barth, 2006). In a productive framing of a conversation it should be possible to discuss the relationship itself even when this appears to be a barrier to one or both parties. Argyris (1990) asserts that 'It is not possible, to my knowledge, to deal with any subject if it is not discussable and if its undiscussability is undiscussable' (p. 29). In a productive relationship there is a mutual wish to overcome such high-risk barriers.

Honesty

This is fundamental to building a trusting relationship. It reflects the integrity and authenticity of the person as characteristics that are trusted. Educational leaders must demonstrate truth-telling in their interactions with others. Faced with a challenging problem, educational leaders will sometimes avoid honesty as the best policy. This feature of human conditioning, the tendency to avoid tackling difficult problems, is often revealed in a mismatch between what we espouse and what we actually do. Tschannen-Moran (2004) refers to how this 'disconnect between the person's actions and words damages trust' (p. 23).

Openness

An aspect of trust that is critical to the quality of 'teacher talk' is that of openness – the sharing of information. In an atmosphere of trust, knowledge is not used to gain power over others, and people feel confident that the information they provide will not be exploited. Tschannen-Moran (2004) distinguishes between personal information (the sharing of joys and fears about life outside the school) and professional information (sharing professional secrets, successful teaching strategies and resources). In both realms, she says, 'openness needs to be tempered with good judgement and care. But a lack of openness can produce a downward spiral of distrust. Without openness, teachers do not have the opportunity to demonstrate benevolence, reliability, and competence to one another' (p. 119).

Reliability

Trusting colleagues to be reliable, whatever the circumstances, is a key aspect of professionalism. In her research, Tschannen-Moran (2004) found that, 'Teachers talked about the importance of being able to depend on other teachers to live up to their commitments or take their responsibilities seriously. Being able to count on colleagues in the midst of unexpected circumstances was important to teachers' (p 119). One of the powerful ways in which trust is generated is 'by individuals doing what they say they will do' (Bottery, 2004, p. 118).

Competence

This facet of trust is particularly important in situations where there is interdependence between teachers and between teachers and leaders – for example, in the case of performance appraisal. Bottery (2004) refers to the demonstration of competence as one of the foundation areas of trust. Teachers make judgements about the professional competence of their peers and leaders all the time because the practice and the results of teaching are relatively transparent. When leaders lack confidence in the professional competence of those being judged, they often resort to unproductive ways of communicating concerns and complex problems of practice remain unsolved. When teachers lack confidence in the competence of leaders, especially those making first line judgements about their performance, they are often unwilling to respect or act upon these judgements, and therefore essential change does not occur.

Meeting the goals of the organisation and simultaneously maintaining positive and trusting relationships with colleagues is the ultimate aim of an educational leader who sets out to be effective in resolving the critical problems that impact on the quality of teaching and learning experienced by students. Educational leadership is predicated on trust because of the high degree of interdependence in the activities that improve teaching and learning. This interdependence between leaders and teachers is rewarding and stimulating when the five facets of trust – benevolence, honesty, openness, reliability and competence – are present in relationships to a high degree. Take these away and trust diminishes. By the time a teacher or leader has encountered a distrusting experience more than once, trust may be lost altogether. The literature is consistent in urging the restoration of trust because of its extreme importance to relationships in individual and group situations (see, for example, Govier, 1998; Tschannen-Moran and Hoy, 2000).

Research evidence points to a link between trust in professional relationships and change that impacts positively on student learning (Bryk and Schneider, 2003). In schools, increasing levels of trust between adults can shift the climate and create opportunities for organisational change and learning. One of the key features of relational trust across all levels of a school is confidence in taking risks related to the responses of others, even when one feels vulnerable. The development of trust lies at the very core of developing and maintaining a sustainable climate for transformative learning both for adults and students.

Organisational learning and student learning outcomes

Leaders and managers in educational organisations want to be in a position to solve the critical problems that act as barriers to achieving purposes that are educational. The knowledge base on organisational learning and the learning organisation provides many pathways to achieving the conditions in organisations that are conducive to the kind of learning that can make a difference when it comes to managing change and improving student learning outcomes.

There is a very small amount of research that refers to educational leadership and organisational learning in tandem. Some studies have adopted a broad view of what constitutes organisational learning (see, for example, the work of Leithwood et al., 1998). Here organisational learning is equated with a notion of collective learning and is not related to the normative theorising of Argyris and Schön (1978). Nevertheless, this research shows that shared understandings can lead to greater commitment to student success and improvements to teaching strategies.

There is further research evidence (Mulford et al., 2004) to show that organisational learning is one factor that can have an impact on teachers' work and consequently on student outcomes. In this study also, the notion of organisational learning in schools is conceptualised in a much broader way than it is in the work of Argyris and Schön (1978) where organisational learning is a process construct linked to processes for double-loop learning to change a theory of action. In their definition of organisational learning, Mulford et al. (2004, p. 5) refer to the sequential building of the following features in schools:

• establishing a trusting and collaborative climate;
• having a shared and monitored mission; and
• taking initiatives and risks.

These features occur within the context of supportive, on-going and relevant professional development for teachers and leaders.

It could be argued that this definition of organisational learning is more akin to the idealistic features of a learning organisation with an emphasis on the leader's ability to transform a culture so that it is enabling and collaborative (Senge, 2006). It is assumed that within a learning organisation the processes of organisational learning are critical and will occur. In contrast, the Mulford et al. study calls for a problem-based learning (PBL) approach to professional development for practitioners that is broad based and does not specifically utilise the learning strategies related to the type of organisational learning skills proposed by Argyris and Schön (1978; 1996).

In current New Zealand research that suggests conditions that can have an impact on teaching quality and, consequently, on student learning outcomes (Robinson et al., 2009), there is acknowledgement of the importance of theories of action in the way an organisation approaches learning and change. When leaders engage with teachers' theories of action and seek to understand these while at the same time being explicit about their own theories of action, they are likely to be more successful in creating lasting change and commitment to new practices. The research also refers to the critical role played by the external facilitators in leading the learning of the participants in a professional development project. If all change and development initiatives were facilitated by trainers who were themselves knowledgeable about the basic tenets of organisational learning and how to engage teachers' theories of action in change processes, there might be an incremental increase of a shared flow of understanding about the potential of this condition in all educational institutions.

While there are many variations of meaning that have been attributed to organisational learning, my alignment with the pioneering work of Argyris and Schön is unwavering and evident throughout this book. In my view the most effective professional development that leaders and teachers can engage in involves the understanding and skill learning related to uncovering a defensive theory of action and adopting a productive theory of action. In the process of developing a learning culture in the organisation, leaders may be more willing to face the sort of problems that persist in spite of efforts to resolve them. Often these take the form of a dilemma the leader has avoided because of its challenging nature. In managing dilemmas – the topic of the next chapter – leaders will need to call on the theoretical resources for organisational learning because these have the potential to build trusting and productive relationships through collaborative engagement in solving the problems that matter most in terms of effective educational leadership and management.

CHAPTER FOUR

MANAGING DILEMMAS THROUGH PRODUCTIVE DIALOGUE

Building productive relationships

Leaders want to resolve the 'people problems' which present major challenges to organisational effectiveness. This is difficult when the problem is in fact a particular kind of dilemma, and the leader is torn between serving organisational and relational needs. Building productive relationships with colleagues who may be part of a dilemma is challenging but worthwhile because it is essential to dilemma resolution. By engaging in productive dialogue, a leader both models and strengthens the productive relationship.

Dilemmas inhibit conversations that require productive dialogue. Leaders often find themselves frustrated because they cannot achieve the resolution they seek when they set out to have conversations with colleagues about difficult issues. This chapter explains the nature of leadership dilemmas and then provides guidance on how to engage in conversations that are productive.

> A leadership dilemma is a particularly complex problem because it contains tensions between what serves the organisation best and what is best for your relationship with the individual involved. In other words you are torn between on the one hand, meeting the needs of the organisation and, on the other hand, meeting the needs of the individual. (Cardno and Reynolds, 2009)

61

An organisation that is able to learn increases its capacity to solve the problems that are most critical in terms of achieving its goals. Leaders in educational organisations are fundamentally concerned about creating conditions to improve the quality of teaching in order to maximise learning outcomes for students. Dilemmas create barriers to achieving high-quality teaching and learning, because they are recurring problems which contain conflict and complexity of a highly challenging nature. The concept of dilemma management contains a body of theory and skill knowledge that offers leaders the opportunity to manage dilemmas to resolution, so that they do *not* recur and block progress towards goal achievement.

The approach to managing and resolving dilemmas presented in this chapter has been my passion for the past 20 years. It subscribes to the notion of organisational learning developed in the seminal work of Argyris and Schön (1974). It draws on research conducted with leaders at all levels in New Zealand schools and early childhood centres. It is both a highly theoretical and highly practical curriculum of theory and tools for the management of dilemmas, so that they can be, and can stay, resolved. And it is a curriculum that focuses on a particular type of dilemma which I have called a 'leadership dilemma'. To understand the nature of a leadership dilemma one must be able to distinguish it from dilemmas in a general sense.

The nature of the leadership dilemma

Dilemmas are complex, tension-fraught problems that arise when a leader is challenged to achieve more than one objective. Leaders typically adopt a stance associated with the most common belief related to resolving dilemmas; that they are irresolvable. Consequently, they avoid having to deal with them. However, if an organisation is to learn, survive and succeed in achieving its goals this can only be accomplished when leaders are prepared to acknowledge and confront dilemmas and attempt their resolution, especially when these dilemmas are associated with the effectiveness of the core work of the organisation.

Educational leaders are under constant pressure to improve the achievement of students. Standards-based reforms all around the world have increased the degree of accountability for leaders, especially in relation to performance management of the professionals responsible for learning and teaching. In this context of performance appraisal a particular type of dilemma emerges when there is conflict between organisational needs, and the needs of an individual. I call this type of dilemma a *leadership dilemma* for several reasons:

1. Those in leadership positions in the organisation have the power to

influence the learning-teaching environment, thus they must own these dilemmas as they alone are in a position to directly lead learning and change in practice. This happens through face-to-face encounters that implicate them wholly in the success or otherwise of the resolution process.

2. These are leadership dilemmas because, once owned by the leader, it is a leader's obligation to publicly declare this ownership as a starting point for dilemma management.

3. In leadership dilemmas there is tension between organisational concerns and a concern for the relationship between the leader and the individual(s) implicated in the dilemma.

This type of dilemma differs from what has been termed an *organisational dilemma* (Hoy and Miskel, 2005), which is a dilemma nevertheless. However the leader may be involved only indirectly, often by exerting a mediating influence on structures and systems by distributing leadership to others who are part of the action-mix surrounding a long-term solution. For example, making decisions about allocating time to different aspects of a curriculum gives rise to dilemmas because no ideal solution can be found.

In contrast, the leadership dilemma arises most often in the context of a leader directly managing the performance of colleagues. For example, if a staff member is reluctant to introduce an agreed new teaching strategy, this is a performance issue because it affects the collective work of a team. If the leader finds it challenging to confront this colleague because they have a poor professional relationship, and this kind of resistance has been encountered on other occasions, it is likely that a leadership dilemma exists.

A leadership dilemma then arises in the course of working with and through others to achieve the organisation's goals. When a colleague's performance jeopardises goals and when it is not possible to resolve the issue collaboratively and without conflict, then the leader could be facing a dilemma. It manifests as tensions between a leader's concern to do what is best for the organisation while at the same time maintaining a positive working relationship with a colleague. Thus, in the context of appraising the performance of others such dilemmas are experienced by educational leaders who are principals, headteachers or academic leaders in smaller institutions or units, and in larger institutions by senior managers who appraise middle managers, and middle managers who appraise staff in their teams. I contend that such dilemmas can be managed to resolution, despite many views to the contrary (see, for example, Cuban, 2001; Dimmock, 1999b). This may well be true of other types of dilemmas, so it is important for leaders to understand how to recognise a general dilemma, in order to distinguish it from a leadership dilemma.

General dilemma characteristics

Every leader is familiar with the sense of finding themselves in a sticky situation or 'between a rock and a hard place'. Whichever way they turn they are likely to have to choose between equally undesirable or conflicted alternatives, and this creates indecisiveness. Thus a dilemma is a complex problem characterised by multiple demands or goals, creating difficult options and presenting irreconcilable choices. These complex problems persist, they resurface or recur, and often our attempts to resolve them only exacerbate the tensions and conflict. To attend to one aspect of the dilemma means sacrificing another aspect. It is not surprising, then, to find that whenever possible the need to resolve the dilemma is avoided. At best, the dilemma may be polarised and one aspect be attended to at the expense of others. The distinction between a problem and a dilemma is that the former can be solved whereas the latter recurs because it has not been dealt with effectively.

In the vast literature that exists on problem-solving and decision-making in organisations, Owens (2004) reminds us that problems are most often categorised into those that lend themselves either to intuitive or to rational models of problem-solving, and those that test the limits of rationality. Rational models, which suggest a step-by-step approach to defining and analysing the problem, developing alternative solutions and then acting on the best solution, are confounded when problems are beset by the uncertainty and ambiguity that are dominant features of the real world of educational management. A crucial issue in leadership learning is to build the capacity of leaders to determine the degree of complexity of a problem by reflecting on the problem holistically 'understanding ... the complexities, interconnections, ambiguity and uncertainty of educational organisations' (Owens, 2004, p. 301). Dilemmas are just such multidimensional problems which require an alternative approach to the one leaders would adopt to address simple, routine problems.

The notion of tame problems versus wicked problems (Argyris and Schön, 1996) provides further clarification of the differences between problems and dilemmas. Cuban (2001) elaborates on this distinction between 'tame problems' which are familiar and frequent situations to which routine procedures and solutions can be applied, whereas wicked problems, he states, are 'ill-defined, ambiguous, complex, interconnected situations packed with potential conflict' (p. 10). According to Cuban these problems are actually dilemmas. Dilemmas that are ethical and organisational in nature are also described in a range of literature.

It is universally appreciated that dilemmas are ever-present, dreaded and particularly complex problems that leaders encounter in organisational life (Cardno, 2001a; Murphy, 2007). Yet, the body of literature that deals with their characteristics in educational organisations provides some mixed messages in terms of labelling these dilemmas and suggesting possibilities that exist for dilemma resolution. Dilemmas are sometimes called organisational dilemmas (Hoy and Miskel, 2005) and are also identified as ethical dilemmas (Dempster and Berry, 2003) which challenge the moral basis of decision-making. Literature about academic leadership in higher education also alludes to a range of 'paradoxes and dilemmas' (Scott et al., 2008). These are portrayed as tensions between, for example, the goals of the university versus the department's goals; the need to achieve a balance between encouraging disagreement and avoiding conflict; achieving a balance between directing staff and consulting them; and balancing accountability of staff with professional independence. These authors describe the dilemma involving, 'being able to figure out where to put the "and" between the two poles of a dilemma or two apparently opposite ways of proceeding' (p. 66).

Within this panorama establishing the 'dilemma' as one of the 'difficult and messy experiential aspects of educational leadership' (Murphy, 2007, p. 4), my own work (Cardno, 1999, 2001a, 2007) has alluded to the leadership dilemma as a particularly challenging problem that must be owned by leaders who are charged with making a difference to the quality of learning and teaching in educational organisations.

Difficulties with recognising dilemmas

Recognising the fact that one is facing a leadership dilemma is the first step along the way to the learning that enables dilemma management. Leaders may resist the idea of describing a complex and challenging problem as a dilemma for several reasons. One reason for this is that the presence of a dilemma overwhelms and creates uncertainty because leaders are unsure about how to proceed. Another reason is that dilemmas trigger negative emotions such as feeling inadequate to the task. Yet another reason is that there are many messages about dilemmas that reinforce the impossibility of resolution, so people feel justified to let the matter rest.

Since we think, when faced with a dilemma, that we have to choose between two equally unattractive options, it is not surprising to believe that dilemmas cannot be resolved. Because dilemmas are exceedingly *complex problems* the very idea that they can be managed is unthinkable. Dimmock (1999b) explains that while a problem may be solved, dilemmas are distinguishable from problems in that they are taken to be irresolvable because, in attending to one element or horn of a dilemma, others are left unresolved. In Cuban's view dilemmas are 'messy, complicated and conflict-filled situations that require undesirable choices between competing, highly-prized values that cannot be simultaneously or fully satisfied' (2001, p. 10). They arise when people:

- compete for limited resources;
- hold conflicting values; or
- wrestle with diverse expectations held by others.

Neither of these authors believes that dilemmas can be resolved. Dimmock asserts that the management of dilemmas begins with the ability 'to conceptualise, reconceptualise and redefine the situation, and then to identify its elements and the values underlying it' (1999b, p. 110). At best, however, the principal can learn to *cope* by having the ability to employ a range of management strategies. In a study of Chinese principals in Hong Kong, this coping takes many forms, such as transfer of a teacher to another school, attempting to compromise, acquiescing with seniors or withdrawing from direct involvement (Dimmock and Walker, 2005). Cuban (2001) is of the view that dilemmas cannot be solved although he believes they can be managed. He conceptualises this management of dilemmas as a form of *satisficing* which requires compromise and helps one to cope with the 'debris of disappointment' (p. 16) that is the consequence of repeated failure and associated guilt. Accordingly if one accepts this limitation then the best a leader can achieve is to continue to create compromises on the understanding that problems are *solved* but dilemmas *recur*. In fact, what we may be seeing here is evidence of various ways in which the confrontation of a dilemma is *avoided*.

In contrast to believing that coping or satisficing are sufficient outcomes in the management of leadership dilemmas, I present an alternative view that leaders can and must manage dilemmas to resolution. A resolved dilemma does not recur. Leadership effectiveness presupposes the ability to address these tough problems in such a way that they remain solved. I am suggesting here a theory of effectiveness that could be extremely challenging for leaders to adopt. In this view of effectiveness, an educational leader makes the following commitment. They commit themselves to making a conscious choice to manage dilemmas and they commit themselves to learning and internalising knowledge that embraces the theory and practice of managing leadership dilemmas. Ultimately, they commit to praxis in theorising about their action as they embrace and enact a productive approach to managing dilemmas every time they are encountered.

A dilemma management approach

In the course of two decades of research, teaching and providing leadership development programmes, I have designed an approach for learning the theory and practice of dilemma management which will be explained in the rest of this chapter. Leaders need recourse to intellectual and practical resources in order to manage leadership dilemmas. These include familiarity with a specific theory base about productive reasoning and development of a set of skills related to productive dialogue or conversations that are productive. Engaging in talk that is productive is the basis for developing a productive relationship with a colleague. Modelling the relationship and being open to continuing learning through practise of productive dialogue sets the scene for others to observe and learn a productive approach. This approach has the following components:

- recognising and articulating the dilemma;
- confronting the dilemma (overcoming avoidance);
- using tools for productive dialogue/conversations;
- reflection-in-action (double-loop learning); and
- creating a dilemma management culture (organisational learning).

When educational leaders understand the theory related to each of the five elements of this dilemma management approach, and become familiar with the tools associated with this challenging demand, then they are able to use this knowledge and the related skills to attend to dilemmas so that they are managed to resolution.

Recognising and articulating the dilemma

Leaders should be able to use both intuition and a holistic understanding of problems to help them to recognise a dilemma when they encounter complex problems which are likely to recur. Senge (2006) promotes the value of a systems-thinking orientation which takes into account the underlying and interconnected patterns of problems that need attention at a deep level to uncover and address their sources. Leadership dilemmas are such problems because unless the beliefs and assumptions that have led to their long and festering life are openly tested, nothing much changes. Hence, the very persistence of a problem is an indicator that it could be a dilemma. Leaders in my New Zealand research settings have provided valuable insights regarding the dilemma recognition issue. For some participants in primary and secondary school research, dilemmas were recognised because they were problems that could not be resolved easily or at all.

One respondent comments that dilemmas are encountered:

because the needs of both parties cannot ever be met.

Another comments that dilemmas are problems solved at a cost:

There is usually a cost in determining a positive solution/resolution and when cost is related to personal relationships it is always difficult.

Yet another stated,

> *Yes, I have dilemmas. These are problematic occurrences that involve a colleague, colleagues or myself, in which I feel helpless to support or solve.*

The recurring nature of a problem is often an indicator that it may be a leadership dilemma. Dilemmas were seen as problems that had not been effectively addressed in the past and hence persisted. Several respondents stated that in their view these problems remained dilemmas because:

> *for me these usually involve issues with professional colleagues that are not new – existed prior to me trying to deal with it.*

> *it was a problem I inherited.*

> *despite trying to address the problems from many different angles they are still problems.*

A study of dilemmas in New Zealand kindergartens (Cardno and Reynolds, 2009) confirms that leadership dilemmas also exist in early childhood settings. The nature of the leadership dilemmas described have been summarised in two broad ways below with the common factor being that invariably *people* appear to be at the centre of the dilemmas:

1. Performance dilemmas:
   (a) teacher not meeting professional expectations (for example, concerns about punctuality, diligence, attitudes);
   (b) team member letting the side down;
   (c) headteacher unable to deal with being a team player and a leader when colleagues did not meet expectations.
2. Value clash dilemmas:
   (a) two teachers unable to agree on standards (related to behaviour of children and/or pedagogy) because of differing beliefs;
   (b) teacher failing to agree with headteacher's pedagogical philosophy.

Although the participants provided examples that resonated with the way leadership dilemmas are described in school settings (Cardno, 2007) none of the respondents were able to articulate the dilemma to isolate the tension between organisational needs, on the one hand, and the need to maintain positive relationships, on the other hand. School practitioners who were asked to identify the issues that created challenging problems for them have revealed that when a problem has aspects that challenge them at a deep level, these trigger the notion that the problem they are dealing with might be a 'hot situation' (Argyris and Schön, 1996, p. 159): in other words, a dilemma.

Again, all of these identified issues dealt with *people* at the centre of a complex problem. Responses have been clustered under three categories: firstly managing people issues; secondly, managing resources for people issues; and thirdly, managing personal issues. Some examples (Cardno, 2007) are provided to illustrate the scope of issues.

1. Managing people issues (focus on performance):
    *   Staff performance – maintaining standards;
    *   Underqualified and ineffective staff member;
    *   Developing an underperforming staff member;
    *   Communication with staff/explaining to staff;
    *   Excellent teacher – poor manager performance issue; and
    *   Trying to change older teachers' practices.
2. Managing resources for people issues (focus on equitable distribution):
    *   Meeting timetable requests with staff shortages;
    *   Work overload/lack of time for change management; and
    *   Meeting needs of organisation and individual (workload).
3. Managing personal issues:
    *   Hate having to deliver hard messages;
    *   Being a leader as well as a friend to staff;
    *   Accepting advice and help without feeling threatened;
    *   Not enough time to focus on the 'big things';
    *   Nervous because of being new to the job; and
    *   Reluctance because people might disagree with my decision.

This kind of evidence confirms the view that the focus on productive relationships between people in the organisation is essential if goals are to be achieved. Every issue for research respondents (in school and early childhood settings) involved people and an interpersonal relationship in which the leader must be willing to take central stage as the initiator of a process to deal with the dilemma. Thus, although it is necessary for a leadership dilemma to be recognised and acknowledged, it is necessary that the dilemma is articulated as a precursor to taking productive action. Equally, while both parties to forging a relationship have their own views about what the dilemma might be, the leader must accept responsibility to act.

Having recognised, acknowledged (and owned) a dilemma, a leader must then be able to articulate it. One part of an effective dialogue about a dilemma is the ability of the leader to *say* to others that the problem is complex, and then to demonstrate their perception of this by mapping the tensions so they declare publicly the concern for meeting *both* organisational needs and individual relationship needs simultaneously. Capable dilemma articulation requires a statement of, on the one hand, the *organisational* strand of the dilemma and its attendant concerns and, on the other hand, the *collegial relationship* strand of the dilemma and its attendant concerns. This also allows the leader to make their views testable and to test the perceptions of others, and encourage them to articulate their assumptions about the dilemma. Leaders engaging in such learning are encouraged to write dilemma maps, which also serve to aid reflection-on-action: that is, looking critically at past attempts and considering how open display of a leadership dilemma might lead to new attempts to put a particular theory into action. A format for mapping a dilemma is presented in Table 4.1.

Table 4.1 A dilemma map

On the one hand there are organisational concerns related to achieving objectives	Yet, on the other hand there are individual concerns related to collegial relationships

In my research I have collected evidence to show that at least in some cases this learning can be transferred to practice. As one school research participant stated:

> *I start with identification of the dilemma. On the one hand ... on the other hand and seek all information that is possible. I have tried to be open about the outcome even if it may not be what I wanted. It is hard to stop going into the resolution with predefined expectations.*

Another stated:

> *The skill is in being able to identify simple problems that can be solved by traditional decision-making processes and dilemmas which need to be treated quite differently.*

Knowing about the nature of a leadership dilemma helps with their recognition as problems of a particular kind that need to be managed using the theory and practice resources that allow them to be confronted rather than avoided.

Learning case for reflection: articulating a leadership dilemma

When a leader thinks that a difficult, recurring problem might actually be a leadership dilemma they need to test out this hunch by trying to analyse the strands of the dilemma that make it complex. A primary school principal's efforts to do this while engaged in a workshop on dilemma management is shown below. To assist people with the articulation of the tensions, I have always guided workshop participants to talk about a dilemma in terms of what is challenging on one hand (*the organisational concern*) and what is challenging on the other hand (*the individual and the relationship concern*). Using the actual language over and over again helps one to internalise a procedure for analysing the dilemma and consequently mapping it.

How Milo views the dilemma

Organisational concern (work goals)	Individual concern (relationship)
On the one hand, as the leader I am concerned because the needs of students in this class are not being met in a manner expected by this school.	*On the other hand, I am aware that this teacher is currently carrying a very heavy personal burden that is now impacting on her performance.*
A second parent has now complained about the poor use being made of homework which on several occasions has not been collected or marked. Another parent has expressed difficulty in arranging an appointment to talk to the teacher about his daughter's progress.	This teacher has been a valued member of the staff for 12 years and I have known her for the last four years as principal.
The team leader has made me aware of difficulties in the team caused by this teacher not meeting expectations for planning and evaluation of their teaching. She has failed to attend several important meetings. Her colleagues on the team are becoming frustrated as her performance is affecting group task completion.	Her partner is seriously ill with a terminal condition but presently in remission. I believe that sensitivity and great consideration has been extended consistently over the last two years by supportive colleagues.
	The teacher has not been approached about the most recent concerns by her team leader because the leader is new to the school (has only been in the position for a year) and is somewhat daunted by the prospect of dealing with a far more experienced and highly respected colleague.

The dilemma for me is that:

On the one hand, I know that something must be done to ensure that team and school expectations are met. I owe it to the parents and the teacher's colleagues to get these concerns communicated and sorted because her difficulties are beginning to impact on students' learning.	On the other hand, I want to be as supportive as possible through this difficult period for the teacher.
	I know I need to tell her about my concerns but I am holding back because I think she will be devastated by this. She may want to leave and will be hard to replace.

(Continues)

(Continued)

Consequently I do nothing	
I have talked about this with the school board chairperson and the deputy principal on several occasions.	I think about what I will say to her a lot – it is now a burden for me and I know I am avoiding the issue.

At this point the principal has had difficulty articulating this dilemma to himself in a way that clarifies the major tensions. He has not shared the view that he has a dilemma with the teacher who is part of the dilemma. Having now written a summary of the key aspects of the dilemma – the next step is for him to convey this to the other party by communicating to them that he has a leadership dilemma.

1 **Why do you think the principal Milo is continuing to prevaricate?**

2 **What exactly should Milo say in opening the conversation?**

3 **Does this scenario ring true for you?**

4 **How would you proceed?**

5 **Does this dilemma also exist for the team leader and how could they be assisted in articulating it?**

Confronting the dilemma (overcoming avoidance)

Leaders faced with the realisation that they are dealing with a leadership dilemma might be able to recognise this and may also be capable of articulating the dilemma clearly. We cannot be sure, however, that they will actually confront the dilemma. To do so involves moving out of a comfort zone into extremely risky or even dangerous ground. It involves meeting with a colleague or other person face to face, or communicating a message about their dilemma in an effective way – so that the issues are mapped for all to see. Knowing what we know about the most common responses to dilemmas, even the most experienced leaders will find ways to do little or nothing, or they could create even more tension around the dilemma by failing in an attempt to resolve it.

Participants in a primary and secondary school study have stated categorically that after learning the theory base, their self-awareness is heightened and they are aware of the fact of avoidance. This takes many forms such as accepting that the problem will remain unaddressed and admitting inability to deal with it. They said, for example:

It is different from less challenging problems as I cannot solve the problem myself. The effects of the problem radiate through the department.

The problem continues – it has become self-perpetuating and therefore destructive.

To date attempts to resolve this problem have been an unmitigated failure.

Certainly I could have given it more time and attention but often that is easier said than done.

The majority of responses in this school study were consistent with what is known in relation to facing up to a complex problem – that it is much thought about, advice may be sought, support may be provided but, for a variety of reasons, action is delayed or avoided altogether. The reasons provided to justify delay and avoidance are related to non-ownership of the dilemma as an issue that the leader has specific responsibility to deal with and the matter of time. The time factor appears to be a big issue in terms of the duration of the problem and the amount of time practitioners believe they will need to spend on resolving the dilemma. The respondents have been painfully honest in their evaluation of their own effectiveness in relation to dealing with a dilemma.

As one participant revealed:

I do know that if I see a problem and do nothing, I am part of the problem.

In early childhood settings, avoidance of dilemmas is also common practice. In our research (Cardno and Reynolds, 2009) we found that after an intervention that provided training in dilemma management, kindergarten head-teachers were able to identify their avoidance of dilemmas. A typical dilemma avoidance response is related to a wish to protect relationships at the cost of meeting organisational goals. One respondent stated:

What stops me is the risk of offending others and breaking down relationships. We are a very small team of three. We need to, and do, depend on each other and need to maintain positive relationships.

And another refers to both her concern for others and things she fears about herself:

Fear of upsetting someone. I ask myself, am I being too hard – setting too high standards? Have I got it right?

Fear of upsetting others is usually accompanied by a fear of threat or embarrassment to oneself, both of which are dominant values in a defensive approach that leads to avoidance in relation to dealing with a dilemma. This feature is commonly identified in other studies of how leaders deal with dilemmas (Argyris, 1990; Cardno, 2007) as the main barrier to leaders' developing courage to confront a dilemma. When leaders' self-awareness of this tendency is heightened, so is their capacity to confront the dilemma and attempt resolution.

A rich and salutary body of research exists around the topic of why leaders do little or nothing to confront the crucial matters of poor performance and incompetence among professional colleagues. Study after study reveals that, when faced by these challenging problems, most leaders are overwhelmed to the extent where they avoid the dilemma or polarise it and hence avoid dealing with its opposing strands simultaneously and effectively (see, for example, Bridges, 1992; Cardno, 1998a). The typical and most common response is to 'do nothing'. Thus the dilemma (and its threat) is avoided, heads are buried in the sand once again, while guilt might be felt about one's ineffectiveness – unless this is job-threatening it too can be relegated to the 'too hard to think about today' basket. When leaders polarise the horns of a dilemma they often adopt a 'be nice' approach where they have decided that relationship preservation is the priority and the organisational goal is sacrificed. Conversely, in a 'be nasty' approach the relationship is sacrificed but achievement of an organisational goal (however temporary, and usually based on compliance not commitment to change) is made the priority. In making these unsatisfactory choices the overarching value that drives practice has been identified as that of *defensiveness*. To overcome the defensiveness associated with confronting and resolving a dilemma, leaders should become aware of the theory associated with defensive reasoning and an alternative which is productive reasoning (Argyris, 1990).

There is no context like performance appraisal for heightening defensiveness, both in those being appraised and those doing the appraising. Yet this is the very context in which leadership dilemmas arise and in which a leader is being exhorted to adopt a non-avoidance stance so that dilemmas are actually confronted. We know a great deal about defensiveness from the work of Argyris and Schön (1996). When individuals on their own behalf, or on behalf of the organisation, are threatened or embarrassed, they become defensive. When conflict and value tensions are present, people invariably act on a 'theory of action' in which the governing values are control and avoidance of unpleasantness. In this programme of behaviour our actions are driven by a wish to win and a wish to protect ourselves and others that overrides what we may espouse as a collaborative style of leadership. This defensive style is not only ineffective but also likely to heighten the defensiveness of others and create barriers to uncovering and examining the assumptions at the source of complex problems such as dilemmas.

What is needed when a leader must confront a dilemma is a theory of action that is productive and governed by an altogether different set of values. In this programme of behaviour our actions are driven by a wish to generate with others the valid information needed to appreciate all dimensions of the problem. In addition this approach values moving towards joint rather than preordained solutions and seeking commitment from both parties that relies on joint monitoring of change. This is a theory of action often espoused as an ideal by leaders. When resistance to change is encountered and when goals are in opposition, this is a difficult theory to put into use and most leaders when faced with a dilemma revert to the default programme that is common to every human being – that of defensive reasoning.

Learning case for reflection: self-analysis of theory into practice

Once you know something about the theory of 'theories of action', and the barriers that you have to overcome to move from a defensive theory-in-use to a productive theory-in-use, you could reflect on why your efforts to attempt resolution of a dilemma might be failing. If you can pinpoint the strategies you are employing in your interpersonal encounters with another person in a dilemma-fraught situation, you may be able to start over with the following thoughts in mind.

Describing a dilemma to self and others

1 Have I been able to map this complex problem as a leadership dilemma?

2 Is the organisational concern dimension clear to me?

3 Is the individual (relationship) concern dimension clear to me?

4 Have I been able to communicate my concerns to the other person using the language that helps to articulate a leadership dilemma?

Reflecting on efforts made to resolve the problem

5 What have I attempted to do to resolve the problem?

Understanding why the dilemma persists

6 Do I understand why the problem persists in spite of efforts to address it?

7 Is its persistence related to a theory of action that is dominated by a wish to control and a wish to cover up/suppress the inherent conflict rather than letting this surface?

Using an alternative approach

8 If I approached this dilemma from a different perspective – where I was prepared to give and get information that makes the conflicting issues discussable – would this make a difference?

(Continues)

(Continued)

9 **What specific strategies would I need to use to do this?**
10 **How could this contribute to dialogue that is productive?**

Conversations involving productive dialogue

The participants in a productive conversation must have recourse to both theory knowledge (about defensive responses) and practice knowledge (about countering defensiveness in a conversation) to participate effectively. When both participants have equal knowledge and skills to conduct a conversation based on productive dialogue, this can be a most empowering experience. When this is not the case then the person initiating the conversation must take the lead and model an approach that provides both (or more) participants with the means to make the conversation open-to-learning. This involves a mental shift towards:

- increasing the use of information by both parties wisely, sensitively and effectively;
- risk-taking to deal with conflict rather than avoiding it; and
- utilising a range of productive dialogue tools to achieve this.

Successful conversations include:

- *Initiating*: letting the other person know why you believe there should be a meeting so that both parties can have a productive dialogue about an issue or concern.
- *Stating*: opening the conversation by stating your perception of the concern and explaining (through illustration or example) why you are reasoning this way.
- *Listening and learning*: providing an opportunity for the other person to listen and learn about your reasoning and thinking related to the issue.
- *Checking*: listening to the other person's perception of the concern and eliciting their explanation (through illustration and example) of their reasoning.
- *Listening and learning*: providing opportunity for you to listen and learn about the other person's reasoning and thinking related to the issue.
- *Sharing*: exploring and finding common ground on which to move forward productively.
- *Agreeing*: making a collaborative commitment to solutions or further conversations.
- *Monitoring*: implementing solutions with both parties committed to regular tracking of change that is agreed.

The nature of a productive dialogue is characterised by:

- an openness to learning displayed by both parties;
- deep listening which is the essence of dialogue;
- honest, forthright communication (always within the limits of common sense);
- evidence-based judgement rather than assumptions left untested; and
- genuine commitment to agreeing and achieving change.

When a leader is challenged by a complex problem and can recognise, in particular, that this is a leadership dilemma they can move forward if they confront the problem and the person rather than avoiding the need for a conversation to take place. Tools to strengthen the possibility of engaging in a dialogue that is productive can be employed.

Using tools for productive dialogue

Two tools that can be employed to learn, practise and engage in productive dialogue are the Triple I approach (Cardno, 1998a, 2001a) and the ladder of inference (Argyris, 1993; Senge et al., 2000). At the point when a conversation takes place these tools can be utilised to create possibilities for productive rather than defensive dialogue to occur. They provide a touchstone – something you can refer to mentally, go back to in your mind, to provide a scaffold for keeping to a productive path rather than straying on to one that is defensive.

The Triple I approach

The Triple I approach can be used as a 'road code' to guide a conversation that subscribes to the theory-in-use associated with a Model 2 (productive theory of action). In this theory-in-use the emphasis is on generating information, agreeing joint solutions and jointly committing to the monitoring of these solutions (Argyris and Schön, 1974). In the 'Triple I' approach, participants are consciously attempting to increase the possibility of valid *information* generation, *illustration* of the basis for judgements and genuine *inquiry,* all of which cater for acknowledgement of *emotions* in interpersonal encounters. Each word beginning with the letter 'I' is associated with a simple rule that can be memorised to help internalise skills needed to engage in a productive dialogue. In this approach the letter 'i' to the power of three is superimposed with the letter 'e'. This is a reminder that if emotions surface they need to be dealt with in the process of informing, illustrating and inquiring. This is captured in the icon used to depict the approach (Figure 4.1).

The guidelines in this approach serve to build the skills for conducting a productive dialogue. These skills are central to internalising the adoption of a theory-in-use that is embedded in productive rather than defensive reasoning. For each letter 'i' and for the letter 'e', there are rules that guide application of the principles (reasons) behind the approach.

Figure 4.1 *The Triple I approach*

The following rules for a productive dialogue are drawn from the original work of Argyris and Schön (1974):

- Say what you think or feel.
- Say why you think or feel this way and provide examples or evidence.
- Check with others.
- Deal with emotions.

By using the rules in conversation and encouraging others to use the rules as well, you are demonstrating the high value placed on generating and utilising information to its fullest extent in problem-solving. Table 4.2 provides examples and explanations for these rules. The more effectively they are applied, the greater the likelihood of success in terms of being productive. It is only through constant practise that people internalise the rules to the extent that this becomes the natural way of initiating and sustaining a dialogue – especially when the subject is likely to threaten or embarrass us and hence create defensiveness.

In order to practise the Triple I approach it is useful to use a prompt sheet with steps to move through like the one in Table 4.3. This practice tool reminds you to state the concern or problem or dilemma clearly and forthrightly, to illustrate the reasons for the concern, and to check the reaction of the other person so that they are allowed to participate in the generation of new information.

If by this point you are close to agreeing what the problem or dilemma is, you may be ready to move on to the step of considering solutions collaboratively. If there is any disagreement at the time you check with others or if perceptions are very different, then this is a new concern and you need to cycle back to the start – to step one where you state this concern, illustrate it, and check further – and keep doing this. Only when both parties to this dialogue agree that there is a shared understanding of the concern, is it possible for you to consider some solutions and evaluate these jointly.

Together you should select a solution and agree on how this will be implemented and monitored by both of you.

Table 4.2 Triple I rules and reasons

Triple I Rules	Reasons for Rules
RULE 1: INFORM ○ **Say what you think or feel. For example:** - 'I feel that I can't rely any longer on your support to revise this programme.' - 'I am worried about upsetting you.' - 'I must tell you that I am very concerned about you not following the guidelines we have for student assessment.' - 'I am feeling vulnerable at this moment.'	**INFORMATION** • **Advocacy is a key demand** • Focus on **giving** quality information Disclose your position or your concerns fully at the outset • **Inquiry is another key demand** • Make efforts to **get** quality information • **Dialogue should demonstrate high levels of advocacy and inquiry** • Give and get information that lets you deal with emotions
RULE 2: ILLUSTRATE ○ **Say why you think or feel this way and provide examples or evidence. For example:** - '… because you didn't attend yesterday's meeting or the one before that.' - '… because on past occasions when I have had to raise difficult issues you have become angry with me.' - '… because I have discovered that the student's work was not internally moderated before it was sent for external examination.'	**ILLUSTRATION** • Always illustrate, explaining the basis used for making judgements and by providing examples to illustrate your reasoning and evaluation of a situation • Seek explanation of others' reasoning and evaluations by asking for illustration • THIS IS AN IMPORTANT ASPECT OF ADVOCACY – clearly stating concerns, being forthright and declaring your position, and encouraging others to do the same
RULE 3: INQUIRE ○ **Check with others. For example:** - 'Where exactly do you stand on this matter?' - 'Have I got my facts right?' - 'Am I judging how you feel correctly?' - 'How do you see it from your perspective?' - 'I need to check your reaction to this.'	**INQUIRY** • Ask relevant questions to seek information, to check others' views and to test your own views • Do not ask questions that control the response of others • Ask questions that check your assumptions about the facts and the emotional responses of others • THIS IS AN IMPORTANT ASPECT OF INQUIRY – getting others to contribute their views and seeking new information

RULE 4: DEAL WITH EMOTIONS
• Be prepared to 'feel' and 'deal' with emotions that attend defensiveness – both your defensive response and the response of others
• Be observant – and acknowledge what you think is happening
• Ask others to help you decide how to proceed
• Do not make assumptions about others' emotional state – check with them

Table 4.3 Steps in conducting a productive dialogue

1	STATE YOUR CONCERN **[Inform]**
2	STATE THE REASONS FOR YOUR CONCERN **[Illustrate]**
3	CHECK OTHERS' REACTIONS **[Inquire]**
4	SUMMARISE SHARED UNDERSTANDING
REPEAT STEPS 1– 4 IF NECESSARY TO ESTABLISH COMMON BASIS FOR MOVING ON	
5	JOINTLY SUGGEST AND EVALUATE SOLUTIONS
6	DECIDE TOGETHER ON A SOLUTION
7	AGREE NEXT STEP AND PLAN JOINT MONITORING

Together, the rules and the steps for a productive dialogue incorporate a theory-in-use called Model 2 that is an alternative to a defensive theory-in-use (Model 1) where the governing values are about winning, protecting self and others and maintaining control. When you find yourself reverting to these defensive values and the strategies that are associated with them, in the middle of practising a productive conversation, you need to engage in something called reflection-in-action which enables double-loop learning to occur (Argyris and Schön, 1996).

In Chapter 3, which deals with the concept of how organisations learn, the theoretical resources for understanding a theory of action approach to organisational learning are provided. To fully internalise the skill-set associated with productive dialogue it is necessary to engage both intellectually and practically so that action is guided by theory and becomes praxis.

The ladder of inference

Argyris proposed a model to explain the way people make inferences when they are reasoning either defensively or productively. He says:

> The ladder of inference is a hypothetical model of how individuals make inferences. They begin by experiencing some relatively observable data such as a conversation. This is rung 1 on the ladder. They make inferences about the meaning embedded in the words (rung 2). They often do this in milliseconds, regardless of whether they agree with the meanings. Then they impose their meanings on the actions they believe the other person intends (rung 3). For example, they may attribute reasons or causes for the actions. They may also evaluate the actions as effective or ineffective. Finally, the attributions or evaluations they make are consistent with their theory-in-use about effective action (rung 4). (Argyris, 1993, p. 57)

The ladder of inference can also be used as a tool that helps with learning the skills of productive dialogue. It can act as a sounding board for checking the extent to which valid information is being generated by the parties involved in a productive dialogue. When people jump to conclusions on the basis of inferring meaning from the selected actions of others (without these beliefs being tested) they are failing to generate valid information in a productive way. The ladder can be used as a reminder for understanding how we ourselves often are implicated in misinterpretation because we do not make our assumptions known in a way that makes them open for others to check. The ladder image becomes a warning signal *not* to make leaps of abstraction up the ladder without obtaining the data needed to really understand what is going on – both with oneself and the other person. So, the ladder is a mental tool for understanding how we reach conclusions about a problem.

As Figure 4.2 depicts, the pool at the bottom of the ladder represents the available data or information that can be used as evidence in our thinking, talking and action. It is available to both parties and as well as using this information ourselves we should encourage others to do this also. The rungs of the ladder represent how we deal with this information. The lowest rung is the point at which we select and describe a particular aspect of the data. The next rung up represents the way in which we interpret and evaluate those data and what we infer from them. At this point we attach our own personal meaning to the observable event or the information. Nearing the top of the ladder, we weave all of this together to draw conclusions based on our interpretations or inferences that we have made about the data. Sometimes these conclusions have little relationship to what the data actually shows or how it could be interpreted by another person. Often action is taken too quickly or without sufficient revisiting of the pool for more data, with consequences that are ineffective.

If we want to have productive conversations and build relationships with others on a basis of trust and truthfulness then we have to let them know the basis on which we are selecting data, interpreting it and drawing conclusions about events in which they are involved. The factors that affect the way we deal with the data are depicted on the left of the ladder in Figure 4.2. We and others need to know the context in which the problem has arisen, we need to let them know how a concern or problem is being framed in our mind – 'where we are coming from' as it were. We owe our colleagues the right to know what values, beliefs and assumptions have had an impact on the data we have selected and interpreted to reach our conclusions. In other words, we need to reveal our selection of data and our thoughts and feelings all the way along the length of the ladder. We need to encourage the other person to do the same. Dipping down regularly and repeatedly to the data pool should become part of every occasion where productive dialogue is practised.

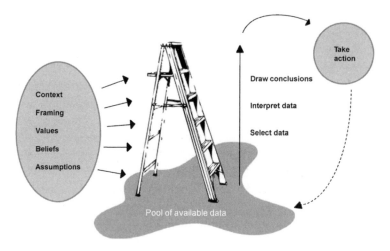

Figure 4.2 *The ladder of inference*

Several strategies can be employed to make use of the ladder of inference notion in the way you present your views on a matter to others. As Figure 4.3 depicts, sharing your own ladder (revealing what is happening as you mentally climb up and down the ladder) is a way of achieving high advocacy. You could use the following strategies to keep advocacy at a high level – giving information to others through:

- stating your view directly;
- presenting your views one at a time;
- presenting your conclusions as options;
- sharing your reasoning; and
- sharing your examples.

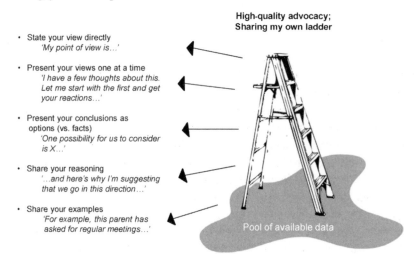

Figure 4.3 *Using the ladder to put forth your own views*

Advocacy needs to be accompanied by inquiry and Figure 4.4 illustrates some of the strategies that can be used to achieve this. Because you are declaring your own conclusions, reasoning and examples, you should ask others to do the same. When these are provided you will be beginning to understand how the ladder is working for the other person and here is a chance to deepen understanding of the issues by:

- testing your understandings of others' conclusions, reasoning and examples; and
- encouraging the other person to ask questions about your conclusions, reasoning and examples.

Thus, both people engaged in the conversation achieve high quality inquiry and gain a better understanding of each other's views.

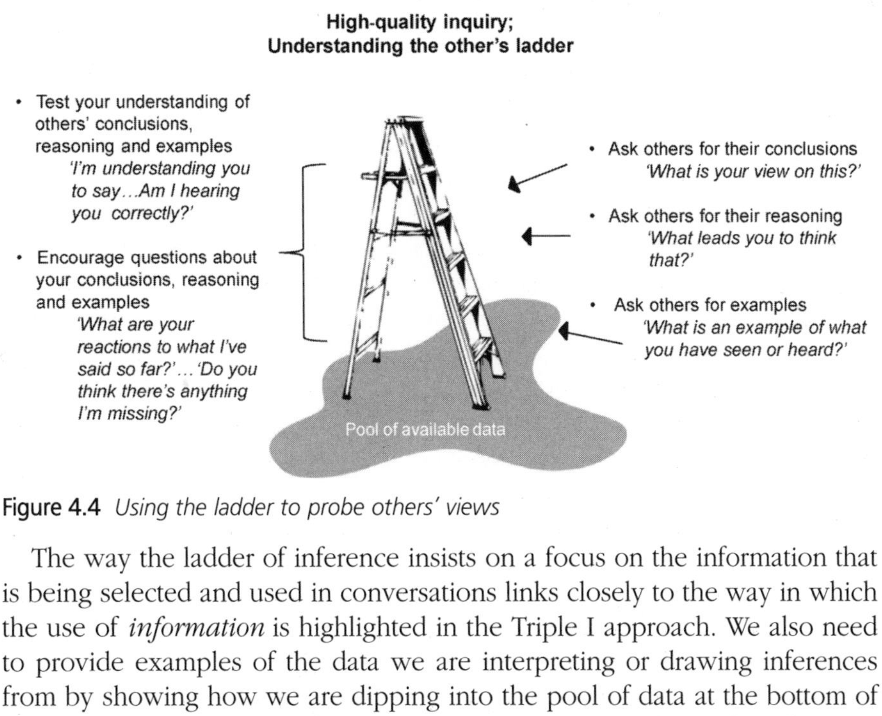

High-quality inquiry;
Understanding the other's ladder

- Test your understanding of others' conclusions, reasoning and examples
  'I'm understanding you to say...Am I hearing you correctly?'

- Encourage questions about your conclusions, reasoning and examples
  'What are your reactions to what I've said so far?'... 'Do you think there's anything I'm missing?'

- Ask others for their conclusions
  'What is your view on this?'

- Ask others for their reasoning
  'What leads you to think that?'

- Ask others for examples
  'What is an example of what you have seen or heard?'

Pool of available data

Figure 4.4 *Using the ladder to probe others' views*

The way the ladder of inference insists on a focus on the information that is being selected and used in conversations links closely to the way in which the use of *information* is highlighted in the Triple I approach. We also need to provide examples of the data we are interpreting or drawing inferences from by showing how we are dipping into the pool of data at the bottom of the ladder. Again, this reinforces the need to use examples and evidence to *illustrate* that is central to the Triple I approach. This is the way the ladder acts as a catalyst to focus on the effectiveness of one's *advocacy*. Finally, we need to make space for the views of others in our inferences. We do this by checking at every rung of the ladder – just as in the Triple I approach *inquiry* is genuinely concerned with testing our assumptions and evaluations. We need to ask others questions that help us to understand the conclusions that have been reached. We need to find out others' reasoning, to understand the evidence that they are basing their reasoning on. We need to ask for examples so that we can get them to work with us close to the bottom of the ladder. This is about effective inquiry and increasing one's ability to learn about the views of others.

As a mental aid, keeping in mind an image of the ladder of inference (and where you or others might be located on the ladder as you move up and down the rungs in making evidence-based or non-evidence based assumptions) is very useful to help self-critique. Checking position on the ladder is a way of slowing down the action or pausing the shot while we are actually in the middle of it. Being able to slow down or stop in mid-action is essential if we wish to reflect-in-action as a precursor to changing both values and action in mid-conversation.

Reflection-in-action (double-loop learning)

Defensive reasoning is sustained by a leadership response that is called single-loop learning (Argyris, 1990). Guided by defensive values, a leader who fails in an attempt to resolve a dilemma tries a variety of different tactics that are consistent with the need to win and keep control unilaterally while avoiding unpleasantness and protecting self and others. To break out of this loop requires a form of praxis based on implementing a new theory of action leading not only to different actions but different actions guided by an alternative set of values; those of providing and receiving honest feedback that is evidence-based, negotiating solutions jointly and both parties making a commitment to monitoring these solutions. Double-loop learning further requires an understanding of and theorising about reflection – and what it really means to be a reflective practitioner (Schön, 1993) in the middle of dealing with a leadership dilemma.

Reflection is something that almost every management text recommends that leaders do. It is associated with notions of deep thinking, critical reflection upon one's own practice and the use of hindsight and theory to conceptualise and reconceptualise issues – especially those related to practice. Many of these exhortations about reflection imply a form of reflection on action which Schön reminds us usually focuses on thinking about action *after* the event and this is often directed towards preparation for the next similar event. This type of reflection does have a place in the range of resources leaders need to manage dilemmas to resolution. However, they also need to engage the more demanding form of reflection which is the ability to *reflect-in-action*. In order to do this one has to bring reasoning informed by theory to bear on the action while in the throes of carrying out that action. This is exactly what dilemma management demands. It is this ability to reflect-in-action *during* a conversation that enables a leader to recognise defensiveness, abandon single-loop learning as inappropriate for the particular situation, and move into a new learning loop (double-loop learning) that is dependent on the adoption of productive values *and* do this in the process of the engagement itself. It calls for the ability to stop action as you theorise and restart with the aim of applying the theory more effectively.

Leaders face several learning demands along the way to becoming adept at conducting conversations that are productive. One of the most challenging aspects of critical self-evaluation in the course of a conversation is finding the appropriate words to use in conjunction with reflection in action. The very thought of having to admit that one needs to stop and revisit the action triggers our defensiveness. The following examples may assist:

You might say: 'Could I please stop our conversation for a moment because I have realised that I have made a judgement here without having enough information?' (This allows you to seek further information before proceeding.) Or, you might say: 'I am sorry, but I need to back-track here, because your response has made me realise that I have not given you an example of what I mean.' (This would allow you to provide the other person with an illustration of your reasoning.)

Table 4.4 illustrates the theory resources that a leader can draw on when they recognise that the conversation is not leading to a productive result because the dialogue is underpinned by values that are defensive.

Several skills have been suggested as the means for achieving reflection-in-action involving double-loop learning. Seemingly simple yet extremely challenging rules of thumb can be applied to generate valid information in a bilateral way. Cardno (1998a, 2001a) has proposed the Triple I approach which uses the prompts information, illustration and inquiry with a constant consideration of emotions to bring productive values into play. It is intended to promote reflection-in-action by encouraging the leader to stop or slow down in mid-action as they move through the steps because this allows them to examine whether their theory-in-use is consistent with a productive model. Argyris (1993) and many others with an interest in generative learning (such as Senge, 1990) propose ways in which the ladder of inference can be used as a tool to implement a theory-in-use that is productive. Each rung of the ladder that one is conscious of climbing can be used as a point to stop and change direction. Argyris (1993) reminds us that most of our inferences are decided in milliseconds and this is counterproductive to any notion of reflection-in-action that demands a slowing down of thinking and acting. Hence, using the ladder model to remind one to go down to the source of evidence (the pool of data) at the bottom of the ladder regularly acts as a mechanism for slowing down the thinking and action to make room for reflection. This is essential if we wish to reflect in action as a precursor to changing both values and action in mid-conversation.

Table 4.4 Theory resources for reflection-in-action

Self-evaluation critical questions about defensive (single-loop learning) values	Self-evaluation critical questions about productive (double-loop learning) values
Are my actions being guided by my wish to win? Have I decided beforehand the direction and conclusion of this discussion? Am I open to this conversation taking a direction that is not predetermined by me? Am I concerned about upsetting the other person but reluctant to reveal this? Am I avoiding raising issues that will lead to conflict surfacing? Have I designed this conversation so that I can maintain control?	Are my actions being guided by a wish to get and give the information needed for both of us to understand our concerns and positions regarding the issue? Am I genuinely prepared to share control with the other person? – Control of the direction of the conversation – Control of the generation of solutions Am I willing to monitor the implementation of solutions jointly with the other person?
Self-evaluation critical questions about defensive strategies	**Self-evaluation critical questions about productive strategies**
Why am I not disclosing my assumptions? Why am I failing to check assumptions that the other person is making? Why am I failing to ask the other person to explain their reasoning? Why am I communicating my messages in a mixed or indirect way? Why am I using questioning in a closed way to control the conversation?	Am I communicating my assumptions (disclosing and explaining my reasoning) so that the other person can respond? Am I encouraging the other person to disclose and explain their assumptions and reasoning? Am I being forthright? Am I asking questions to genuinely seek information?

Creating a dilemma-management culture (organisational learning)

Schein (2010) asserts that culture is closely related to the way in which an organisation or group goes about solving its problems. If an organisation is capable of detecting and correcting errors, it is developing capacity for organisational learning (Argyris and Schön, 1996) which is a matter of individual learning that can become embedded in the norms of an organisation and thus create a learning culture. Leaders play a key role in modelling such learning and transferring norms associated with the effective resolution of dilemmas to the culture of the organisation. The concepts of organisational culture and organisational learning are based on a fundamental premise of organisational memory that is carried by individuals and taught to new members of the group. Thus, for dilemma management to become embedded in the way the organisation attends to complex problems it needs to be taught as both theory and skills to all members of the organisation, both those who lead and those dependent on effective leadership practice, for the health and success of the organisation as a whole.

Embedding the notion of and the values of organisational learning within a school's culture of problem-solving is neither quick nor easy. This does not make the aspiration to create a learning culture any less important. In fact, of all the conditions that an educational leader can influence or create, I strongly believe that laying the foundation for the organisation to learn through an understanding of dilemmas and how they can be managed is a goal worth pursuing – however many learning challenges arise (Cardno, 2010). It is only through commitment to utilise the skills of productive conversations in everyday situations that a sense of how this is the 'right' way to deal with a complex problem will start to pervade the thinking and behaviour of the members of an organisation. It will become a cultural norm, continually strengthened and valued only through practice, practice and more practice, that is underpinned by a sound knowledge of the theory base.

CHAPTER FIVE

MANAGING AND DEVELOPING PROFESSIONAL PERFORMANCE

Building productive relationships

A fundamental tension between the developmental and accountability purposes of performance appraisal creates leadership dilemmas. Leaders manage these dilemmas by paying simultaneous attention to organisational and relational concerns. Productive rather than defensive dialogue achieves the resolution of these complex problems. A holistic approach to professional development enables leaders at all levels in the organisation to acquire the knowledge and skills needed to resolve dilemmas through productive dialogue.

Managing performance

Educational leaders can influence the direction and effectiveness of an organisation if they focus their activity on solving problems that act as barriers to improving student achievement. When they make the supervision and evaluation of teaching and teachers (performance appraisal) a priority this is likely to have an impact on student learning. In the rhetoric that surrounds the imperative for appraisal of professional performance in educational settings, there is consistent reference to the purpose of appraisal being the improvement of teaching and learning. This is underpinned by two aims:

- making teachers accountable for their performance; and
- using appraisal information for staff development and progression.

As the prime educational or instructional leader in the organisation, a principal is expected to employ performance appraisal as a mechanism for improving teaching and learning. Yet, it is interesting to note the international concerns that are expressed about the very loose linkage between the appraisal activities of principals as instructional leaders and improved student learning (see, for example, Ellett and Teddlie, 2003). A study by Sinnema and Robinson (2007) also shows that only a very small percentage of teachers discussed the relationship between a particular aspect of their teaching and student learning during appraisal discussions. Most of these discussions appeared to be focused on goals that had little or nothing specifically to do with student learning. Leaders who are committed to making a difference to student learning outcomes should heed the messages in the literature that point to the value of this activity when its focus is firmly fixed on evaluating and improving teaching and learning.

Both the organisation and the individual benefit from staff performance appraisal because it can lead to affirmation that performance expectations are being met, and to the identification of areas for improvement. It has dual purposes in that it provides a means of demonstrating accountability and a means for targeting development needs. 'Appraisal' is a complex evaluative process involving a number of activities. In essence, it involves participants in a continuous conversation about performance data, which provides a basis for making judgements and considering what needs to be improved. This conversation begins when a staff member enters the school and is continued through formal and informal processes which examine performance, and provide feedback and the opportunity for professional development under an umbrella of what is termed 'performance management'.

Performance management

Macky and Johnson (2000) remind us that the term 'performance management' has several meanings attached to it. It emerges from the language of the human resources management (HRM) movement that was evident in business management from the 1970s onwards. From one perspective performance management has a narrow meaning that is synonymous with a performance appraisal process requiring five fundamental activities. According to Armstrong (2000, pp. 17, 18) these are:

- role definition;
- performance agreement (or contract);
- personal development plan;

- managing performance throughout the year; and
- performance review.

Another perspective defines performance management as a very broad set of activities that spans the organisation's relationship with an individual from their entry to the time they exit the organisation. Rudman (2002) describes performance as the effectiveness of focused behaviour, that is, behaviour focused on doing a job in the context of specific objectives. The behaviours or activities that constitute a job must be set out in a *job description*, together with an indication of the expectations that are held of the particular person performing the job, so that the standards to be met or the results to be achieved are clear from the outset and are related to a specific context or situation. From the perspective of the individual, performance management is built around answers to two basic questions which we all have as employees:

1. What is the job that you want me to do?
2. How well am I doing the job?

This view of performance management presents it as an integrated and diverse set of organisational activities that are aimed at achieving strategic organisational ends. The breadth of this concept, which locates appraisal and development as central elements of a system, is shown in Table 5.1.

Table 5.1 Elements in a performance management system

- Strategic personnel planning
- Operational personnel planning
- The recruitment, selection and appointment of staff
- The remuneration of staff
- The induction and initial monitoring of staff
- The appraisal of staff
- The professional development of staff
- The promotion and reward of staff
- The discipline of staff
- The dismissal of staff
- The exit of staff from the organisation

It is this conception of performance management that is common to most education settings. Performance appraisal is one of the three personnel management functions that are inseparably central to performance management (see shaded section in Table 5.1). These three functions, of induction, ongoing appraisal and related staff development, define the scope of performance appraisal. They should *not* be viewed in isolation from the other functions, because they are all closely connected and interlinked in an effective performance management system.

Fundamentally, effective performance appraisal rests on the mutual agreement of the appraiser and the appraisee about what is expected in terms of performance, opportunity to receive feedback about performance and to improve this. In many international contexts school teachers and managers are provided with clear direction regarding expectations for quality of teaching and managing through professional standards that are developed by the profession and employers in tandem. Professional standards for principals, middle managers and teachers may be found in several international settings including New Zealand. In England and Wales for example, the Department for Education and Skills (2004) has promulgated national standards for headteachers and teachers. In Australia and the USA professional standards are an embedded feature of professional accountability in performance management at both country-wide and district or state level. However, unlike the school sector, higher education professionals do not appear to have developed formal professional standards, but they utilise position and job descriptions in a similar way.

An integrated view of appraisal

Many people appear to have a limited view of what appraisal actually involves. I have often heard people say things like, 'I am having my appraisal tomorrow', or, 'I really must get ready for the Deputy Principal's appraisal'. What has happened, I believe, is that these people have understood (or actually misunderstood) a formal review meeting or appraisal interview to constitute the whole of 'appraisal'. This is a very common situation in my experience, and is mentioned at the outset because it illustrates how easy it is for the appraisal process to be reduced to rare opportunities for some formal dialogue about performance. Appraisal is *not* an occasional formal meeting, although such meetings are an integral part of the process. It is a process that is linked to almost all personnel management functions – in a performance management system. Furthermore, it involves a very specific range of essential activities. These activities are listed below, to give an overview of the scope of appraisal.

Performance appraisal involves:

- the development and negotiation of a working, dynamic job description and/or performance agreement in a partnership between the appraiser and appraisee;
- clarification of how the professional standards for teachers and managers (in the case of schools and kindergartens) are linked to expectations;
- supervision of performance through regular monitoring, classroom observation, data gathering and meetings in which there is dialogue about performance and its improvement;
- formal occasions to review performance on the basis of databased judge-

ments made by self and others in the framework of the job description;
- coaching, mentoring and support for professional development;
- consideration of constraints that might be affecting performance and efforts to remedy these;
- planning for development and for changes in the job.

All of these activities create a context in which the purposes of appraisal can be achieved. Appraisal does not fulfil a single purpose nor is it a single activity. It is a comprehensive and complex process involving multiple purposes and activities that are integrated to benefit both the organisation and the individual. An effective approach to appraisal transparently integrates the dual accountability and developmental purposes.

Dual purposes of appraisal – accountability and development

For appraisal to be an effective form of evaluation, it should encompass both its developmental (formative) and accountability (summative) aspects (Cardno and Piggot-Irvine, 1997). Therefore, it should include a focus on teachers and the organisation being accountable for their performance, and a focus on how the organisation and the individuals who work within it can develop. This integrated approach sees appraisal happening all the way along a continuum:

Integrated appraisal goals

Accountability goals ←—————————————————————→ Development goals

Many attempts to introduce effective appraisal systems appear to have failed because they make a strong distinction between values that underpin accountability and values that promote development. Furthermore, these systems need to adopt a clear focus on the overarching aim of appraisal in educational settings, which is, the improvement of teaching and learning. In order to achieve this aim, the approach to all activities related to appraisal should focus on making a connection between teaching and management practices and student learning.

In order to adopt an appraisal system that integrates both accountability and development with a focus on improving teaching and learning, that system must have several essential elements. In this integrated approach, therefore, there is:

- reciprocal accountability between the manager and the staff member;
- concern with individual performance based on negotiated and agreed expectations for both accountability and development;
- goal setting that is specifically related to teaching and learning;

- development needs identification and alignment at the individual, departmental, and organisational level;
- developmental activity strengthened by expert mentoring and coaching;
- hierarchy (management) support, with strategic and operational resource links;
- open acknowledgement of contentious issues and joint effort to find solutions to problems of practice;
- no comparative element; and
- data-based judgement (through the collection of evaluation material including information about student learning outcomes).

Learning case for reflection: analysing accountability and development features in your appraisal system

It is to be hoped that your appraisal system will be regularly reviewed. If appraisal is to be an effective mechanism for improving learning and teaching and achieving both accountability and development purposes, then it requires leadership attention to what the system demands, how it works in practice and whether it is meeting its stated purposes. In a workshop with the senior management team of a secondary school, I used the questions below to check understanding of how the current appraisal system was meeting their needs in terms of both accountability and development.

Accountability

How do unit heads demonstrate their accountability for implementing an appraisal system?

Is the format of current staff job descriptions adequate for documenting accountability?

What other reports achieve accountability in the appraisal system?

To whom do staff account for their performance?

Is there confusion about limits or levels of accountability?

Who is accountable for the effectiveness of a staff development programme?

How does dialogue about accountability build trust?

Development

Are individual and team development goals linked to teaching and learning?

Is there an annual programme for professional development?

How does the programme link with professional development needs identified in an individual's appraisal process?

(Continues)

(Continued)

How could the links between professional development and staff appraisal be made more explicit?

How is the organisation's strategic plan linked to department and individual plans for development?

How are individual development goals monitored and reported?

How does dialogue about development build productive relationships?

When appraisal occurs in a system that integrates accountability and development in a framework of improving teaching and learning, the key activity that must occur is *dialogue* at all points of enacting the system. It is through productive dialogue about establishing expectations, observing practice, setting and monitoring development goals and reporting achievement that possibilities for change are explored. If the participants in appraisal are aware of the tensions and dilemmas that might arise, and develop the skills to consider and alter theories of action that might hinder change, then they are capable of forging the sort of productive relationships that are needed to improve practice and consequently improve learning outcomes for students. It is an educational leader's responsibility to establish the learning conditions that make such change possible through professional development practices that incrementally engage all participants in appraisal processes that can build productive relationships (Cardno, 2010).

An appraisal cycle

When all the elements of appraisal are assembled in an annual cycle of appraisal-related activity it should be possible to achieve a number of purposes that span accountability and development. In the example of an appraisal cycle (Figure 5.1) there are three essential aims that are accomplished through meetings.

In a calendar year, a normal appraisal cycle would start with an *initial meeting* in order to confirm performance expectations, that is, the nature of the job. This is usually done by confirming the job description or professional standards that apply, if appropriate. It is also a chance to confirm agreement about a development plan that contains objectives for improvement. Because in schools, the focus should be on teaching and learning goals, the individual objectives set by teachers should be about this. The appraiser should arrange further regular formal meeting times throughout the year. In general, three meetings are considered adequate. However, as data are collected, analysed and discussed, additional and perhaps less formal

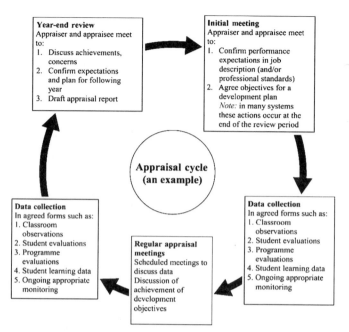

Figure 5.1 *A cycle of appraisal activity*

meetings will also occur. The cycle depicts ongoing data collection that becomes the basis for dialogue between the appraiser and appraisee. If there is opportunity for dialogue throughout the cycle of appraisal and this leads to adjustments and further monitoring of practice then this is productive – resulting in 'no surprises' at the time for formal discussion at the end of the cycle. A final appraisal meeting for a year-end review brings the cycle to a close, but it is also closely linked to a roll-on of activity that starts the new cycle and is hence seamless in this way.

Data collecting takes a variety of forms in the context of performance appraisal as the following examples illustrate:

Classroom observation
The most common form of collecting evidence of teaching practice is for the manager to arrange to observe classroom practice. Teachers in all types of institutions are familiar with this type of data collection event. It requires a pre-observation agreement of intent, observation record keeping and feedback in a post-observation conference. A higher education example is a Learning and Teaching Advisor conducting an observation of postgraduate students participating in a groupwork exercise.

Student evaluation of teaching
These data capture 'student voice' and are typically used with older students in secondary school and higher education settings. Institutions of higher education often require the evaluation by students of every course they have enrolled in.

Document evaluation
Teaching and learning documents (teaching and lesson plans, student achievement data, reports of student learning and achievement) provide evidence for conversations about performance.

Learning case for reflection: I do not like surprises!

Thomas was really excited at the start of the year to take up his first position as head of the maths department in a small secondary school. He was particularly looking forward to working with his new team of three colleagues and felt he had a real obligation to them in relation to his role as their appraiser. Because he was keen to get things right, Thomas carefully read the school policy on staff appraisal and was pretty confident about how to proceed because in the previous year he had attended a two-day workshop on effective appraisal practice. So, he embarked on a schedule of regular meetings and reciprocal classroom observations and hoped for the best. By the time he had his second formal meeting with the most experienced staff member on his team, he was aware that somehow he was not 'hitting it off' with Connie. Her student results from the previous year were outstanding and she had agreed to mentor the newest teacher in the team. All very positive, yet Thomas felt she was not happy with his leadership for some reason and was worried that in spite of dropping hints about his willingness to listen to anything that concerned her, he was not hearing what he needed to. At his own appraisal meeting with the deputy principal (DP) a month later, Thomas was surprised to hear the DP relay to him the principal's concern that the maths department was not a happy place. Instantly defensive, he retaliated with his concern that the DP and the principal could have informed him of this much earlier so that it could have been acted on. He had a hunch, after all, that something was not right. For Thomas, the failure of his own appraiser to let him know about something that was being discussed at senior management level without his knowledge had created an unpleasant 'surprise'.

This kind of scenario is common to appraisal practice. What may have been a simple need to be kept informed has actually escalated to a level of complexity that will take some unravelling. I believe that there is a leadership dilemma tucked away here that is owned by the deputy principal who appraises Thomas.

1 If you were the deputy principal in this case, what might the dilemma be for you?

How should you proceed?

2 If you were Thomas in this case, what might the dilemma be for you?

(Continues)

(Continued)

How should you proceed?

**3 If you were the experienced teacher (Connie) in this situation
what might the dilemma be for you?**

How should you proceed?

Developing performance

Professional development is a corollary of performance appraisal. If we
know how well we are performing our job and how well students are learning, then we might be in a position to pinpoint the areas in our performance
that could be improved. The literature that deals with effective educational
leadership clearly signals the importance of developing staff professionally.
Several studies indicate the considerable effect on student learning brought
about through active leadership of professional development by the principal (see for example, Blase and Blase, 2000). This rich literature base
confirms the significance of the principal's role in creating conditions conducive to effective professional learning and development for staff. As
Robinson et al. state:

> Principals have a key role to play in increasing the prevalence of pedagogi-
> cal leadership practices in their schools. They do this by endorsing the
> leadership of teachers with relevant expertise, creating a culture of collective
> responsibility for student achievement and well being, and leading and par-
> ticipating in teacher professional learning. (2009, p. 207)

While educational leaders of small organisations may be able to personally
participate in and provide professional development, this is not a realistic
scenario for larger schools and in particular for secondary and higher education settings (Dempster et al., 2009). In these larger settings, leaders
influence practice more indirectly and strategically. They can do this most
effectively through a holistic approach.

Holistic professional development

Educational leaders significantly influence the development of people and,
consequently, improve the effectiveness of an organisation when they harness the potential of professional development in a holistic way (Cardno,
2005). In the holistic model that is outlined here, development is strongly
linked to the achievement of strategic goals, is underpinned by sound prin-

ciples of educational leadership at all levels and, above all, is considered as a planned and cohesive programme with the process of performance appraisal placed at its centre. This may require changing the way educational leaders think about what constitutes professional development. A scrutiny of some current practices reveals many advances but also some shortcomings in school settings.

A snapshot of current practice

In school-based research and consultancy work with New Zealand schools, I regularly encounter great similarities in the organisation of provision of professional development. This broad analysis of experience identifies commendable aspects of practice. In both primary and secondary schools there is evidence of considered co-ordination of professional development activity. In most secondary schools a senior- or middle-level manager is usually charged with responsibility for overseeing a budget and programme. Primary school principals commonly take on (and sometimes delegate) this responsibility. An increasing emphasis on school-based change projects rather than one-off training events is another positive feature (Education Review Office, 2000a). The critical challenge for schools is how they go about achieving links between the evaluation of practice and its development through, for example, performance appraisal (Cardno and Piggot-Irvine, 1997). Many of the current efforts to co-ordinate professional development fall short of a holistic conception of this vital aspect of educational leadership. Some examples have been selected to showcase these ineffective approaches:

1. *The smörgåsbord approach.* In this approach, schools set aside a budget for professional development and staff choose what they wish to do from a broad array of advertised events. The approach is associated with notions of off-site in-service training courses for individual teachers, usually of one-day duration and often funded by the Ministry of Education in relation to curriculum contracts. The values guiding this approach are that staff have a right to a share of professional development resourcing and that they should be able to choose what they want to do.
2. *The do-it-all approach.* This approach is characterised by the belief that the school should respond to all opportunities for professional development, especially those offered to support the implementation of a plethora of improvement initiatives that are arguably part of a government-driven agenda. As a consequence many schools, concerned that they will 'miss out' if they do not register to participate, have chosen to involve teachers in too much professional development, resulting in overload and disenchantment with what should be a positive and rewarding experience.

In the above approaches, professional development is usually viewed as something that must be done because it has been budgeted for or can be cheaply accessed. It is often seen as an 'add on' and its connection to school change initiatives is seldom discernible. New thinking about the very nature of professional development is apparent in a marked language shift that has occurred in recent times. One example of this is evident in New Zealand where usage of the term 'in-service training' (Education Review Office, 2000a) has now been replaced with the term 'professional learning and development' (Education Review Office, 2009a). The international literature strongly represents the notion of teacher learning being central to a concept of professional development in educational organisations (Darling-Hammond and Richardson, 2009). While acknowledging the critical importance of teacher learning, professional development needs to be viewed as having a wider scope. Guskey's (2000) definition of professional development as 'those processes and activities designed to enhance the professional knowledge, skills and attitudes of educators so that they might, in turn, improve the learning of students' (p. 16) does this. It goes beyond the notion of teacher development to embrace management development, acknowledging that student learning can be improved through direct and indirect influences.

Reconceptualising professional development holistically

In suggesting that an approach to professional development can be more holistic, I am advocating a reconsideration of its scope to ensure that it:

- caters for teachers and managers;
- meets school-wide, team and individual needs;
- is strongly linked to the achievement of strategic goals;
- is underpinned by sound principles of educational leadership; and
- is organised as a planned and cohesive programme.

The model depicted in Figure 5.2 provides a conceptual framework that educational leaders can use to frame their thinking when they design a holistic programme of professional development for an organisation. According to Pritchard and Marshall (2002) there appears to be no particular model of professional development that has been 'verified by research as the most effective for schools' (p. 117). This holistic model for planning a professional development programme is relevant for all education sectors. It comprises three fundamental elements that interact with professional development:

- sound educational leadership to underpin the model;
- effective performance appraisal at the centre; and
- strategic management and review as an overarching leadership activity to guide and evaluate planning.

Figure 5.2 *A model of holistic professional development (source: C. Cardno, 2005, p. 296, 'Leadership and professional development: the quiet revolution',* International Journal of Educational Management, *19(4), with the permission of Emerald Publishing Group)*

In addition, the model suggests that at least four dimensions of professional development should feature in an effective programme:

- school development;
- curriculum development;
- management development; and
- personal development.

It should be noted that the equal emphasis on each quadrant as illustrated is not intended to be fixed but shifts according to strategic and immediate priorities. Furthermore, as the model continues to be tested in practice, further dimensions might well emerge.

The infrastructure for a holistic approach

Educational leadership

An appreciation of context underpins the model. Whether the context is a higher education department, or a school or early childhood centre, an appropriate form of *educational leadership* is required to initiate and support change through professional development. Research shows that effective educational leaders create a culture of learning that supports professional growth (Cardno, 2010; Scott et al., 2008). As Day (1999) reminds us, the leader's ability to create a learning culture for both adults and students is a critical variable in determining whether staff view professional development as just another demand or whether it becomes integral to the way the school community views long-term improvement. The model assumes that educational leadership will be practised by several people, spreading this task beyond the preserve of the senior leader. Leaders of large organisations need to take heed of newer and purportedly more effective forms of disbursed educational leadership that rely on middle managers to play the role of leading teacher and expect principals to be 'leaders of leaders' (Childs-Bowen et al., 2000, p. 30). This means that school leaders should invest energy in developing the capacity of others to influence the critically important issues of teacher quality and student achievement.

Research into teachers' perspectives of effective educational leadership reveals that teachers value school leaders who promote professional growth and facilitate dialogue about professional practice (Blase and Blase, 2000). Conversations about practice should be embedded in activity related to performance appraisal. When difficult situations arise and leaders recognise these as dilemmas, they need to be addressed using the skills of productive dialogue.

Enacting educational leadership in a way that directly or indirectly influences both teacher and student learning includes:

- knowing how to create conditions that make it possible to recognise and resolve leadership dilemmas through productive dialogue;
- leading others to lead by delegating to them (particularly middle managers) the responsibility to improve teacher quality and student achievement;
- providing an infrastructure to sustain a *system for performance appraisal* that identifies needs, meets goals of accountability and development and is linked to strategic initiatives that are in turn, linked to teaching and learning;
- dealing with immediate and future needs through a planned, professional development programme that is strategically aligned with the school's vision.

Performance appraisal

At the heart of any effective professional development programme is the means by which we get to know what needs to be improved and why, before we set about the task of deciding how we will do this. In short, appraisal is about being able to demonstrate accountability. It is also about being able to evaluate and make judgements about performance so that developmental objectives can be set and achieved. An effective appraisal system gains staff commitment and is valued. It allows colleagues to engage in dialogue that leads to learning and change, and is the pivot for mounting a professional development programme that can meet the needs of individuals, teams and the whole school. This is achieved when appraisal activity generates information and insights that guide decision-making about professional development. Leaders, who are expected to nurture and communicate the vision and long-term plans, should be able to rely on appraisal information to judge the capacity of the organisation to achieve these.

For performance appraisal to be effective it should achieve four things:

1. Provide honest and objective feedback.
2. Make dialogue about improvement possible.
3. Identify professional development needs.
4. Bring about agreed and desired change.

Learning case for reflection: making relationships discussable

Sashi, who is the principal of a primary school, believes that the appraisal system is generally working well and is valued by staff because, in addition to many opportunities for informal feedback, they have recourse to formal occasions for dialogue that is focused on a variety of data collected at various points in the appraisal cycle. The principal himself appraises Millie, the deputy principal, and three team leaders, who in turn appraise the staff in their learning level teams. Millie was instrumental in setting up the system and overviews its implementation. Sashi intends to undertake a review of the system in the coming months and is having a meeting with Millie to consider the way in which they will go about sharing this task and what they need to find out about the effectiveness of their current system. Recently, Sashi has become aware of a change in Millie's attitude towards helping him with initiatives which in the past she willingly and enthusiastically engaged in. He has not talked to her about this and hopes that she will not create difficulties about participating in the proposed review.

Millie has a very different view about the way the appraisal system is working. First, she has not had a good experience herself because the principal has cancelled two appraisal meetings recently and has not yet written her appraisal report for the previous year or confirmed her development plan. He is not demonstrating a commitment to the practices he expects of others, in Millie's view. Second, tensions between herself and the principal have contributed to a relationship that is somewhat shaky at present, to say the least. Millie does not feel valued (the lack of attention to her own appraisal by the principal has made her feel resentful) and she finds it

(Continues)

(Continued)

difficult to talk to the principal about administrative problems because he is often implicated in these. Consequently, trust is being eroded and Millie is currently actively looking for positions elsewhere.

This is undoubtedly a leadership dilemma for the principal. On the one hand, he wants to be confident about the effectiveness of the appraisal system, yet, on the other hand, he knows that the deputy is a key player in this and he is uncertain about her commitment and the level of trust in their relationship. It is also a dilemma for the deputy because she monitors the system, on the one hand, and, on the other hand, believes the principal himself is undermining the integrity of the system and she is loath to tell him this directly.

This is a particularly difficult scenario in terms of dilemma management because at the heart of this dilemma is a relationship issue for both players. It is particularly difficult for the deputy to broach the relationship issue with her superior. There is a power imbalance that makes her reluctant to do this. On both sides there is a lack of trust, which will be exacerbated as time goes on unless one of them takes a courageous stance and actually raises the relationship within their dialogue.

1 **What might make it possible for the principal to make their relationship part of a productive dialogue?**

2 **What defensive barriers would Sashi need to surmount in order to do this?**

3 **What might make it possible for Millie to make their relationship part of a productive dialogue?**

4 **What defensive barriers would she need to surmount in order to do this?**

Strategic management and review

An overarching concern in establishing a professional development programme should be the extent to which the long-term goals of the organisation both influence, and are influenced by, the development of staff. Thinking and catering strategically for the management of human resources (Macky and Johnson, 2000), including their development, is something that leaders cannot ignore. In fact, the importance of strategic resourcing as a key dimension of educational leadership is highlighted in literature that points to decisions about staff quality being the most crucial decisions a school leader can make in terms of strategic human resource management (Miles and Frank, 2008; Robinson et al., 2009).

The ability of educational leaders to engage in strategic management (by paying attention to both strategic planning for the long term and the implementation of annual operational plans) is increasingly viewed as a central aspect of effective leadership (Preedy et al., 2003). A further expectation is that planning will be informed and shaped by the results of regular reviews at both the strategic and operational levels. A holistic programme of professional development that draws on the recommendations of systematic and comprehensive reviews of programmes and policy has potential to impact on strategic improvement.

Balancing dimensions of professional development

Balanced professional development programmes pay attention to all four dimensions in the model (see Figure 5.2). The two dimensions in the top half of the circle – curriculum development and school development – are possibly the ones that always have and still feature most significantly as professional development foci. The two dimensions in the bottom half of the circle – personal development and management development – are paid far less attention in the views of several cohorts of postgraduate students who I have approached to undertake reviews of their organisational practice.

Dimension 1: curriculum development

This dimension is related to both large national policy imperatives and smaller teacher-initiated efforts to improve curriculum delivery and assessment – in other words it relates to teacher pedagogical learning about teaching and learning (Timperley et al., 2007). It has traditionally and currently been accorded a very high priority both nationally and locally, so much so that it invariably dominates the way professional development is planned as the largest or only focus. While this is rightly so and it is essential that teacher professional learning and development should focus predominantly on pedagogical matters related to the core task of teaching and learning, it should not subsume other dimensions.

Dimension 2: school development

The inclusion of school-wide development initiatives in a professional development programme serves to broaden the scope of what professional development means. In general this involves an organisational development approach to initiating and sustaining a change strategy. Groups of teachers and managers in schools can engage in a cyclic process of problem identification, planned change and evaluation akin to action learning with the help of outside facilitators (Cardno, 1996). Action research is increasingly valued as a vehicle for collaborative and critical evaluation and change of practice in relation to school-wide management (Cardno, 2003). On a cautionary note, school development initiatives should be reserved for major innovations and interventions. Leaders should not aspire to foster demanding engagement in these substantial change efforts without consideration of the time and resources needed to achieve change effectively. They should, however, be knowledgeable about systematic approaches to change and able to judge when it is appropriate to apply them.

Dimension 3: personal development

This dimension is related to the need for both teachers and managers to acknowledge and develop the skills that enable effective communication and problem-solving in everyday encounters with other people. The set of skills related to strengthening interpersonal relationships within the organisation is crucial. As patterns of educational leadership change to accommodate more distributed forms, the range of management tasks, such as performance appraisal, become more widely shared. As middle-level leaders become more accountable for appraising the performance of staff in their teams, they need to develop in their people the critical skills for managing productive relationships. Appraisers and appraisees need opportunities to engage with a curriculum for dilemma management that includes the skills of productive dialogue. These are the skills needed to participate as the managed or the managers in the performance appraisal activities related to supervising, evaluating, mentoring and coaching, giving and receiving performance feedback and solving performance problems (Cardno, 2007).

The development of personal skills also takes on particular significance when people become responsible for the achievements of those they manage. It could be said that the development of personal skills in relation to any form of management or leadership development is essential. In particular, a focus on the self-development of managers to build their capacity for self-awareness and self-management is viewed as a precursor to becoming interpersonally aware and able to manage others. Goleman (1998) has assembled these elements of personal and interpersonal skill learning in a framework of what he calls the *emotional intelligence* quotient, which can be measured to determine capability for managing self and others with emotional awareness. This concept has a bridging ability to closely link our intrapersonal awareness capability with capability in building and harnessing productive interpersonal relationships in our work with and through others.

Dimension 4: management development

All staff in management positions should be motivated and supported to access the body of information, theory and skills needed to work with and through others to accomplish organisational goals. Around the world there is evidence that education systems have recognised and responded to the need for leadership and management development of aspiring, newly appointed and experienced school principals (Wildy et al., 2009). For other managers at senior and middle management levels a picture of inconsistency emerges. As Bush (2009) asserts, some countries such as Singapore cater formally for middle manager development. North American settings vary in requiring qualifications for assistant and deputy principals but, in general, the preparation of mid-level managers for their roles and their ongoing development once appointed is a major area of concern. There is now strong research evidence that supports a focus on developing mid-level leaders as well as principals to increase the indirect effects of instructional leadership on student learning (Seashore Louis et al., 2010).

Leaders at this middle level are significant players in the business of creating and maintaining effective organisations. They are also the likely recipients in any distribution of educational leadership or its delegation in terms of both authority and accountability. By far the most unrecognised dimension of professional development in school programmes appears in my experience to be that of management development. I believe the same may be true in many higher education institutions. An appreciation at the highest level of organisational leadership of the nature and benefits of this dimension in relation to developing other leaders in the organisation is possibly the most crucial aspect that needs to change in thinking about the concept of professional development holistically.

Features of management development

Historically, management development is portrayed as a special form of professional development. It is related to the specialised body of knowledge and skills that emerges from the discipline of generic management (Woodall and Winstanley, 1998) and the associated field of educational administration, management and leadership. This, in turn, draws on concepts from education, philosophy, sociology, psychology and business management. Management development assists the personal and professional growth of managers so that they develop competencies and cognitive capabilities to perform their role effectively. In most cases there are three major demands placed on managers:

1. the management of people for whom they are responsible;

2. the management of systems (which invariably also involve people in their operation); and
3. the management of self (because so much of the work is about inter-actions with others that reflect one's own behaviour).

Management (or leadership) development is a broad concept that embraces a number of elements and is impacted upon by a number of agencies in school systems. It incorporates management training, management education and management support (Rudman, 2002).

Management training This is described as a process by which managers develop hands-on or skill development through practice which is guided by formal structured means. In education settings it has also become synony-mous with the notion of in-service courses – short, practical training sessions which individuals attend – usually delivered off site and often unconnected with wider school development issues. For example, senior staff might par-ticipate in a one-off training course related to time management and delegation. Training activity usually has an individual focus, although there are several schools that employ consultants to deliver tailor-made school-based training events in management-related areas such as team development or planning.

Management education This is the term used to describe the type of learn-ing that takes place in a structured, formal, institutional framework and leads to a qualification. For example, in many countries master's and doctoral level qualifications are offered in educational administration, educational manage-ment and educational leadership. In some settings, such as the USA, a master's-level qualification in the specialised field of educational administra-tion is a requirement for appointment to a senior leadership position in a school.

Management support This refers to opportunities both on the job and off the job that lead to professional growth. But the most effective management support is often delivered in the one-to-one processes of coaching and men-toring and relies on experienced mangers being able and willing to assist new managers to reflect on their practice and learn.

- *On-the-job support opportunities* are those that the organisation can pro-vide in various forms, but the coaching that occurs in a formal relationship between the manager and the person they report to in an appraisal process is deemed to be the most relevant and effective learning oppor-tunity. In addition to coaching, job rotation and promotion also provide opportunities for learning, understudying roles and succession planning.

- *Off-the-job support opportunities* are those that increase learning opportunities for a manager. Mentoring, which is a form of collegial guidance less formal than coaching, can be provided by colleagues inside or outside the organisation. Management mentors are senior, experienced staff who are willing to build a learning relationship with a junior colleague without the formal need to judge their performance. Other activities include membership of local, national and international educational management associations; attendance at professional and research conferences that include papers on leadership and management issues; subscribing to educational management periodicals to keep abreast of research and best practice.

Management development cannot occur in a culture that is unaware of what it is and unprepared to resource it so that it can flourish. It is an aspect of professional development that demands time and money to demonstrate that there is a real commitment to growing management capability across the organisation. Management development is not the preserve of the principal or senior leadership alone, yet it must be recognised that an enlightened principal or dean has the power to open doors for others.

Leading and actively managing professional development

Educational leadership, variously termed professional, instructional or academic leadership, includes responsibility for the 'professional learning culture' (Day, 1999, p. 83). We know from the research conducted by Blase and Blase (2000) that teachers value educational leaders who promote and participate in professional development. The role of educational leaders in leading professional learning is a central focus of a synthesis of best evidence on teacher professional learning and development (Timperley et al., 2007). Across a number of studies, these researchers found that leadership played a very important role that took different forms. They say:

> We have identified four different roles that leaders may adopt: developing a vision of how teaching might impact on student outcomes, managing the professional learning environment, promoting a culture of learning within the school, and developing the leadership of others in relation to curriculum or pedagogy (Timperley et al., 2007, p. 196).

These are important messages for leaders to take on board in their efforts to make professional development effective, and for effective professional development to have outcomes for teachers that result in improved outcomes for learners. Leadership activity also relays messages about what is important. When systems and processes for performance appraisal and professional development are well established and well operated, they shape the culture of the organisation.

One significant way in which leaders can indirectly influence student learning is to nurture this sort of culture. To do this they must create conditions that are conducive to organisational learning and the management of leadership dilemmas which, if resolved productively, can in turn lead to an improved learning environment for students. If leaders pay attention to the often ignored dimensions of personal and management development and use these dimensions to increase the capability of all staff to engage in productive dialogue about problems of practice, this could benefit everyone in the education community.

CHAPTER SIX

MANAGING DECISION-MAKING COLLABORATIVELY

Building productive relationships

Collaboration in decision-making can occur at a macro organisational level involving teachers and the wider community in making key organisational decisions. At the micro level, leaders and managers have opportunities to interact with individuals and teams in collaborative and productive ways to solve problems of practice. In an organisational culture where collaborative decision-making is the norm there is likely to be a high level of trust in leaders and greater possibility for complex problems like leadership dilemmas to be managed through productive dialogue that is inherently collaborative.

The core work of educational leaders: solving problems and making decisions

Leaders and managers in education systems and organisations constantly engage in decision-making to solve problems of policy and practice. Solving these problems constitutes the 'daily bread' of their work. Decision-making about educational problems occurs at the highest level of policy-making concerning the administration of education and the laws and regulations that shape its form and delivery. At the organisational level, governance decisions

about strategy and policy guide institutional direction and goal establishment. At all institutional management levels leaders and managers engage
daily in attempts to resolve real problems in the most effective way. In short,
managing, when it is viewed as working with and through other people to
achieve an organisation's goals, involves at its heart the activity of decision-
making. As Hoy and Miskel (2001) assert, 'decision-making is a major
responsibility of all administrators' (p. 325), it pervades all formal organisations which are in fact decision-making structures.

Some of the earliest descriptions of management place decision-making as
the central activity because it links to all other activities. For example, Peter
Drucker, in his work that defines the 'meaning of management' (1955) highlights the need for managers to make decisions in relation to every facet of their
key tasks which comprise planning, organising, monitoring, communicating
and motivating, and developing staff. Further, Drucker (1966) draws attention
to two basic kinds of decisions – generic or unique – and argues that a manager must be able to identify and then deal appropriately with a particular kind
of decision. Generic decisions belong to a general group of organisational problems and comprise the major work of the leader of a team or the organisation.
The regular, recurring and routine problems that arise out of principles, policies
and rules that an organisation has established and, in most cases, applying the
appropriate principle, policy or rule is what is required. Unique decisions are
those that call for creative decision-making in circumstances where there are no
established guidelines. Although completely unique situations are rare, they are
demanding and in these cases decision-makers need to explore all ideas that
are relevant to the problem. It is important in this kind of decision-making to
understand the very nature of problems in order to distinguish simple problems
from those that are complex and that, therefore, do not lend themselves to routine or simple solutions.

Understanding the nature of problems

Problems that require decisions to be made about their solution are of many
types. One description of a problem as 'a gap between an existing and a
desired state of affairs' is proposed by Robinson (1993. p. 25). She further elaborates on the nature of problems that are neutral and those that are negative.
Neutral problems are described as puzzles or challenges that need to be tackled. For example, a neutral problem could be related to a need to establish a
new programme to meet the specific needs of a group of learners, such as
Chinese immigrant children. Or it could be that an organisation lacks a system
for tracking staff absences. When such problems are inadequately solved they
become negative problems. This notion is also expressed by Hoy and Miskel
(2008) who say that, 'decision-making is a dynamic process that solves some
organisational problems and, in the process, often creates others' (p. 324).

Managers are expected to possess the ability to recognise and define problems. This may lead to an urge to define and solve problems quickly and superficially, most often leading to only partial solutions being found. Simple, straightforward problems may lend themselves to solutions guided by rational problem-solving behaviour, using prescribed steps in an organised way or finding answers in regulation and precedent. It is most likely, however, that managers will encounter problems that are complex, have several facets, and are often hard to define. Complex problems can be described in many ways, in contrast to simple problems.

Well-structured problems have clear solution criteria, specific information requirements and straightforward procedures for reaching a solution (Simon, 1973). They are simple, routine problems, which in turn, resonate with the problem type proposed by Drucker (1966) as needing a form of generic decision-making. Generic problems occur frequently in organisations and can normally be handled by applying the appropriate formula, rule or policy. Problem complexity, on the other hand, is evident in problems called organisational dilemmas where tensions abound (Murphy, 2007), ethical dilemmas (Cranston et al., 2006) and leadership dilemmas (Cardno, 2007). Dilemmas are problems fraught with conflict between opposing goals and, like ill-defined problems (Robinson, 1993), may be subject to multiple interpretations and solutions. Ill-structured problems can sometimes be addressed by attending to a part of the problem and transforming this into a well-structured smaller problem. Yet the larger problem may well continue to exist or recur. Drucker (1966) describes these problems that are challenging and require creative decisions as unique. Distinguishing between routine and unique problems helps the manager to avoid mistakes. One mistake is to treat a routine situation as if it were a unique event; another is to treat a new event as if it were just an old problem to which old procedures could be applied.

Managers can better understand problem complexity through awareness of these views of what problems are and the forms they take. This is especially the case in situations where their decision-making is not only failing to solve an existing problem but is leading to the creation of new ones. Decision-making and problem-solving go hand-in-hand. The terms are sometimes used interchangeably because the problems prompt the decisions.

Decision-making models

Early leadership and management theorists such as Simon (1973), who recognised that decision-making was at the heart of organisation and administration, searched for the ideals of 'correct' decision-making. Contemporary decision-making theorists admit,

> There is no best decision-making model, just as there is no best way to organize, to teach, to do research, or to do a myriad of other things. As in many complex events, the best approach is the one that best fits the circumstances (Hoy and Tartar, 2008, p. 86).

Beliefs about the rationality of both the means and the ends underpinned classical models of decision-making. It was assumed that if the leader went about the process in a controlled and systematic way, considering all the options and selecting the best alternative, this constituted good administration. The models concerned primarily with optimising (best solution finding) or with satisficing (compromising) commonly defined steps for problem recognition, analysis, solution seeking and planning action. The notion of the participation of 'others' alongside the leader in the decision-making process was completely absent in these models. They generally referred to the leader's interactions with people in terms of conflict and co-operation (Hoy and Tartar, 2008). Later models such as those proposed by Tannenbaum and Schmidt (1973) presented the management of participation in decision-making as a way of improving the quality of decisions. They also promoted participation as a means of increasing the acceptance of decisions by others within the framework of the contingency approach to decision-making (Hersey and Blanchard, 1982).

Shared decision-making

Shared decision-making is promoted widely in the literature that deals with problem-solving and decision-making in educational settings (Hoy and Tartar, 2008; Owens, 2004). Including others in collaborative decision-making processes is valuable for several reasons:

- Collaboration utilises the expertise of others and thus can lead to better decisions being made.
- Collaboration gains commitment to implementing decisions when others are involved to varying degrees.
- Collaboration is underpinned by a democratic ideal – giving prominence to the voices of all in a collective.

The literature employs several terms such as collegial decision-making, participative decision-making, and collaborative decision-making to indicate the inclusion of others. In relation to higher education settings, Bush (2011) alludes to the origin of collegial models, the British universities of Oxford and Cambridge, where collegium occurs in structures where members have equal authority to participate in decisions which are binding on all. He asserts, however, that a consequence of the rapid growth of higher educa-tion in the past two decades 'may have made it more difficult for the collegial aspects of universities to maintain their previous significance in the decision-making process' (p. 76). Generally, collegiality assumes that there will always be discussion and consensus and that power is shared, yet several aspects of what Bush (2011) describes as collegial models bear similarities to the notion of collaborative decision-making, which is also strongly aligned with values of shared decision-making proposed, for example, by Cardno (1990) and Hallinger and Heck (2010). Collaboration encompasses a wide view of par-ticipation embracing ideals of inclusion in decision-making, co-operation, working together collaboratively and the spreading or distributing of leader-ship across a number of levels, groups and individuals.

Without doubt, the notion of collaboration is an ideal, and espousals of com-mitment to a collaborative management approach are often not reflected in the theory-in-use of practices within an organisation. One research study has estab-lished a considerable gap between what co-operation and collaboration in elementary and secondary schools' practices should be to enable change and what these practices are in reality (Jenni and Mauriel, 2004). If collaborative practices are to find their way into the fabric of organisational life, it will be as a result of the commitment of leaders to the notion of including others in the decision-making and problem-solving processes. Sharing leadership itself is a further challenge for educational leaders because of the currently popular idea of viewing this as something that can be distributed among many.

Distributing leadership and management

There is now a rich literature and lively ongoing debate about the influential notion of distributing leadership beyond the boundaries of singular forms of leadership (Woods and Gronn, 2009). Spillane and Diamond (2007) assert that the notion has caught the attention of policy-makers, researchers, prac-titioners and philanthropists, and that it has come to mean many things for many people. In their view it is 'Frequently used as a synonym for demo-cratic leadership, shared leadership, collaborative leadership' (p. 1) and the idea 'acknowledges that the work of leading and managing schools involves multiple individuals' (p. 7). From a distributed perspective, leadership is stretched over the work of multiple leaders, some with formally designated positions and others who informally take responsibility for leadership. Proponents of distributed leadership claim there are many benefits. These are summarised by Woods and Gronn (2009, p. 438) as follows:

- School improvement and effectiveness are associated with democratic and participative styles of leadership.

- Organisational capability is enhanced by tapping the ideas, creativity, skills and energy which exist throughout the organisation.
- Challenges of complexity, work intensification, and the burden of leadership could be reduced if they were shared.

One strong description of the distribution of leadership is contained in seeing it as 'numerically multiple actions' (Gronn, 2003, p. 34) that are dispersed among some or all members of the organisation. Gronn asserts that this multiple sense of distributed leadership is the most common implying many levels of leadership. In fact, a single individual does not need to perform all of the essential leadership functions. These can be shared by several members of a group or by a set of people who can perform these functions collectively, providing leadership through the sum of its parts. But Gronn also points to another description of distributed leadership which is 'as conduct comprising joint or concertive action, rather than aggregated or individual acts' (2003, p. 35). According to him this kind of distributed leadership is characterised by:

1. Collaborative engagement that arises spontaneously in the workplace showing that leadership is evident in the interaction of many leaders.
2. Intuitive understanding that develops as part of close working relationships in units and teams where high trust abounds.
3. Collaborative practices used within the organisation including structures and institutional arrangements that enable collaboration.

It is clear that both the multiple and concertive forms of distributing leadership have implications for collaborative decision-making in educational organisations. Gronn (2008) suggests that a coalescing of hierarchical and heterarchical elements might produce a hybrid form of distributed human conduct in organisations as an alternative way of understanding the decision-making practices of leaders and managers.

The purpose of encouraging distributed forms of leadership is inherently pragmatic (Bush, 2011; Gronn, 2003) but is also purported to be concerned with improving student learning. In research that has studied the impact of collaborative leadership (Hallinger and Heck, 2010) and distributed leadership (Seashore Louis et al., 2010) on schools and students, there is evidence of how sharing leadership can increase its indirect effect on student learning. The research on school leadership effects is consistent in proposing that leadership can no longer be viewed as just an individual phenomenon but should be seen as an organisational phenomenon with an emphasis shifting from a study of *the leader* to *leadership*. Distributed leadership takes many forms that may be formal or informal – making it a very complex concept that manifests in a variety of patterns when it is distinctly linked to leadership construed in terms of influence.

When we talk about leadership and management being distributed, this may occur in several ways and the research that has searched for links between leadership distribution and student learning confirms that 'no single pattern of leadership distribution is consistently linked to student learning' (Seashore Louis et al., 2010, p. 54). This significant study points to implications that should be of interest to policy-makers and practitioners alike:

- Actual distributive behaviours and practices associated with core leadership practices (setting directions, developing people, redesigning the organisation and managing the instructional programme) need to be explored to identify specific patterns of distribution that are effective. Merely exhorting principals to distribute leadership is meaningless.
- There is some evidence to suggest that sharing leadership with others around planned student learning improvement issues may be worthwhile.
- A preliminary task is to nurture in principals a disposition towards distributing leadership. Their beliefs about this and how they feel about others' expertise and participation is fundamental to the way they enact their leadership roles.
- The distribution of leadership more widely in schools should not be viewed as a means of reducing the principal's workload. Principals are involved in a great many leadership tasks and initiatives. Sharing leadership with others is normally associated with specific goals or initiatives and the principal needs to retain a co-ordinating role.

A focus on management

As with so many new stars that appear on the educational leadership theory horizon, the notion of distributing leadership is illuminating a wide landscape yet to be explored. This is related to how *leadership* is conceived and enacted in order to most effectively impact student learning. In this chapter the focus is on *managing* collaborative decision-making, which implies a much tighter and very practical focus. In relation to the power of distributed leadership practices in enabling effective decision-making, it is useful here to pause to consider some definitional issues raised by Spillane and Diamond (2007), who say:

> Management activity maintains, hopefully efficiently and effectively, current organizational arrangements and ways of doing school business; it centers on maintenance. Leadership activity, in contrast, involves influencing others to achieve new, hopefully desirable, ends; it frequently involves initiating changes designed to achieve existing or new goals. (p. 4)

Spillane and Diamond also warn against an oversimplification of the differences. While management is often about preserving things and leadership about changing things, these efforts to change and preserve are often blended to meet both management and leadership goals. It is also salutary to note that while the management versus leadership distinction is often a useful theoretical tool, in practice it is very difficult to identify activity as managing or leading. In talking about 'leadership' and 'management', I prefer to make no distinction between these two terms because I subscribe to the view that the most essential element of effective management is leadership. An effective manager can utilise their personal decisions about the distribution of work as a way of influencing the quality of that work.

Delegation as collaborative work distribution

At its most practical level, shared decision-making and problem-solving occurs in the form of distributing work through a very well known management technique called 'delegation'. First, this occurs formally within the framework of the hierarchical structure of the organisation. Most delegations relate to tasks that cascade through levels of responsibility and authority and are recorded as permanent expectations in job or position descriptions. Secondly, this occurs when specific organisational goals or initiatives require the delegation of their management to others. These are random, one-off events where the expertise of others can be harnessed and, in reality, these sorts of delegated tasks may well be associated with transferring a leader's workload to appropriate others.

In a nutshell, managers who do not delegate are neglecting one of the most indispensable tools of management. Even when they do employ this technique, it is often poorly practised; one of the reasons for this being that it is relegated to the level of a basic skill that does not need attention because it is so self-evident. What is evident in management practice, however, is that generally most managers do not delegate enough (Stott and Walker, 1992). Good delegation rests on understanding the principle of what can and cannot be delegated in relation to accountability, responsibility, authority and resources. Attending to all of these matters lays a sound foundation for a delegation to be effective.

The principles of good delegation are:

- *Accountability:* which cannot be delegated and rests with the person who is formally accountable for the task within the bounds of their job description;
- *Responsibility:* which is what is accepted in a delegated task;
- *Authority:* which is given along with a delegation to enable the person to accomplish the task; and
- *Resources:* which must be provided along with the delegation.

Considerations that should be foremost in relation to delegation include the clarity of the delegation and the style of collaboration used to manage it.

Delegation implies that the task is to be trusted to another, hence in judging the effectiveness of a delegation there is a bilateral obligation that comes into play. What is important to the delagatee is that the task has been clearly explained; responsibility for decision-making has been clarified; sufficient authority to act has been given; the way the leader will oversee the delegation to maintain accountability has been communicated; and adequate resources have been provided. If the delegator attends to all of these aspects before the delegation is undertaken it is more likely to be successful and should help to build a trusting relationship.

Stott and Walker (1992) have identified several reasons why managers bypass the opportunity to delegate. Among these is a reluctance to 'let go'. Managers who pride themselves on their particular expertise are often reluctant to utilise the expertise of others. It is interesting to note that Seashore Louis et al. (2010) note that beliefs and feelings influence a leader's disposition towards employing the expertise of others. If they are not disposed to a collaborative approach in the first place they may also be reluctant to trust others enough to delegate.

Learning case for reflection: I don't know if I can delegate

Jody is a middle manager in a higher education institution where she has been the academic leader of a most successful postgraduate programme. For the past 18 months she has felt overloaded and has not been able to find sufficient time to attend to her personal research goals. She leads a team of six extremely capable lecturers who know how burdened she feels at present. Two of these team members have dropped hints that they would be happy to help with some of the major tasks that have to be accomplished by the end of the first semester. To date, Jody has been reluctant to take up their offers – in fact, she has been too busy to even consider how she might ask them to help. When she did give the matter some thought – especially in relation to a periodic programme review scheduled for later in the year – her initial reasoning was as follows:

I know I keep putting off making a start on the programme review task because I am so busy with other things – I have not had time to think about it.

Also, I am the only person in the team who has experienced a programme review before – I don't think any of the others could do the job as well as I can. I enjoy getting these things sorted.

I could work alongside one of the others but I'm reluctant to just give away my hard-earned expertise.

(Continues)

(Continued)

Yet, I am the one who often grumbles that no one on my team seems to come forward or take the initiative in seeking new experiences that would help them to develop their own leadership capability.

Basically, Jody has talked herself out of delegating the task. But because she is also very honest with herself she has asked to meet with the head of department, Jack, to seek some help with how to formally approach her team to seek help. This is what Jack has suggested in the form of a check-list that can be used with the team to decide the nature of the task and how it can be delegated.

Delegation checklist

1 Explain the task and the sort of expertise needed to complete it.

2 Clarify responsibility including deadlines.

3 Discuss authority limits and resources that accompany the delegation.

4 Explain how you will maintain accountability (regular checks on progress, for example).

If you were a member of Jody's team would you be prepared to volunteer to take on a delegated task after working through the checklist?

What concerns might you have about the success of the delegation?

If you were Jody (with all her reservations) what would you expect if this delegation were to succeed?

It is assumed that collaborative decision-making can lead to better decisions and greater commitment and can be particularly effective when harnessed to implement initiatives for improving student outcomes. We know that the existing authority structure in schools creates barriers to some modes of distribution being enacted such as ceding formal authority to others (Bush, 2011). Another barrier is the attitude of the principal in a school, or head of department in a higher education institution, who may not be disposed to anything that diminishes the power of a singular style of leadership. The leader's preferred style (no matter what they may espouse) is a key determiner in developing a disposition towards being collaborative and the considerations, demands, time and energy that this involves. In short, the feelings and beliefs that leaders have in relation to sharing leadership and their style of including others (or not) in decision-making is demonstrated in the theory-in-use of their actual practice.

Decision-making and leadership style

Discussion about decision-making is often centred on the personal style of a manager. For example, as Owens (2004) asserts:

> there is the widely held expectation that persons in administrative positions will personally "be decisive". What that means is far from clear, but it is often taken to mean making decisions swiftly, without delay or temporizing, and clearly with minimal ambiguity (p. 288).

However, because managers work with and through other people to achieve the organisation's goals it is important to include a perspective of decision-making as a collective, organisational activity.

A leader's personal disposition invariably determines their adoption of a particular style of decision-making. In organisational settings, the expectation is that they will also be knowledgeable about the situational factors that affect a decision-making context. This implies the need for understanding and responding to a situation appropriately. Thus, deciding how to handle a decision-making situation is a fundamental leadership skill. Leaders can adopt styles that are autocratic, democratic or laissez-faire to determine the extent to which they make individual decisions or draw others into the decision-making activity. This is depicted in the work of Tannenbaum and Schmidt (1973) in relation to a *continuum of leadership behaviour,* illustrated in Figure 6.1.

Continuum of leadership behaviour

The continuum of leadership behaviour does two things. First, it describes dominant styles that leaders and managers subscribe to because of their personal qualities. Secondly, it offers insights into the possible range of styles that can be adopted to meet specific situations. An effective manager is one who is prepared to utilise a variety of styles according to the nature of the problem being solved. The axis depicted in Figure 6.1 represents the behaviours associated with an authoritarian style (telling and selling) where the manager acts without including others, a democratic style (testing, consulting, joining) where the manager includes consideration of others' views, and the laissez-faire style (leaving) where the manager gives staff the freedom to act.

The two extremes of this continuum are governed by principles that are not democratic. The manager's use of authority alone to make and convey decisions indicates an approach that does not factor in the needs of others to be included in decision-making. The laissez-faire leader abrogates the role of decision-maker in providing an area of freedom for staff to make decisions on their own. In the democratic space that occupies the middle of this continuum, democratic principles are applied in various degrees. When ideas are tested with others with the possibility of review, this involves a sharing of the problem information as well as a potential decision. When ideas are presented as options or alternatives and recommendations are sought, others' views are being valued. When the manager joins with staff in solving a problem this is a collaborative effort. This notion of a continuum of behaviour that spans a variety of styles indicates the need for leaders and managers to vary their decision-making style according to the nature of the problem or the situation in which the problem is located.

Situational leadership (the contingency model)

In the *situational leadership model* proposed by Hersey and Blanchard (1982), the style of a leader is contingent upon several situational factors that can also be associated with making decisions:

- the amount of guidance a leader gives in relation to a task or decision;
- the amount of relational support the leader provides; and
- the readiness or maturity level of followers to achieve objectives.

Based on these factors, a leader can be highly directive, highly collaborative or highly distributive in relation to a specific task. Basically, the leader is expected to understand the value of choosing an appropriate style according to the degree of collaboration that a situation warrants.

The factors that are important in making decisions about who to involve and how they should be involved in decisions according to the situational leadership model, have links to the sort of decisions that a leader should make in relation to employing delegation as a tool for dispersing work across many people. Delegation is one of several options about the form of leadership to adopt according to a situation that is determined by analysing the relationship (support and communication) between leader and follower and the task capability (maturity) of the follower. As a consequence, four scenarios emerge (Bolman and Deal, 2008). In the ideal situational style, a leader chooses to delegate and leave the task entirely to the follower; the other three style choices are directing, coaching and supporting, which are akin to the seminal styles of telling, selling and participating proposed by Tannenbaum and Schmidt (1973).

Choosing an appropriate situational leadership style:

- Leadership through directing should be used when followers are unable and unwilling or insecure.
- Leadership through coaching should be used when followers are unable but are willing or motivated.
- Leadership through supporting should be used when followers are able but unwilling or insecure.
- Leadership through delegating should be used when followers are able and willing or motivated.

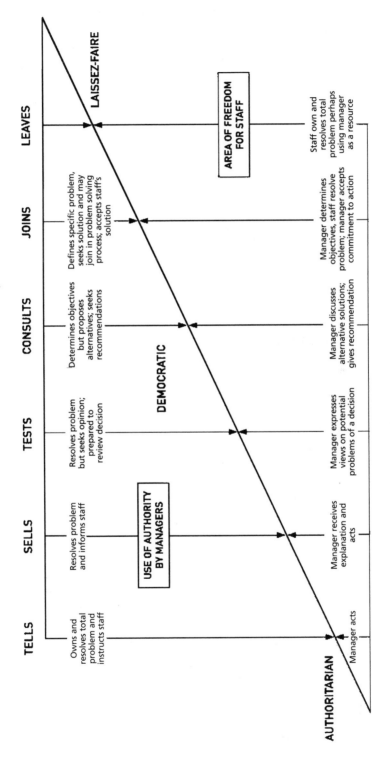

Figure 6.1 *Continuum of leadership behaviour (adapted from R. Tannenbaum and W.H. Schmidt, 1973, 'Continuum of leadership behaviour: how to choose a leadership pattern', Vol. 51, Harvard Business Review, with the permission of Harvard Business Review)*

In terms of decision-making styles, the situational leadership model reinvests the art of delegation with considerable importance. One weakness of the model lies in the notion that the leader alone makes constant judgements about the ability and attitudes of followers. In placing this demand within a productive relationship framework where information and reasoning are openly shared to reach a sound decision, an expectation would be that the leader was able to check assumptions about a follower with them directly. This would create an opportunity for dialogue that could result in higher trust, greater commitment and ultimately better delegations.

One key advantage of the situational leadership model is the focus on relationships. However, although currently popular in management training, the successful application of the model in commercial settings is not well researched. If the decisions of the leader alone are to direct their style in a particular situation, then I believe the model will be unable to achieve the effective decision-making it purports to make possible. Relationships need to be tested and it will take engagement in dialogue that is productive to achieve this, and such dialogue is inherently collaborative.

The concept of collaboration

The terms 'collaborative' and 'participative' are used here in their widest and most similar sense to denote inclusiveness of others in management processes for decision-making. Collaboration is the term employed to 'express partnership, co-operation, agreement, consent, and working in combination to accomplish institutional objectives. It is bound to notions of consultation, involvement and participation; shared goals, shared vision, openness, trust and democratic ideals' (Cardno, 1990, p. 1). In transporting the concept to the educational arena it is necessary to distinguish between internal and external collaboration.

> An *internal collaborative partnership* between the educational leader and staff can be built as a result of values and structures fostered and facilitated by aware and active leaders. Such leaders understand the culture of the organisation and are prepared to manage change, manage productive relationships and promote staff participation in planning and decision-making.

> An *external collaborative partnership* can be fostered between the organisation, the community and the system based on relevant and appropriate consultation and involvement of those outside the school who can and wish to contribute. Again, relationship building with external stakeholders is critical to a productive partnership which, in turn, is enacted through collaborative practices.

No matter how differently or at what pace the norms and processes of collaboration are introduced, they should be viewed as the means to achieving educational ends and not as the ends in themselves. Features of collaborative practice in educational organisations may be identified as contributing to professionalism and collegiality, and to partnership and wider community commitment to institutional goals that are ultimately focused on improving student achievement.

In a collaborative educational organisation:

- there is sound leadership and direction;
- staff are knowledgeable about the organisation's goals;
- teamwork is evident at all levels;
- roles and responsibilities are clearly defined;
- mechanisms for participation exist and operate;
- emphasis is placed on the development of communication skills;
- problem-solving is related to organisational development;
- professional development is given a high profile; and
- internal and external collaboration are managed.

A fundamental aspect in developing and sustaining a culture of collaboration is a need to *manage* collaborative management. In essence, the success of collaborative practice rests on the ability and skill of the leader to actively manage the participation of others in decision-making. Collaboration is described and promoted as a desirable aspect of professional work and purported to be an important mechanism in a school's efforts towards achieving excellence (Fauske, 2002; Tschannen-Moran, 2001). Yet, accounts of skilful use of collaborative practice are not evident in the literature. One reason for this may be that leaders are daunted by the overwhelming nature of a commitment to collaborative decision-making and need a better understanding of the complexity they will be expected to manage.

Managing collaborative management: a conceptual framework

The theory and practice of the effective management of collaborative decision-making is bound up in a conceptual framework of *leadership decisions*. Leaders should be wary about embarking on any collaborative experiments until they are prepared to ask the essential leadership questions about decision-making. Four leadership decision areas constitute the framework. These are: *why* decisions, *who* decisions, *how much* decisions and *how to* decisions. Essential leadership questions flow from these decision areas in this framework. Leaders pose these questions to themselves to prepare for effective shared decision-making – and they do this every time they are faced with a non-routine decision.

1. 'Why' decisions – leaders consider whether collaborative management is the appropriate approach in a particular situation. They must be knowledgeable about the many myths associated with collaboration. They also need to be committed to the values of collaboration, and able to communicate these to others.
2. 'Who' decisions – if the problem requires a collaborative process the next question a leader must address is who will be included. Several models of shared decision-making can be called on to provide guidelines.
3. 'How much' decisions – are about how much collaboration will be appropriate. There are many degrees of collaborative activity. Sharing information may be all that is needed in one instance, yet at other times it is essential to invite people to participate to a much greater extent in the decision-making and beyond this to implement the decision.
4. 'How to' decisions – leaders consider how existing (or potential) structures, processes and techniques can be employed to include others in a collaborative decision-making process.

Although the conceptual framework for leadership decisions about collaboration was developed in a school context, the ideas are transferable to both early childhood and higher education settings in which complex problems challenge the leader to ask these reflective questions of themselves:

Why collaborate?
Who should be included?
How much collaboration is appropriate?
How should we collaborate?

Leadership question 1: why collaborate?

Leaders need to know the arguments for and against collaborative decision-making which are reflected in the huge literature on problem-solving, change management and participative decision-making. This literature tells us that in educational organisations seeking to succeed and improve, co-operation and collaboration are critical functions (Jenni and Mauriel, 2004). The fundamental education imperative to improve student learning and achievement has also been associated with collaborative leadership practices (Hallinger and Heck, 2010). Collaboration is a way of life in many early childhood and primary school settings where teachers work together closely and expect a collaborative culture. In secondary school and higher education settings, the expectation to participate, especially in decision-making related to curriculum and student issues is strong. In short, collaborative approaches are anticipated as the norm in most education settings. That they may also lead to better decisions and better student learning outcomes are added advantages. But collaboration also has its downside, being hugely time-consuming, making demands on the leaders and participants that need to be clearly justified. Hence, I have taken a position that requires that this immensely challenging and often unwieldy commitment to collaborate is *managed* by the leaders who unleash it in education settings.

This implies that others who will participate in these processes will also need to be informed about what constitutes a *managed* collaborative approach. At this point, if the leader (and others in key positions) believe strongly that the organisation will benefit from increased collaboration in decision-making, then the review of current beliefs and practices, the modification of structures such as meeting cycles, and the associated training of staff (regarding structures, processes, potential and pitfalls) could be useful pragmatic starting points.

Change and collaboration

Change management and collaborative management are two concepts which are inextricably entwined. Moss Kanter (1983) conveys a message that is timeless, familiar and challenging. She asserts that any change is disturbing when it is done to us, but can be exhilarating when it is done by us, that is, when we are included in the momentum and excitement of innovation or change. She says, therefore, that, 'masters of change are also masters of the art of participation' (p. 241). But, effective participation entails a lot more than just additional committee meetings or the establishment of another task group to deal with a problem. In Moss Kanter's terms, 'Participation, it is clear needs to be managed just as carefully as any other organisation system, and it creates new problems demanding attention in the course of solving others' (p. 242). The potential for participative or collaborative decision-making to impact positively on change is huge. But, it also has its pitfalls.

On the positive side, collaborative decision-making:

- is organisationally sound as it permits decisions to be made as close to the point of implementation as possible;
- is consistent with democratic principles based on the premise that those affected by decisions should have a voice in making them;
- contributes to staff satisfaction, and higher levels of motivation, morale and commitment;
- is closely related to trust and effective collaboration can foster trust;
- can improve the quality of decisions, and allow error correction and perception checks leading to greater understanding and acceptance;
- permits the utilisation of a broad base of expertise;

- can indirectly have a positive impact on student learning by creating conditions that foster academic capacity building; and
- is a mechanism that is associated with management in effective schools.

On the negative side, collaborative decision-making:

- is extremely time consuming and energy intensive;
- can become unwieldy if the structure and processes are too complex;
- is often mistakenly viewed as being synonymous with unanimity;
- can lead to frustration if staff expectations to be directly involved in consensus decision-making are not fulfilled;
- can lead to resentment if staff experience overload;
- may become an end in itself rather than a means of achieving organisational goals;
- highlights limitations of staff competence to contribute;
- demands skills and necessitates training for all concerned;
- encroaches on the territory of higher level managers; and
- demands an extremely high level of ability and skill from leaders who must manage the decision-making process.

Dispelling myths about collaboration

When a leader has to make a decision about *why* it is necessary to approach a particular decision-making situation collaboratively, they are likely to encounter strong beliefs in others about what it means to be collaborative. Because there are various myths associated with the notion of collaborative practice, it is important to share ideas and create opportunities to discuss expectations and realities. The reality is often one in which staff have a view of collaboration that is quite different to the leader's view and, consequently, they are expecting practices of a particular type. If a leader is committed to introducing the principles and practices of managed collaboration an initial (and essential) step is to present to staff an explanation of what collaboration can and cannot consist of in practical terms.

Myth 1: that managed collaboration is the same thing as collegiality. While several authors write about collegiality and collaboration as if they were actually one and the same thing (Bush, 2011), there are distinctions that need to be drawn. For example, Brundrett (1998) provides a definition of collegiality which sees 'teachers conferring and collaborating with other teachers' (p. 305). This implies collegial activity amongst professionals in their daily work and the value of respecting co-professionals (colleagues) as equals in decisions about teaching. Bush (2011) emphasises the democratic impulse that guides collegial behaviour, saying that collegial models of educational leadership 'assume that organizations determine policy and make decisions through a process of discussion leading to consensus' (p. 72). This implies that in a collegial model all staff will participate formally in all decision-making processes through official representation. In contrast, the model of collaborative decision-making that I am advocating in relation to managed collaboration embraces several degrees of collaborative activity (incorporating informing and consulting) that include others in a variety of ways.

Myth 2: that managed collaboration depends on consensus based on unanimity. When the value of collaborating in decision-making is espoused, it raises expectations that unanimous decisions will carry the day. It is important to dispel the myth that reaching a consensus is the same thing as unanimity. In some decision-making situations it may be appropriate to use a deeper level of collaboration that involves discussion in order to seek consensus. Employing this deep level of collaboration is a leadership decision in managed collaboration and requires considered examination and debate about issues before there is agreement to abide by the best solution despite personal disagreement. The essence of consensus is that the minority agree to the majority view to implement a solution on the understanding that this will be evaluated in due course in order to test its effectiveness.

Myth 3: that decisions will be made using majority agreement. Most people are familiar with parliamentary arrangement techniques for decision-making that require voting and majority agreement. It is not surprising for staff to expect that a collaborative decision-making process might require voting for preferred options. It is important to let people know that this will not be the case except in rare circumstances. For example, it could be useful to ask the staff to provide a show of hands to test unanimity or a move towards consensus.

Trust and collaboration

A very important reason for a leadership commitment to collaborative decision-making is its link to trust. Tschannen-Moran (2001) says that the processes of collaboration and trust are reciprocal because they depend upon and foster one another. Genuine collaboration cannot exist unless trust exists alongside it. We build trust by being honest and respecting the capacity of others to appreciate the need for information sharing. If a culture of collaboration is to be built then the organisation's leaders must be prepared to explain the purposes and the limitations around a collaborative but managed approach to decision-making. If presenting a rationale for proceeding is the cause of contention for participants then the sources of this contention should be surfaced through ongoing dialogue. If collaboration is to be truly valued as purposeful and effective then its shortcomings need to be openly and productively addressed in order to enable all participants to trust and value its intent and processes.

Leadership question 2: who should be included?

Who should be invited to participate in decision-making? Good intentions can be so easily misapplied unless these decisions are carefully and consistently made by leaders. It also pays to involve other senior managers in helping you to make these decisions. In this case there is no doubt that many minds are better than one! Collaborative decision-making is not a case of involving everyone all of the time and, in fact, there is nothing staff dislike more than being involved in decision-making that they believe is the principal's prerogative, or being involved but not being able to influence a decision. These are cases of 'false collaboration' and contribute to resentment and lack of trust. Making leadership-level decisions about who to include in the decision-making process may be helped by knowing about some of the models that have been developed to guide effective decision-making. Several models for shared decision-making exist. Two of these models, the *zone of acceptance model* and the *Vroom–Yetton decision-making tree,* are presented here to stimulate leaders to rely on more than intelligent intuition to make this preliminary decision about collaboration.

Zone of acceptance model

So, how does one best make decisions about who to include and to what degree they should be included? One of the most useful tools in this case was developed by Bridges (1967) to define boundaries between participation and non-participation. It involves a concept called *zone of acceptance,* illustrated in Figure 6.2. Briefly, it is assumed that within the zone of acceptance will fall decisions and directives which staff will accept as the leader's prerogative. Beyond this zone staff will want to be part of the decision-making process. The degree to which this occurs is put to two tests: the test of relevance and the test of expertise.

1. *The test of relevance.* If an issue is highly relevant for staff, that is, they have a stake in the outcome or are likely to be directly affected by the decision, then involvement should be considered.
2. *The test of expertise.* If staff can contribute meaningfully to the decision, by providing expertise or drawing on substantive experience, then their involvement should be considered.

These two tests should be applied in every situation that calls for consideration of who should be involved.

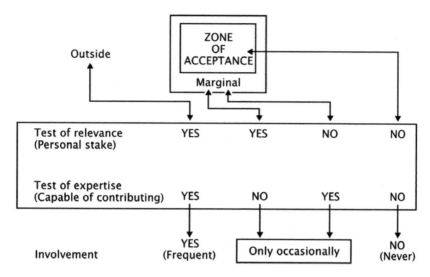

Figure 6.2 *Zone of acceptance (adapted from figure 9.3, p. 342 in W. Hoy and C. Miskel, 2001,* Educational Administration: Theory, Research and Practice, *with the permission of McGraw-Hill)*

Using the tests: applying rules of thumb

- Never involve staff if the issue lies within their zone of acceptance (for example, decisions about the brand of photocopying paper the school will purchase).
- Always involve staff to at least some degree if it is an issue outside the zone of acceptance and if it has high relevance and staff can contribute in a significant way (for example, a curriculum decision, or decisions related to student welfare).
- Occasionally and selectively involve staff when an issue is marginal to their zone of acceptance (another decision for the leader!) and if there is either high personal stake or high capability of contribution present.

When these tests are applied effectively, and particularly when leaders begin to internalise their use and apply them automatically to all non-routine decisions, the benefits can be great in terms of trust-building that leads to better decisions and relationships.

One further test which can be applied in leadership decisions of this nature is the *test of jurisdiction* suggested by Owens (2004). It may be appropriate to consider who has jurisdiction to make and implement a decision, because to suggest staff or stakeholder participation in a decision-making scenario outside their official jurisdiction can only lead to frustration as great as that produced by non-participation. An example of how the promise of collaboration can turn sour for some people is when a member of the board of trustees of a school might be invited to participate in making a management or a teaching-learning decision that is not within their jurisdiction as a member of a governing body.

Vroom–Yetton decision-making tree

Closely related to the theories about adapting style to situation, is this model for shared decision-making proposed by Vroom and Yetton (1973). These authors suggest that it is up to the leader to analyse the contingencies in each situation and then behave in the most effective manner. Five leadership styles were identified as fitting under the broad categories of autocratic, democratic and laissez-faire (see the earlier Tannenbaum and Schmidt, 1973, continuum model).

A decision-making tree (Figure 6.3) allows the leader to proceed from step to step by asking pertinent questions that lead ultimately to the adoption of one of the five styles.

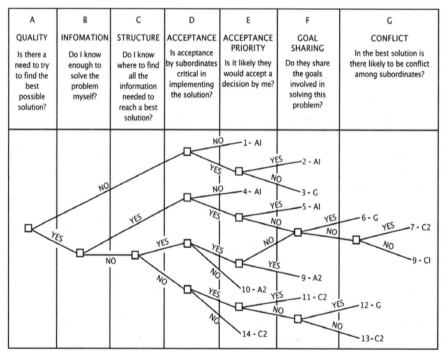

Figure 6.3 *Vroom–Yetton decision-making tree (adapted from R.G. Owens (2004, p. 295)* Organisational Behaviour in Education, *with the permission of McGraw-Hill)*

Answering the questions in the decision-making tree

A. *Is there a need to try to find the best possible solution?* (This is a *quality* of decision concern which could be related to time or lack of time to consult, need to stimulate trust, or keeping people informed through participation.)

B. *Do I know enough to solve the problem myself?* (This is an *information* concern.)
C. *Do I know where to find all the information needed to reach a best solution?* (This is a problem *structure* concern.)
D. *Is acceptance by subordinates critical in implementing the solution?* (This is an *acceptance* concern.)
E. *Is it likely they would accept a decision by me?* (This concerns the *priority* accorded to acceptance.)
F. *Do they share the goals involved in solving this problem?* (This is a *goal-sharing* concern.)
G. *In the best solution is there likely to be conflict among subordinates?* (This is a concern about ongoing *conflict*).

Using the branches of the tree as a flow chart at each point of questioning allows the leader to arrive at a proposed process related to one of the decision-making styles in this model. The style codes are as follows:

Autocratice process
A1:   Leader makes decision using whatever information is available.
A2:   Leader secures necessary information from members of the group then makes the decision.
Consultative process
C1:   Leader shares the problem with relevant members of the group, then leader makes the decision.
C2:   Leader shares the problem with members as a group at a meeting, then decides.
Group process
G: Leader chairs a group meeting and facilitates a consensus. Leader does not try to 'sell' a particular decision.

While it is unlikely that leaders will formally use these models when confronted with issues of who to involve in collaborative decision-making, the theories associated with effective shared decision-making have some value. The main contribution of these theory models is to provide leaders with more than intuition to rely on; the models provide tools for critical reflection. While Owens (2004) confirms the usefulness of the flow chart for showing the logic of using a variety of styles to suit circumstances, he is also critical. Research shows that managers (including high school principals) go about decision-making in ways that are not even remotely related to the models. Thus there is an evident gap between the theory and practice of shared decision-making.

Leadership question 3: how much collaboration is appropriate?

Once a commitment to collaborative decision-making has been made, the leader must accept that the one thing that will never diminish is the need to constantly make decisions about the appropriate way to go about decision-making. A vital question that a leader must consider, is the degree of collaboration that will be appropriate for a particular situation. The model of categories of collaboration in Table 6.1 was a model I developed to deal with the challenging issue of including the school community in the development and review of charters (Cardno, 1990, p. 101). In practice, and through the experiences of many schools who have used this model, I now believe that it is extremely pertinent in any decision-making context when a leader is faced with the wish to be inclusive of others, but does not wish to encounter the pitfalls of either too much or too little collaboration. The message of the model is simple. Collaboration is a multidimensional concept and it is equally effective if it engages people at category one, informing, as it is at the fifth category, participation. It is important to choose the category that is appropriate and then to make effective use of the particular degree of collaboration chosen.

One of the key pitfalls of collaborative decision-making practice relates to leadership decisions that are *not* made about the type or degree of collaboration that is appropriate in a particular situation. The assumption that you are being collaborative only when you involve others in the deepest degrees of collaboration (such as the fourth and fifth degrees depicted) is one that should be tested in every decision-making case. Staff become frustrated when they are engaged beyond the degree to which they need to be involved and in many cases they just want to be informed and, where necessary, given the opportunity to provide feedback about the information – hence there is no need to involve them beyond the first and second degrees depicted in Table 6.1.

Table 6.1 Categories of collaboration

1 **Information**	*Letting people know* what is happening by all available means and accepting feedback	
2 **Consultation**	*Seeking response* or advice formally or informally from individuals and groups	
3 **Discussion**	Presenting information and arranging forums to *facilitate debate* which presents a plurality of views, and serves to increase understanding and encourage questioning	
4 **Involvement**	*Inviting people* as subscribers to participate in the review processes incorporating planning, decision-making and evaluating	
5 **Participation**	*Taking part* in policy and programme implementation as contributors and active participants	

Leadership question 4: how should we collaborate?

How can an organisation go about establishing the structures and introducing the processes which make it possible to practise collaboration?

Educational leaders need to become familiar with a range of methods for increasing the contribution others can make.

The first thing to do is to review current structures to determine conditions that may help or hinder the goal of collaborative practice. Do staff meetings occur in ways that allow teams at various levels of the organisation to be informed, to comment or to make recommendations to the leader? Are there too few teams, or too many? Do teams know the ground rules for effectively contributing to decisions? Do they understand their limits in terms of making, rather than contributing to, decisions? All these questions need to be addressed at the outset so that there are clear guidelines for all and a structure that enables rather than restricts making the very best decisions.

Once structures are examined, and modified if necessary, the next thing to attend to is the development of processes that can be used easily and quickly when needed. There are numerous techniques for participative decision-making. Any major text on management will provide pointers. Here are some techniques currently in general use:

- Making use of scheduled meetings to explore issues (department teams, curriculum committee, whole staff, senior management team, board of trustees, and so on).
- Establishing task groups to investigate an issue and make recommendations.
- Delphi method – as an alternative to meetings, participants comment on an issue in writing, these are tabulated and circulated as a report to all concerned who are asked for further comment. A further tabulation occurs to summarise similarities and deviances, and these are discussed at a meeting.
- Ringi – a Japanese exercise which is simpler than the Delphi method and involves circulating ideas on a notice among a group of staff and asking each one to comment before passing it on. It can also be effective as noticeboard Ringi – placing on a notice board a suggestion for change and asking staff to note their comments.

Teachers in all education sectors are familiar with classroom strategies for group work that enable and encourage participation. These techniques can be employed in meetings and forums to facilitate discussion and debate. The most practical approach overall, however, is to employ the first two categories of collaboration – informing and consulting others – to the fullest extent possible whenever appropriate.

Productive collaboration

If the potential and possibilities inherent in effective collaboration do not cross a leader's mind, it is unlikely that the values that create a collaborative culture will be fostered in an organisation or any part of it. Seashore Louis et al. (2010) refer to this proclivity towards collaboration as developing a disposition towards distributing leadership. Thinking about and espousing a commitment towards collaborative approaches to decision-making is one thing. Doing it is another. Developing an understanding of the pathways to productive collaboration is a first step towards taking action. Leaders can build on this and progress along this pathway when they adopt theories of action that demonstrate openness to information. When these theories of action are shared and enacted they can produce sustaining conditions for collaborative learning and change (Fauske, 2002). Primary among such conditions, in my view, is the organisation's ability to learn about complex problems in order to resolve them. Solving problems collaboratively is in essence a celebration of bilateral rather than unilateral decision-making. A commitment to resolving the really complex problems of practice requires a leader to understand and be willing to resolve leadership dilemmas that arise when our problem-solving efforts are not effective. This demands a focus on intrapersonal, interpersonal and organisational learning, and the development of specific skills that enable productive relationships and productive decision-making to flourish.

Learning case for reflection: did I make the right decision?

Dave is deputy principal in a large secondary school and his key portfolio is the management of the pastoral care system, including staff with special responsibilities for year-level pastoral care and discipline. In all, he manages 15 deans assigned to five year-levels whose role is to support teachers with student discipline and pastoral care issues. All of these staff teach in a variety of subjects and approximately half of their time is dedicated to deans' duties. Over the last three pastoral care team meetings an agenda item has been one related to time out students. These are students who have misbehaved in class and teachers have sent them out of the classroom to report to the year-level dean. The deans are frustrated because in spite of several attempts to discuss the problem and arrive at some lasting solutions, other items on agendas have taken precedence and the problem is not only persisting but now it is escalating with 22 students referred to the deans on the previous Friday.

David feels he is out of his depth here. Every time his team has tackled this issue there have been many bright ideas and these have been conveyed in notices to the whole staff at morning briefing meetings. The teachers have been given notice to do the following, for example:

> Do not send a student to the dean without another, reliable student accompanying them.

Always send the student with a written note explaining why you have initiated time out.

Please come and see the dean as soon as you can after each incident.

Neither David nor his team members are confident that they are going about addressing the problem effectively. And, at this stage, David is aware that he does not know enough about the underlying causes of the problem and is grasping desperately at some sticking plaster solutions. In the meantime the relationship between teachers and deans is developing into a blaming and naming situation and the principal has become aware of this strained relationship and has alerted Dave. What he does know is that without the co-operation and collaboration of all staff in resolving this problem he cannot meet the expectations held of him to deal with it.

If you were in Dave's shoes, what sort of questions would you be posing to yourself and the team in order to:

choose who to involve in an effort to understand the problem and gather necessary information using the tests of relevance and expertise;

choose the degree of collaboration that is most appropriate in including others using categories of collaboration as a guide;

choose the form that collaboration would take in relation to who will be involved and to what extent?

CHAPTER SEVEN

PRODUCTIVE TEAMWORK

Building productive relationships

Teamwork provides the context for resolving many of the complex problems that act as barriers to the achievement of educational goals. When productive relationships exist between members a team is more likely to be effective. Hence, the ability of the team to learn as individuals and as a collective is central to teamwork. Team members and team leaders alike need to develop and practise the skills of productive dialogue that enable learning to occur and productive relationships to be built.

Understanding the nature of teams

Teams now have a significant role to play in the structure of modern organisations in terms of work arrangements and organisational problem-solving. A vast literature exists in relation to the role, function, development and effectiveness of teams, confirming that teaming is very prevalent in organisations. Although teams in educational settings are viewed as an essential element for structuring the work of the organisation, the value of teams is often assumed as a 'given' and many of the assumptions we make about the contribution of teams remain untested.

While we may be able to claim in many areas of leadership and management theory and practice that there is a sound body of knowledge that specifically covers the context of education, this is not true about teams. This could be because the study of groups and teams is inherently interdisciplinary (Weingart and Cronin, 2009). These authors contend that many of the concepts emerging through research on teams are often 'dusted off' existing concepts from various core disciplines. An example of this is the way authors have revisited the notion of team effectiveness linked to team learning (see, for example, Senge, 2006). It is important to recognise that the 'grand theories' about teams have a long history in the domains of psychology, organisational psychology and business management. This is one topic in which we need to recognise the dearth of specific research into team behaviour, team effectiveness and team learning in the educational sphere of practice.

Much of the work in organisations is done in groups or teams and educational organisations in particular are commonly structured so that teams play a significant part in the achievement of the organisation's goals. At the outset, knowledge about what distinguishes a *team* from just any *group* of people who work together is essential. There are many groups that can be identified in educational organisations; whether or not they meet the fundamental characteristics of being a team is another matter. For example, Bolman and Deal (2008) assert that, 'A key ingredient of a top-notch team is an appropriate blueprint of roles and relationships set in motion to attain common goals' (p. 101). This message is conveyed by many other writers about teams as opposed to groups.

O'Neill (1997) asserts that while the concept of the team is now firmly embedded in the educational management literature, it 'may be that "team" status is awarded unconditionally by practitioners to any number of different functioning groups within the organisation' (p. 76). Groupings of people abound in an organisation, in terms of coming together for common interests such as a curriculum committee of middle-level leaders or governing groups such as institutional councils or boards of trustees. These groups are not necessarily teams. A team is not created by merely giving the label 'team' to people sharing a common title such as 'Head of Department' or 'Senior Manager'. Teams in educational organisations are seen to be very different when contrasted with the nature of, for example, sports teams. In sport, teams demonstrate the characteristics of high-performing teams: networked connections; interdependence; intense focus on goal achievement and commitment to development. In education settings there is often a blurring between teams that work together to achieve common goals and groups that are formed to contribute to collaborative decision-making. An example of the former is a teaching team in a subject area or a level of teaching. An example of the latter is a committee constituted of middle-level leaders to advise senior leadership decision-making. So, while a collection of people could be a team, what distinguishes a team from a group is that it generally has the following distinctive features:

- common service goals;
- ground rules;
- meshing functions; and
- leadership.

There is a difference between *real* teams and *self-styled* teams. Walker and Stott (1993) in their study of senior management teams ask several questions which are related to determining the norms of effective teams. These relate to the purpose of the team, team roles, decision-making practices and team development. Determining what constitutes a real team is a particularly pertinent issue in the light of the increasing demands being made on educational leaders and the consequential reliance on teams to perform both delegated and distributed leadership tasks. In addition, expectations of collaborative practices and decision-making may lead to a greater reliance on the team as a unit of leadership and management.

So, what then is bona fide teamwork? Bell (1992, p. 45) provides a succinct standard for judging teamwork. He cautions that reaching this standard is not something which will happen automatically because teamwork has to be managed and developed if it is to be effective. According to Bell, teamwork is about a group of people working together on the basis of:

- shared perceptions;
- a common purpose;
- agreed procedures;
- commitment;
- co-operation; and
- resolving disagreements openly by discussion.

Teams and groups are not, therefore, synonymous terms because the notion of a group is much looser than that ascribed to a team. A team is a body established to accomplish specific tasks and its members have skills which fit with those of others to produce an overall pattern of effective performance (Adair, 1986). Furthermore, as Coleman and Bush (1994) assert, teams need to be nurtured and developed if they are to be an effective vehicle for organising work. They claim:

> There is a substantial gap between labelling a group and a team and creating an effective work team which is able to function in a total quality environment. Too often teams are established and expected to operate simply by virtue of having delegated tasks – little consideration is given to the way the team functions. (p. 267)

Types of teams

There are basically three predominant types of real teams (as opposed to the groups that self-style themselves as a team). These are *permanent* teams, built into the organisation's structure, and *project* teams that are short-life teams because once they achieve the task the team dissolves. Teams that are *self-managed* are also identified in the literature.

Permanent teams

In a study of New Zealand schools (Cardno, 1998b) there is evidence that teams (self-styled) proliferated in both large and small primary and secondary schools. Permanent teams such as a senior management team existed in more than 80 per cent of all schools and in 96.5 per cent of secondary schools. More than half of all schools claimed to have other permanent teams in the form of subject (or teaching) teams, curriculum committees and professional development committees. Student services teams existed in only a few primary schools, in half of the small secondary schools and in all of the large secondary schools. So, regardless of size, most schools were reliant on permanent teams within the organisational structure. These teams are usually predetermined because of member expertise. Leaders of such teams seldom have the luxury of being able to select team members and the challenge with permanent teams according to Adair (1997) lies in transforming an assembly of people into a team.

Project teams

In addition to permanent teams, nearly 50 per cent of all schools in the New Zealand study (Cardno, 1998b) indicated that they created short-life work teams, variously named as task teams, project teams or working groups. The study revealed that the highest incidence of this type of team occurred in large primary schools (91 per cent) where several such short-life teams were established each year – in some cases as many as 10 – to carry out specific tasks such as evaluation of a programme or managing a school event. An important implication of project team proliferation is the overburdening of staff who are already members of several permanent teams at the same time.

It is a considerable commitment to be a member of a real, active and effective team. This is especially so when membership of a permanent team such as the senior management team or a teaching team constitutes the core work. Teamwork is embedded in the culture of sharing and collaboration that is often attributed to educational organisations, and especially schools (Bush and Middlewood, 2005). Leithwood (1998) attributes an increase in teamwork to school restructuring and the growth of site-based management which in turn assumes some form of participatory decision-making. Teamwork is also often viewed as a response to work intensification in the form of sharing and distributing leadership (Gronn, 2003). For these reasons, and particularly in the world of commerce, the importance of self-managed teams has increased.

Self-managed teams

This type of team may have no formal external or internal leadership and is often associated with 'fast-forming project teams having members operating at the same position level' (Goodwin et al., 2009, p. 88). In schools, self-management authority has been identified in senior management teams where the principal is both the line manager and the formal leader of the team (Wallace and Huckman, 1999). The other key team in schools that is often self-managed is the teaching team. Similar patterns of teaming are to be seen in higher education settings where the department team is the key operating unit. Again, line managers are most often the formal leaders of such teams. They have an organisational link to senior managers while retaining considerable self-leadership authority for the functioning of the team. This differs from the way self-managed teams are conceptualised in the generic literature about teams. Here they are portrayed as groups of employees who manage themselves, share the leadership role, schedule their own work and job assignments, and make decisions to remedy their own problems (Bolman and Deal, 2008). In the case of educational settings, even when teams have some of the features of a self-managing team there is usually some kind of external accountability link to a higher level in the hierarchy that typifies structures in this context. In educational settings, the issue of whether groups working together are merely self-styled teams, or real teams (meeting some essential standards for effective teamwork) is not very well researched. Nevertheless, a useful starting point for teams wanting to improve their performance is knowledge about what constitutes an effective team.

Team effectiveness

Teamwork requires a focus on three essential elements: achieving the task, building and maintaining the team and developing the individual. These elements need to be integrated and this is achieved through leadership of the team. In short, the most important aspect of an effective team is its leadership. According to Adair (1986), 'These elements – task, team and individual – constitute the core responsibility of the leader' (p. 121) and are at the heart of productive teamwork (Figure 7.1).

The literature on teams abounds with lists that encapsulate what effective teamwork is about (see, for example, Hensey, 2001; Preskill and Torres, 1999). There is a very high degree of concurrence among those who propose a set of characteristics for effective teamwork, even though the priority they accord to these characteristics may differ. All of these characteristics need to be present for a team to function effectively. Adair (1986) proposes a set of characteristics that I have chosen to frame the analysis below because it ranges over the three domains of:

- attention to achieving the task;
- attention to maintaining the operation of the team; and
- attention to the development of individual team members.

Figure 7.1 *Elements of teamwork leadership (source: J. Adair, 1986, p. 121,* Effective Teambuilding, *with the permission of Peters, Fraser and Dunlop publishing)*

The characteristics of effective teams are presented here as building blocks (Figure 7.2) which must all exist to some degree to hold up the structure and enable team processes to work well.

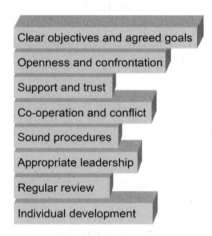

Clear objectives and agreed goals

Openness and confrontation

Support and trust

Co-operation and conflict

Sound procedures

Appropriate leadership

Regular review

Individual development

Figure 7.2 *Team building blocks*

If the team 'building blocks' are necessary for a team to work effectively then teams must be given the opportunity to develop as a team. Adair (1997) suggests that review is a powerful tool for team-building and should systematically follow task completion and development activity. Taking time to reflect on what has been achieved and what has been learnt supports and sustains team development. It is salutary to note that results of a research study of teams in New Zealand schools (Cardno, 1998b) show a marked gap in relation to the use of review in team development. In this study a disparity was evident between a high degree of formality and accountability, on the one hand, and a low to moderate degree of development and review, on the other hand. Teams in this study were not sufficiently required or supported to engage in review and development. The literature abounds with practical advice and resources for team development: building teams, balancing teams, managing teams and most recently, emphasis on the notions of team learning and the emotional intelligence of teams. A key player in teamwork and team development is the team's leader because who, otherwise, will take responsibility for developing the team's capacity to effectively achieve its task? In dealing with tasks and individuals in teamwork, leaders encounter relational issues. When relationships are sound it is easy to apply team theory to practice. When relationships are challenging then the focus of leadership must shift to surfacing and addressing leadership dilemmas that often lie at the heart of distressed relationships (Cardno, 2007).

Task-focused effectiveness characteristics

The primary need for a team is to accomplish a task. 'The task is *what* the group is talking about or working on. The task is usually seen in terms of *things* rather than people' (Adair, 1986, p. 61). Teams in the workplace are *purposeful* groups with intermeshing functions that are employed to achieve work tasks. Hence a primary characteristic for an 'on-task team' is its knowledge of that task. Accordingly, effective teams must have clear goals and objectives that are agreed. In addition, in such teams there is evidence of:

- shared purpose and direction;
- acceptance of the goals (targets) by all team members;
- sound procedures for team operation including planning;
- understanding by team members of their roles and how they fit into the overall framework of both the team and the organisation;
- accountability in reporting team achievements;
- regular team review.

Leaders are responsible for ensuring that the team knows and agrees its goals, establishing sound procedures, and taking stock (reviewing) team practice. Without periodic reflection on its direction and goals, and the team's capability to achieve these, a team will stagnate (Adair, 1986). Research into the practices of teams in New Zealand schools (Cardno, 1998b) showed that, while there was a high degree of accountability displayed in terms of documented objectives and reporting (75 per cent of respondents), there was a low to moderate response (40 per cent) to confirmation of engagement in regular team review practices.

Team function and team role

The way a person contributes to a team can be defined in two ways. First, a *functional contribution* is required in relation to the positions or designations of members. A person's function in the team is determined by their job, expertise and qualifications to perform that function. Some teams have a formal place in the structure of the organisation – such as senior management teams, programme teams or teaching teams. It is important for such teams to know where they fit strategically and how they contribute to the achievement of institutional vision and goals. Project or short-life teams are particularly vulnerable to ineffective practice if they are not given clear direction. This is because such teams are often comprised of multifunctional members. These teams should establish their 'terms of reference' in relation to purpose and functioning. Otherwise, they may well exhibit what Preskill and Torres (1999, p. 33) identify as the characteristics of ineffective teams, which are outlined below.

Ineffective teams:

- waste time, are disorganised and inconclusive;
- make members feel isolated; allow individuals to dominate;
- have poor process facilitation;
- focus on irrelevant information;
- do not establish a clear role for team members;
- avoid conflict at any cost;
- do not value members' ideas;
- develop subgroups or cliques within the team;
- allow hidden agendas and power politics to take precedence;
- overemphasise process to the exclusion of content; and
- have members who do not value teamwork.

Every team member needs to know their function in the team. This is a critical condition in terms of every member being able to contribute effectively. It also allows for a variety of related functions to be communicated and intermeshed to achieve the team goal. Once again, it is a leadership responsibility to achieve the synergy within the team that is needed to accomplish a common task.

Secondly, every team member adopts a *relational role* in a team which is connected to how they behave, interrelate and connect with other people in the team as they go about accomplishing the task. This is the part they play in relation to the process of teamwork. It is part of their personality and is determined by the way they work with other members of the team. Belbin's (1993, 2010) research into the roles that team members adopt as their preferred way of working resulted in the classification of team roles into the following broad typical types:

1. *Completer finisher*: this person is a perfectionist – someone who likes to make sure that all the fine details are attended to. Their high standards can be useful in urging accuracy and the completing of a task before the team embarks on something new.

2. *Coordinator*: confident and able to become the unofficial chairperson. This person encourages everyone to contribute and imparts a sense of purpose to the team.
3. *Implementer*: a person who is seen as loyal to the team or company – sometimes called the company worker. They are efficient, take on difficult tasks and help the team to turn ideas into actions.
4. *Monitor evaluator*: this person likes to delve deeply into problems and to analyse data. They are able to stand back and see a variety of options but also have a tendency to move slowly and sometimes dampen enthusiasm.
5. *Plant*: this person is creative and loves to generate ideas. Someone playing a creative role will be very positive and will constantly be coming up with new ideas for the team to develop. Sometimes has difficulty communicating ideas to others.
6. *Resource investigator*: someone who likes to deal with other people in the organisation and so can make sure that the team has all the information it needs. They perform an important liaison function especially in project teams where specialist expertise might lie outside the team itself.
7. *Shaper*: a task-focused leader who organises things and people and gets things moving. Too many shapers in a team might be a cause for conflict.
8. *Specialist*: this person is a self-starter. They are dedicated to their specialism and provide expert knowledge in a narrow field. Specialists are often criticised for getting caught up in the technicalities of an issue.
9. *Teamworker*: a person who enhances group cohesion and helps generate a team spirit by a 'let's all pull together' approach. They are good listeners, and good at smoothing over dissent.

Belbin created a self-perception inventory as a management self-development tool which allows people to work out their own natural role in terms of the nine major role types defined above. Several websites exist where adaptations of his original work can be found, such as http://www.belbin.com. The web-based material offers access to the self-perception tool for use in self-development and team development.

The key purpose of increasing self-awareness and group awareness of the preferred role that is played by individuals in the team is to *balance* the team. Team balance is a key to the success of project management teams because it is an approach that leaders can take to assemble team members who bring a variety of strengths to teamwork. There are some limitations, however, on perfectly balancing team roles. One is that in many permanent teams the functions performed by members are central to their membership and the leader cannot choose who will be in the team. Another is that even when a project team is being assembled, it may not be possible to have all team roles represented. A leader who is knowledgeable about the advantages of a balanced team may have to compensate for role deficiencies themselves in such a case. For example, if no team member is a perfectionist, then the leader must be especially focused on taking care that attention is paid to detail, accuracy and task completion. In summary, awareness of both their function and their relational roles in the team should be fostered by team leaders.

Balancing focus on task and team

An understanding of team relational roles contributes to achieving a balanced team and also indicates that a leader is focused on the task and the team maintenance dimension of leadership in unison. Balancing concern for the team (its socio-relational interactions) and the task (its work objectives) is a constant challenge for leaders. Self-reflection on how this balance is being achieved is the first step to improving leadership practice. An exercise called 'Understanding your leadership behaviour' is provided here to aid reflection.

Reflective exercise: understanding your leadership behaviour

(From Napier, R.A. and Gershenfeld, M.K. (1988) *Making Groups Work: A Guide for Group Leaders.* Boston, MA: Houghton Mifflin. Reproduced with permission of R.A. Napier on behalf of the authors)

EXERCISE

Leaders need to focus on both tasks and people in their work. Any action which helps a group complete its task is a leadership action. Any action that helps maintain effective working relationships among people in the group is a leadership action. When you are leading a group, what leadership actions do you engage in? How do you influence other group members to complete the task and maintain collaborative relationships with the people involved?

This TASK-MAINTENANCE model for discovering leadership style has been developed to examine the task orientation and maintenance (people) orientation you display. The purpose of this exercise is to make you more aware of your typical leadership behaviour.

THE PROCEDURE IS AS FOLLOWS

1 Working by yourself, complete the questionnaire on the following page.

2 Determine your score and place it on the task-maintenance grid below.

3 Reflect on how this pattern may be improved – see explanation below.

UNDERSTANDING YOUR LEADERSHIP BEHAVIOUR – A DIAGNOSTIC EXERCISE

Each of the diagnostic items numbered 1–12 describes a leadership action. In the space next to each item write a score between 1–5 assigned as outlined below:

    5 if you always behave that way

    4 if you frequently behave that way

    3 if you occasionally behave that way

    2 if you seldom behave that way and

    1 if you never behave that way.

DIAGNOSTIC ITEMS

When I am a member of a group –

_____   1   I offer facts and give my opinions, ideas, feelings and information in order to help the group discussion.

_____   2   I warmly encourage all members of the group to participate. I am open to their ideas. I let them know I value their contributions to the group.

_____   3   I ask for facts, information, opinions, ideas and feelings from the other group members in order to help the group discussion.

_____   4   I help communicate among group members by using good communication skills. I make sure that each group member understands what the others say.

_____   5   I give direction to the group by planning how to go on with the group work and by calling attention to the tasks that need to be done. I assign responsibilities to different group members.

_____   6   I tell jokes and suggest interesting ways of doing the work in order to reduce tension in the group and increase the fun we have working together.

_____   7   I pull together related ideas or suggestions made by group members and restate and summarise the major points discussed by the group.

_____   8   I observe the way the group is working and use my observations to help discuss how the group can work together better.

_____   9   I give the group energy. I encourage group members to work together better.

_____ 10   I promote the open discussion of conflicts among group members in order to resolve disagreements and increase group cohesiveness. I mediate conflicts among members when they seem unable to resolve them directly.

_____ 11   I ask to summarise what the group has been discussing in order to ensure that they understand group decisions and comprehend the material being discussed by the group.

_____ 12   I express support, acceptance, and liking for other members of the group and give appropriate praise when another member has taken a constructive action in the group.

(A)

Task action

___ 1 information and opinion giver

___ 3 information and opinion seeker

___ 5 direction and role definer

___ 7 summariser

___ 9 energiser

___11 comprehension checker

___ *Total for task actions*

Plot this total using the grid horizontally

(B)

Maintenance action

___ 2 encourager of participation

___ 4 communication facilitator

___ 6 tension reliever

___ 8 process observer

___10 interpersonal problem solver

___12 supporter and praiser

___ *Total for maintenance actions*

Plot this total using the grid vertically

USE GRID BELOW TO PLOT TOTALS

GRID PLOTTING

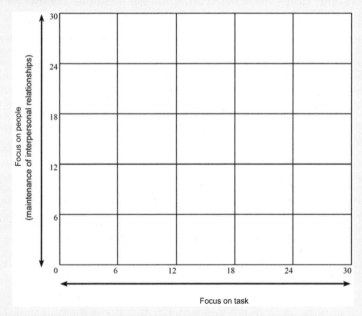

Description of Task-Maintenance Patterns

(6,6) Only minimum effort is given to getting the required work done. There is general non-involvement with other group members. The person with this score may well be saying 'To hell with it all'. Or he or she may be so inactive in the group as to have no influence whatsoever on other group members.

(6,30) High value is placed on keeping good relationships within the group. Thoughtful attention is given to the needs of other members. The person with this score helps create a comfortable, friendly atmosphere and work tempo. However, he or she may never help the group get any work accomplished.

(30,6)   Getting the job done is emphasised in a way that shows very little concern with group maintenance. Work is seen as important, and relationships among group members are ignored. The person with this score may take an army-drillmaster approach to leadership.

(18,18) The task and maintenance needs of the group are balanced. The person with this score continually makes compromises between task needs and maintenance needs. Though a great compromiser, this person does not look for or find ways to creatively integrate task and maintenance activities for optimal productivity.

(30,30) When everyone plans and makes decisions together, all the members become committed to getting the task done as they build relationships of trust and respect. A high value is placed on sound, creative decisions that result in understanding and agreement. Ideas and opinions are sought and listened to, even when they differ from one's own. The group as a whole defines the task and works to get it done. The creative combining of both task and maintenance needs is encouraged.

Team-focused effectiveness characteristics

In addition to a focus on the task itself, the group or team need to develop and maintain working relationships among the members so that the group task can be accomplished. This is called the maintenance need of the group. Adair (1986, p. 61) says that, 'Maintenance refers primarily to *people* and their relationships with each other' (original emphasis). Maintaining the team is a responsibility that all team members shoulder, but in formally led teams, this should be a key concern of the leader-manager. At the heart of the effective management of a team is its leadership. Leaders need to understand that teamwork requires a constant focus on all three elements – the task, the team and the individual – simultaneously as the team strives to achieve its goals. Team management can be both highly rewarding and extremely demanding as leaders attempt to utilise the strengths of the team and deal with the challenges. A team can be a powerful force in bringing about change but unless the team itself is robust and unless the change is managed, teams can fail to be effective.

Team leadership

The primary characteristic of an effective team is that it is led. Team leadership is essential whether this leadership is individual or shared. The leader(s) must nevertheless take responsibility for building and maintaining effective team operations. In an effective team there is a formal leader who has, as a significant responsibility, the fostering of shared and distributed leadership within the team (Zaccaro et al., 2009). In short-life project teams, the team often does not exist long enough for the leader to have a significant impact on the development of others. In permanent teams, provided the leadership is not subject to short-term rotation, leaders are able to develop not only their own skills as leaders, but also the skills of members, thus creating shared expertise.

Effective team operation is characterised by:

- appropriate leadership (individual or shared) determined by the nature and purpose of the team;
- an established climate of support and trust;
- open, honest communication;
- ability to deal openly with conflict and work through differences rather than avoiding or suppressing these;
- learning from mistakes by confronting them;
- the ability of the team to be both co-operative and collaborative; and
- developing team skills to maintain effectiveness.

A leader's performance of their key task to develop the team, as a team involves building the team, establishing structures for teamwork and engaging in processes such as meetings and productive communication that enhance teamwork.

Team-building

Team-building is one of the key dimensions of team leadership. This aspect of developing the team is often overlooked when teams come into being as a result of setting up or restructuring an organisation. It is essential to have some understanding of how a team grows to become a high-performing team. Leaders adopt a limited view in thinking that bringing the team together for regular social functions is the primary way to develop teaming. A wider view includes knowledge of the stages of development that a team goes through before it becomes effective.

Hensey (2001) refers to four stages through which a group passes before it becomes an effective team:

Stage 1: Collection – the gathering together of people who gather to perform a collective task;
Stage 2: Group – the collection establishes some boundaries for membership and feels that it has a group identity;
Stage 3: Developing team – the group creates a sense of teaming by putting in place the rules and processes that guide their work as a team

with a particular focus on the inter-dependency of team members. The function, goals and leadership of the team are clearly identified; and Stage 4: High-performing team – where the team demonstrates all the characteristics of an effective team.

The notion of developing an effective team was presented in the seminal research of Tuckerman (1965) who described four stages through which a loose group of people might be converted into an effective team. This development process incorporates:

• team forming;
• team storming;
• team norming; and
• team performing.

Every time a team is established (or re-established with the addition or loss of members) it has the potential to develop from a gathering of people to a highly performing unit that achieves its goals. In the first instance people come together to undertake work as a group in which there are both individual and collective contributions. Thus a team is *formed* in name. Tuckerman's research showed that in its early stages team members go through a *stormy* period of unsettled differences while getting to know the views and values of others in the team. Beyond this stage, where some of the normal conflict that arises in teams is settled (but often recurs) is the stage of reaching agreement on the key values and standards that the team adopts as a whole. This stage of *norming* – settling differences in the course of agreeing common goals and commonly valued processes – leads to the final stage of a team having the capacity to *perform* their common task at a high level.

Another representation of the development process is shown in the following list that comes from the Henley School of Management in the UK (Dunham, 1995). It again represents the team-building process of getting to know one another, jockeying for position as the members become more familiar with one another, risk-taking as trust and confidence grow and, finally, working together effectively. It is also important for the team to know that every time a new member joins, the process will begin all over again with:

• ritual sniffing – testing out and getting acquainted;
• infighting – sorting out the pecking order;
• experimentation – identifying strengths and weaknesses;
• effectiveness – relationships established and skills utilised; and
• maturity – effective work methods in operation in a climate of trust.

At the point of maturity, the team is once again subject to influences that could jeopardise its effective operation. A very mature team can slip over the edge of effectiveness into lethargy. It is also at this point that teams can become victims of *groupthink*, a condition that allows complacency and comfort to rule the day rather than the sharper and more effective elements of conflict and debate.

Groupthink

Sometimes groups that have worked together for a long time slip into a habit of concurrence rather than allowing their decisions to be challenged. Some signs of groupthink (Gronn, 2003; Preskill and Torres, 1999) are that members strive for unanimity rather than exploring alternatives and seeking new information. Alternatively, they uncritically accept the team's decision even when it is a poor one. In other words, the comfort and complacency of socio-emotional cohesion is paramount and the group becomes overconfident in risk-taking and less effective over time. While suggesting that groupthink is a negative aspect of teamwork, Neck and Manz (1994) propose a positive way of thinking and talking which they have labelled *teamthink*.

Teamthink

Teamthink is bound up with the notion of team members talking to one another in ways that encourage divergent views and lead to an open discussion of collective doubts. In the words of the concept originators, teamthink is advantageous for teams because, 'a group pattern of thinking emerges, that is more than the existence of a simple collection of individual minds' (Neck and Manz, 1994, p. 935). The belief that there is merit in subsuming individual thinking for teamthink is not without its critics. For example, Preskill and Torres (1999, pp. 38, 39) point to the critical role that is played by those who facilitate such team dialogue. They say, 'In fostering teamthink, the facilitator strives to maintain a balance of team cohesiveness while still valuing the individual. Instead of seeing continuous consensus, the facilitator should help the team to come to periodic consensus'. Managing such conversations is no simple task and as Gronn (2003, p. 126) asserts there is 'a vital role for "the" team leader in engineering teamthink'. A negative aspect of managed teamthink is that taken at face value, it could read like mind control.

If not the leader, then who will be on the alert for detecting team practices that indicate either a slippage into groupthink or a team that is being pushed into teamthink? The leadership and management development of team leaders-managers is one of the highest priorities for an organisation that wants to improve teamwork. And, as we know, the team is now strongly established as the most evident and effective work unit in most organisations.

These teams need leadership that can build and develop the team. As a team lives its way through these developmental processes they grow to know one another's strengths and weaknesses, learn how to harness the capacity of the team and can then be said to be engaging in *teamwork*. Leaders also inherit or create the functional framework for teamwork. These are the structures and processes that allow the team to function.

Team structures

Teams are a critical factor in a collaborative decision-making structure. A common ideal surrounding teamwork is that the team provides the means for collective, collegial, collaborative practices (Cardno, 2002). It is also often assumed that the organisation has a culture in which values of trust, openness, honesty and sound interpersonal relationships exist. If an organisation does not have the means for collaborative teams to contribute meaningfully to achievement of its goals, then teamwork is often only window dressing. When organisational leaders fail to pay sufficient attention to the systems and structures that are needed to support the involvement of staff in teams, their work often fails to produce the results that are required (Preskill and Torres, 1999). Furthermore, teams have to engage in processes that create commitment and synergy which impacts on improvement if they are to justify the belief that so many writers appear to have in their potential.

An infrastructure that supports teams will require a formal allocation of time to teamwork. Most teams do much of their decision-making work in meetings. A structure for scheduled team meetings needs to underpin a system of teamwork. Most teams have a relationship to other teams. For example, a team of middle managers would have a link to senior management and also a link to their core functional team such as a subject team. The flow of communication, clarity of decision-making authority and feedback loops between teams should reflect a carefully thought out system. Team members should be able to distinguish between their core work teams of which membership is mandatory and optional team membership of other teams. They should also be able to control their membership of task or project teams beyond the permanent teams they belong to. Research in New Zealand schools has shown that teachers (and especially those with leader-manager roles) belong to a large number of teams. This raises the question of how many teams it is feasible to belong to if the goal is team effectiveness.

Team process – meetings

Teamwork is predominantly done in team meetings. Without doubt the team meeting is one of the most significant performance indicators of a team's development and effectiveness (Dunham, 1995). Meetings are the context in which the team operates as a team. Between meetings many tasks are carried out by sub-teams or individuals. So, for the team leader, the greatest opportunity to build and develop the team lies within the framework of meetings. Furthermore, effective meetings are the foundation for effective teamwork. Team leaders can utilise meetings to achieve successful outcomes when there is good planning, good organisation, good interaction between members and follow-through on decisions. Staff can feel let down if valuable time is spent at meetings that are unproductive. Everard and Morris (1985, cited in Dunham, 1995, p. 56) say that, 'Meetings are vehicles for communication and action rather than for confusion and frustration'. The leader must develop an important skill, which is to carefully judge the need for a meeting before one is called. There are many less time-consuming ways to communicate with a team. Rather than requiring a number of people to dedicate precious time, information can be circulated electronically, for example. Some tried and true characteristics of good meetings are listed below to alert the leader to making the most of the team's most precious resource: time.

Characteristics of good team meetings:

- They are managed.
- Terms of reference for a team should contain details of meeting commitment.
- Leaders should consider the developmental advantages for rotating the chairing of the meeting and introduce this if appropriate.
- Someone should take the role of recording decisions (or formal minute-taking).
- The agenda should be managed but open to additional items.
- People should be invited to provide a position statement about an agenda item and lead discussion.
- The group should be aware of interactions and support the chair in facilitating contributions from all members.

In summary, team meetings that are well planned and well run create the context for effective teamwork. Leaders who are knowledgeable about the need to initially and continually build the team's capacity should also value the meeting as a forum for achieving developmental objectives including time for team self-review.

Team process – conversation

The process that enables team learning and development is the conversation that occurs during and beyond team meetings. The means by which the team makes decisions and solves its problems in relation to achieving the task is team talk. It is the process that aligns, enlivens and binds a team. Team talk is a group activity but it is the capability of individuals in the team to engage in productive, rather than defensive, talk that opens up the possibility of the team learning and growing together. Team leaders need to be skilled in group management skills and also capable of dealing with complex inter-personal relationships to utilise communication processes to integrate the focus on task, team and individual. It is here that an understanding of pro-ductive rather than defensive ways of dealing with interpersonal issues is likely to be of great use. It is in this highly complex and sometimes conflicted context of group interaction that the team needs to be able to talk in ways that assist listening and learning. This requires that the team as a unit and the individuals in the team are able to discover the underlying sources of problems and resolve these openly and honestly. When such problems are leadership dilemmas (Cardno, 2007), there is an even greater need for the team to build trust in its ability to create and maintain productive relation-ships through productive conversations. How the team learns to do this is outlined in the next section.

Individual-focused effectiveness characteristics

Teams in the workplace are made up of individuals brought together because they have the capacity to carry out an individual function that can be meshed with the interacting functions of others to create concertive action. Adair (1986) reminds us that the needs of individuals come with them into group life. Capable individuals need quality relationships in their work life; they need respect from others and self-respect; and they have a need for self-actualisation, the fulfilment of one's potential by growth. Adair contends that, 'If such needs can be met *along with* and not *at the expense of* the group task and maintenance needs, then the group will tend to be more effective' (original emphasis, p. 61). Communication is the key to allowing individuals and the team to engage in learning.

Team learning

The literature on team learning appears to be dominated by two particular approaches. One features the collective team learning processes as the way forward (Manz and Neck, 1997). The other highlights a constant need to remember that teams are collections of individuals. It is the development of the individual that contributes directly to the development of the team. It is the individual who learns and who, in turn, contributes to *team learning* (Senge, 2006).

The first approach emanates from the framework for constructive thought patterns in a group provided by Neck and Manz (1994). In their research, these authors have found that collective learning can take place in a team if thought patterns can be changed. It is, however, at the personal level that thought patterns are influenced and this is then carried into teamwork, and also has the potential to affect organisational performance. Manz and Neck (1997) propose that in self-managing teams, members need to develop strategies to analyse and manage the following while engaging in *teamthink*:

- beliefs and assumptions (with teamthink dominant group beliefs are identified and challenged);
- internal dialogues (self-talk) (team self-talk should be constructive and allow for a challenge of the status quo); and
- mental images (visualising successful interaction and achievement – creating a common view of what can be accomplished).

Together, these elements interact to produce team thought patterns as integrated patterns that then tend to be repeated when similar circumstances arise. An effective self-managing team can learn how to adopt positive rather than negative thought patterns. For example, 'opportunity thinking' focuses on constructive problem-solving while 'obstacle thinking' fosters a retreat from problems (Manz and Neck, 1997). The role of leadership in fostering the sort of learning (and teamthink training), that leads to positive and productive thought patterns in teams that have a more hierarchical structure, is not easy to discern in the literature. However, Leithwood (1998) suggests that to explore collective team learning the notion of 'team mind' could be considered. The question of whether 'such a collective mind could be conceptualised?' (p. 208) is indeed a thorny one. In furthering the debate about collective team learning, he offers two perspectives from which teams can adopt a learning stance. One is organisational or team culture that shapes the interactions of team members and helps with the learning challenge of building shared memory and telling stories to pass on organisational knowledge to new members. The other learning challenge that all members face as individuals is deciding how to act in order to adapt their contributions to the team's collective actions. This is a way in which the individual learns from the team and vice versa. As Leithwood (1998, p. 214) states:

> Collective team learning entails a change in these patterns of action through processes of mutual adaptation. These are processes in which individual members adapt their contribution to the team partly in response to their understanding of the new challenge facing the team and partly in response to the responses of their fellow team members' actions. In this way the team's learning has the potential to both precede and to contribute to the individual member's learning.

The second approach to team learning is connected to the notion of *organisational learning*. Team learning that requires deep and significant learning on the part of individual team members emanates from theories about how organisations learn to solve their problems (Argyris and Schön, 1978). Senge (2006) proposes that while organisations may be slow to discover and correct mistakes, teams hold out great potential for learning that can, in turn, impact on the organisation. My own research in New Zealand (Cardno, 2002) shows that team learning can be both welcomed and feared by team leaders. As I have stated:

> The particular set of skills associated with effective communication that leads to organisational learning are those associated with the confrontation and elimination of defensive dialogue and the use of productive dialogue in teams. For many leaders of teams, this is an inordinate challenge that fits the adage of 'taking the tiger by the tail' because it appeals on the one hand and yet, on the other hand, is fraught with danger. As the learning capacity of the team grows, so exponentially does the challenge for the leader who must be capable of modelling personal openness to learning and have the ability to effectively utilise team strength even though this might challenge their own goals and capability. (p. 221)

From this perspective, the 'discipline of team learning involves mastering the practices of dialogue and discussion, the two distinct ways that teams converse' (Senge, 2006, p. 220). The kind of talk that a team engages in makes all the difference in this context of team learning. Teams need to learn communication skills that move their talk from the arena of discussion to the arena of dialogue in order to overcome defensive routines (Argyris, 1985). Senge (2006) draws attention to two primary types of discourse: 'dialogue' and 'discussion' (attributing this distinctive contribution to Bohm, 1965). He points out that the word discussion has the same root as percussion and concussion. It has connotations of sallying back and forth from opposite sides, with an underlying principle of needing to win. By contrast, dialogue comes from the Greek word dialogos. *Dia* means through, *logos* means word or meaning. Dialogue contributes to a pool of 'common meaning' that can be accessed collectively. Winning is not a paramount principle and people are not in opposition, but are participators in widening the common meaning pool, which explores issues from many viewpoints. The key to this kind of communication is the suspension (or revealing) in front of others the assumptions that are usually not shared. This demands a high degree of trust because it requires one to, first, refrain from imposing views on others and, secondly, to avoid suppressing what they think. Furthermore, in team dialogue, assumptions must be suspended collectively – not an easy task, because as Senge et al. (1994) assert, 'Hanging your assumptions in front of you so that you and others can reflect on them is a delicate and powerful art' (p. 378).

In a collegial atmosphere both dialogue (to explore complex issues) and discussion (presenting and debating different views and making decisions) can and should occur. In addition, the team should be able to acknowledge the different goals of each. They should also seek to balance high levels of both advocacy and inquiry. When a team practises genuine advocacy (laying out reasoning and thinking for others to see) and inquiry (encouraging others to challenge views and reveal their own assumptions) this is powerful and productive communication. Its purpose should be aligned with values of increasing valid information for all. Teams able to achieve this become effective in terms of engaging in productive rather than defensive dialogue.

Learning case for reflection: challenging the team to suspend assumptions

Corrine and Dan have been joint programme leaders for a higher education programme in adult literacy. They co-manage a team of 12 people who in the main work part-time. In fact, they are the only full-time members of this teaching team. Team communication has been an issue for the last six months or so and team meetings are fraught with difficulties such as low attendance because staff have other major work commitments that need to be juggled. The joint managers are currently concerned about individuals who are not correctly using existing systems for student attendance and assessment recording. Corrine is convinced that they need a face-to-face meeting with all members to develop a shared understanding of team commitment to common practices. In particular, two of the longest serving team members are the worst offenders and appear to be cavalier in the manner in which they attend to these tasks. Dan, however, believes that they need to communicate directly with the two people who are at the heart of this concern.

In their dialogue with each other about this issue Corrine was able to share her assumptions with Dan. She suspended these thoughts:

I think we need to do this as a team because Tom and Jerry need the pressure of being accountable to the whole team to get them on board. I don't think they will admit to us if they are struggling but they may do this with another team member and rely on a colleague to coach them. I assume that if we are too pointed in our criticism they will be upset and they are so important to the programme.

Dan's assumptions about Tom and Jerry were suspended as follows:

As always they will agree with everything we suggest in front of the team and then go their own merry way. I think they are struggling with the system and hate having to admit this. I guess that because we have not confronted them before they are hoping we will let this slide. They know how much we rely on them for other key tasks and probably think we will continue to cover up for their shortcomings.

What Corrine and Dan are dealing with is a leadership dilemma where the concern is both about organisational objectives being met and relationships being maintained. They have both been able to suspend their assumptions about Tom and Jerry to one another. The next step is to confront these staff members in a team or individual setting and *include them* in the suspension of assumptions.

In your view do you think that the suspension of these assumptions and the ensuing dialogue will be effective in a team or an individual meeting?

If you were to apply the steps for a productive dialogue in this situation, what would you convey at each of the following steps?

1 Saying what you think/feel (suspending your assumptions)

2 Saying why you think/feel this way (showing how you reached these assumptions)

3 Checking others' response to your assumptions (and hearing their assumptions)

4 Using suspended assumptions to establish common understanding of the issue

5 Using common understanding to propose solutions jointly.

Tools for team and team leader development

If the potential of a team as an agent for organisational learning is to be realised, then the critical issue of team development must be addressed. Furthermore, it must be addressed in such a way that it impacts on the manner in which a team deals with conflict and learns from mistakes. This requires a particular type of team leadership in which conflict and disagreement are harnessed to enable learning. Failure to deal with conflict is one of the main ways in which individual and team learning is blocked. Conflicts that go unresolved can seriously damage a team's functioning and learning. Leaders should be alerted to these consequences because, 'When conflict between individuals is not addressed adequately, people begin to lose trust not only in the process but also in each other' (Preskill and Torres, 1999, p. 36).

A productive dialogue tool for teams

One tool that provides skill awareness and skill learning through practice is double-loop learning (Argyris and Schön, 1978). The skills of double-loop learning are underpinned by self-awareness of our tendencies to be defensive and the wish to suppress conflict rather than allowing it to surface and be dealt with. It calls for a special kind of dialogue. It also requires a high degree of knowledge about dealing with defensiveness. Hence in Senge's view it 'also involves learning how to deal creatively with the powerful forces opposing productive dialogue and discussion in working teams' (2006, p. 220). Countering these forces involves a praxis of theory and action. This is needed to learn how to overcome the pitfalls of single-loop learning which lead to only a change of action without a change of the fundamental values that make working relationships productive. If teams and their leaders learn how to apply tools such as the Triple I approach (Cardno, 2007) in everyday practice, they move towards the use of productive dialogue which, in turn, becomes the cornerstone of productive relationships.

An emotional intelligence tool for teams

Goleman's (1996) ground-breaking introduction of the concept of *emotional intelligence* signals the importance of both personal competence (self-awareness and self-management) coupled with social competence (social awareness and relationship management). This notion of managers needing to be emotionally intelligent in order to work effectively with other people is built on a foundation of *resonance*. Resonant leaders know how to articulate and synchronise a mission that resonates with the values of those they lead. According to Goleman et al. (2002) a resonant leader is strongly connected to and is honest about their own emotions in order to be connected to others. They need to be exceptionally self-knowledgeable to engage in effective interpersonal relationships. The following exercise is based on the elements that create both personal and social competence. Teams can also develop individual and collective emotional intelligence strengths (Druskat and Wolff, 2001) which create a foundation for effective teamwork.

A useful team development exercise, which also provides insights for self-development, involves a self-rating of one's perceived capability in the two domains of personal competence and social competence. The reflective exercise allows one to score a range of competence indicators. When the scored exercise is shared in a team situation it provides an opportunity for members to discuss implications for the team. It should be noted that the use of such exercises for team development requires conditions of high trust and highly skilled facilitation. When these conditions are not present, the self-reflection demand may make people defensive and render the exercise ineffective or even damaging rather than developmental. Team leaders in particular could benefit from the sort of critical reflection such an exercise provides.

Reflective exercise: Self-Assessment of Emotional Intelligence Domains

(Adapted from D. Goleman, R. Boyzatis and A. McKee (2002) p. 39, *The New Leaders: Transforming the Art of Leadership into the Science of Results,* with the permission of Little, Brown Publishers)

	THE CAPABILITIES	SELF-RATING 1 ←——→ 5 LOW HIGH
PERSONAL COMPETENCE These capabilities determine how we manage ourselves	Self-awareness **Emotional self-awareness** – *reading one's own emotions and recognising their impact; using 'gut sense' to guide decisions* **Accurate self-assessment** – *knowing one's strengths and limits* **Self-confidence** – *a sound sense of one's self-worth and capabilities* Self-management **Emotional self-control** – *keeping disruptive emotions and impulses under control* **Transparency** – *displaying honesty and integrity; trustworthiness* **Adaptability** – *flexibility in adapting to changing situations or overcoming obstacles* **Achievement** – *the drive to improve performance to meet inner standards of excellence* **Initiative** – *readiness to act and seize opportunities* **Optimism** – *seeing the upside in events*	
SOCIAL COMPETENCE These capabilities determine how we manage relationships	Social awareness **Empathy** – *sensing others' emotions, understanding their perspective, and taking an active interest in their concerns* **Organisational awareness** – *reading the currents, decision networks, and politics at organisational level* **Service orientation** – *recognising and meeting follower, client and customer needs* Relationship management **Inspirational leadership** – *guiding and motivating with a compelling vision* **Influence** – *wielding a range of tactics for persuasion* **Developing others** – *bolstering others' abilities through feedback and guidance* **Change catalyst** – *initiating, managing and leading in a new direction* **Conflict management** – *resolving disagreements* **Building bonds** – *cultivating and maintaining a web of relationships* **Teamwork and collaboration** – *co-operation and teambuilding*	
	SELF-RATING TOTAL (out of possible total of 95)	

CHAPTER EIGHT

STRATEGIC LEADERSHIP AND MANAGEMENT

Building productive relationships

In formulating strategy and developing vision, leaders are building myriad relationships with external and internal stakeholders. Educational organisations have multiple stakeholders creating a range of goals that are often in tension. It is the leader's responsibility to forge unity from disparity in the process of strategic decision-making. In order to do this, the leader needs to build a culture in which collaboration and mutual commitment to common goals can flourish. This is achieved through strategic thinking, analysis review and planning. Strategy must also be implemented. In the course of strategy implementation, leaders depend upon productive relationships to align organisational and individual needs in order to achieve educational purposes.

Some limitations to being strategic

Leadership is most often associated with long-range, big picture and futuristic thinking and this notion of visionary leadership is strongly promoted in both generic and educational management conceptions of effective leadership (Bush et al., 2010). Setting direction and establishing goals for an organisation are undoubtedly the major ways in which educational leaders lead. It could be argued that in contrast to business and commercial enterprises, educational organisations strategise in a far more limited way. Planning is promoted as an essential facet of leadership in all settings, be they early childhood centres, schools or higher education institutions. However, in spite of the rhetoric that this activity is strategic, there are significant restrictions to the creation of vision and the formulation of strategy in educational organisations.

First, government-funded schools will meet state imposed directions or boundaries around their proposed strategic initiatives. In other words, their vision and strategy could be curtailed by larger system-driven policy expectations. Over the past two decades, educational research in the UK in particular has created a surge of interest in the degree to which government-driven agendas have created a new form of strategic planning in schools where the 'purpose of planning has now become that of ensuring that schools implement initiatives that are devolved to them by central government' (Bell, 2002, p. 412). In higher education, too, centrally developed vision statements and strategies are the norm and funding for higher education providers is usually contingent upon their institutional goals and objectives being in alignment with these broad directions. So there are some limits to the notion of visionary leadership in the way strategy is broadly managed in relation to education. Bush et al. (2010) suggest a need to be cautious about embracing the rhetoric of vision when it is likely to be constrained by an overlay of vision created by central government. Nevertheless, even within restricted boundaries, which are much wider in higher education than in the other sectors, planning in a framework that is strategic is a fundamental aspect of effective educational leadership.

Secondly, in many systems educational organisations are required to plan in a particular way to encapsulate targets specifically related to student learning outcomes within their plans. An example of this is annual target setting related to improving student achievement that is a requirement of strategic planning for New Zealand schools (Government of New Zealand, 2001). While this may be viewed as a restriction of visionary thinking, the explicit focus on student learning can also be seen as a way of making strategic management and leadership more tightly focused on educational endeavour. Robinson et al. (2009) highlight goal-setting and strategic resourcing as dimensions of educational leadership though which leaders can strategically influence the improvement of learning and teaching. A meta-analysis of several studies shows these factors have an impact (albeit moderate and indirect) on improving student outcomes. Both of these leadership activities are implicit in any conceptualisation of strategic leadership and management (Bryson, 1995; Morden, 2007).

Therefore, despite what may be seen as limitations to the way in which strategic management and leadership are played out in many educational organisations, effective leadership requires effective management of strategy.

Effective leadership in education requires that the focus of strategic management is unwaveringly on teaching and learning and that its ultimate concern is the improvement of student learning outcomes. In the context of developing and implementing strategy a leader must work with other people both within and beyond the organisation, and forge relationships that are a positive and productive foundation for turning strategy into action. Unless leaders in educational organisations are well informed about the concept of strategy and its potential and pitfalls, they will not be in a position to judge whether this major aspect of decision-making is something they can embrace to improve their leadership and management or whether it is as Bell (2002, p. 407) suggests, 'full of sound and fury, signifying nothing' – a hollow exercise because real strategising does not lie within the power of leaders at institutional level.

The concepts of strategy and quality management with links to educational marketing have been drawn into education over the last two decades from the field of generic management theory (Foskett, 2002; Murgatroyd and Morgan, 1992). The educational management literature that promotes the adoption of strategic leadership and management in educational settings believes it has much to offer (see, for example, Davies and Davies, 2004; Fidler, 1996). Planning has been identified as one of the facets of effective management since the earliest attempts to analyse and define the meaning of the term management (Drucker, 1955). In its widest sense, planning encompasses two management dimensions. One dimension is embedded in the present and concerned with current tasks and operations. The other dimension is concerned with what will be different. The *strategic management* paradigm brings both strategic planning and strategic implementation together. It is concerned with strategy formulation, and long-term strategic planning at the macro or big-picture level. It is also concerned with short-term operational planning for implementing strategy at the micro level (Cardno, 2001b; Middlewood, 1998).

The evolution of strategic management and leadership

A number of approaches to long-range planning emerged in the 1960s when the logic of strategic planning was born. The strategic planning model was intended to deal with the organisation as a whole and relate it to its environment, so that in times of rapid change and universal competitiveness, management could become more proactive. A problem, however, was that it offered no guidance as to how to make the strategic processes work in a given context (Limerick and Cunnington, 1993). There is no specific model of *strategic management* or *strategic planning,* as it is variously referred to in the literature, that has been particularly designed for educational settings. All of the ideas that have been borrowed come from the generic management literature.

Bowman et al. (2002) remind us that the field of strategic management has come a long way in the 40 or so years of its existence. They identify three major influences in the field, the earliest being a strong practice element with researchers focusing on rich descriptions of practice from top management perspectives. The work of Porter (1980) exemplifies the next wave of influence – coming from economists – in the late 1970s and the 1980s, and characterised by a competitive framework. A third set of influences is identified as coming from the behavioural scientists including the ground-breaking work of Argyris (1985) for example. This school of research focuses on the functioning and survival of organisations and the behaviour of the people in them – with an emphasis on co-operative networks. All of these influences have advanced and enriched the field of strategic management and continue to provide rich ground for the development of theory and the understanding of practice as it continues to challenge managers in organisations.

In transferring the best ideas and practices of strategic management to education settings, the one aspect common to strategic leadership and educational leadership is goal-setting. The major research studies of educational leadership over the past 30 years have searched for evidence of leadership behaviour that leads to school effectiveness measured in terms of student learning achievement. At least four of these studies have acted as way-posts over several decades to confirm the importance of setting academic goals and then monitoring their implementation (Seashore Louis et al., 2010; Weber, 1987). Goal-setting is at the heart of effective educational leadership and a core activity of strategic leadership. When these goals lead to action that impacts on improving student learning outcomes then strategic educational management and leadership occur.

While educational organisations are aware of the importance of planning, understanding of the nature of strategic management and planning is often treated as irrelevant because of its evolution within business practice and research (Bryson, 1995). However, recent insights into the significance of goal setting and strategic resourcing as desirable knowledge and skills in the context of school leadership and management may awaken interest in these dimensions of leadership that overlap with strategic management.

When educational leaders are introduced to or reflect on the value of strategic management, the pedagogical focus of goal-setting needs to be highlighted and the concept of strategic human resource management needs to be actualised in everyday practice. In both of these strategic management activities there is potential for relationships with internal and external stakeholders to be built and utilised effectively.

Pedagogical goal-setting as part of strategic educational leadership

In the best evidence synthesis (BES) on school leadership there is confirmation within the research evidence that 'the content of goals may be as important as the process by which they are set' (Robinson et al., 2009, p. 97) and this content must be *pedagogical* in nature and specific if the impact is to be effective in terms of improving student learning. Leaders must be able to establish the importance of selected goals and do this by making links to moral and philosophical commitments, thus securing the type of alignment that is essential between vision, its translation into goals and the actualisation of goals through setting and achieving objectives. Robinson et al. (2009) comment on the importance of articulate goal-setting. They say, 'one of the requirements for effectiveness is that goals are clear and unambiguous. … Goals are clearer when they include a target and a timeframe' (p. 108). These authors also assert that the importance of building capability for setting and reviewing goals extends across all levels of leadership and includes teachers. This is because, 'Goal setting – for both teacher and student learning – is part of a cycle of evidence-based assessment, analysis and determination of next steps' (p. 109).

Educational organisations are beset by many complexities that affect the application of the logic of strategic management without careful consideration of contextual challenges. First, there are multiple stakeholders: the state or institutional owners, community, parents, students and staff. Goal-setting for strategic purposes is not straightforward. The agendas of various stakeholders may sometimes be in conflict, and tensions between differing stakeholder values create a challenge for leaders in goal-setting. Secondly, education serves many purposes and a strategic approach can be overwhelmed by having too many goals. The ability to formulate and prioritise goals that will secure commitment and have a tight fit with what the organisation values highly (Rudman, 2002) hinges on the capability of leaders to create opportunities for stakeholders to understand the goals, including the beliefs and values that underpin them. When goals are valued they are more likely to gain commitment and be achieved (Latham and Locke, 2006).

Learning case for reflection: internal stakeholder commitment to goals

I was recently approached to facilitate a one-day workshop on planning and goal-setting for 17 heads of department in a large co-educational secondary school. The principal wanted me to run this professional development session because he had an ambitious aim: improving strategic management in the school. He was disappointed with the quality of planning at the middle management level and wanted school-wide goals and department goals to be better aligned and to be used as a basis for review. Basically, however, what he wanted was for the department heads

(Continues)

(Continued)

to produce technically well formulated plans to which they would be bound in accounting for the performance of the department.

I found myself in a difficult situation because I had to reveal to Jeff that spending a day with these middle managers with the objective of having them produce well-documented plans at the end of the day would not meet his long-term aim of improving strategic management. A strategic journey is an inherently collaborative one. It needs to collect and convey people to a common destination. Above all, it requires the journeyers to have a clear understanding of what the destination is. In this case, the principal would need to set out at the head of the travellers. He had to be absolutely clear about the nature of the school-wide strategy and, in a New Zealand setting, strategic decisions are intended to be a governance function. Consequently, the school's board of trustees would need to participate in the school-wide activities of visioning and goal-setting. Only when this level of strategic planning had been achieved by the governing board and senior management would it be right to expect mid-level managers to plan in a coherent and aligned manner. I communicated my view to Jeff and he agreed that he, personally, and his board chairperson had much to do in preparation for an expectation of improved mid-level planning. He acknowledged that above all he wanted his mid-level managers to be motivated about planning and knowledgeable about how to go about this. He also acknowledged that he needed to meet their expectations which related to developing a school strategic plan as the umbrella plan for mid-level planning. Furthermore, he realised that the department heads themselves should be involved appropriately in this planning as they were without doubt the most important internal stakeholders whose commitment he needed to gain to achieve his own aim.

Jeff then asked me to help him to formulate some critically reflective questions to guide the actions he would take to strengthen a collaborative approach to strategic management in the school. These questions could assist others with a similar aim.

1 **Do we as a school have a clear statement of our purpose, values and goals that permanently guide what we do – and how do we review this?**
2 **Have the governors and senior management undertaken adequate strategic analysis to consider the need to formulate a vision that creates a different future for this school?**
3 **How well have we identified and involved stakeholders in visionary thinking?**

> **4** How well have we included middle-level managers as key stake-
> holders in considering the future and the way present goals
> impact on their own department's performance?
>
> **5** Have we achieved a clear distinction between strategic and oper-
> ational planning?
>
> **6** How will we (senior and middle managers) align department-
> level goals with school-level goals and then with strategic
> initiatives?
>
> **7** How robust are our systems and practices for review and does
> review link to strategic and operational planning?

As awareness of the critical importance of goal-setting and evaluation of goal achievement is raised in relation to educational leadership, this may also create an appreciation of how the generic principles and practices of strategic management can be adapted to be more relevant, and more applicable in educational settings with the constant aim of aligning organisational endeavour to achieve improved learning outcomes – for leadership, for teachers and for students.

Strategic management is also inextricably aligned with other management practices that focus on improvement – such as performance appraisal. To make it possible for a strategic initiative to permeate all organisational practice it must be featured in the goals of individuals. Hence, teacher goal-setting must have a pedagogical focus as the primary concern. Staff performance appraisal systems provide a mechanism for motivating staff to set development goals that are aligned with the organisation's pedagogical aspirations. When issues arise in relation to concerns about staff performance and achievement of goals at this level, then leaders will need to have the skills that enable them to have conversations with staff about goal achievement. Such conversations are easy when there is an atmosphere of trust and support. However, when relationships are strained, attempts to have productive conversations (Cardno, 2007) may fail. Leaders who are able to recognise the complexity of such situations will draw on resources for managing dilemmas as a way forward. Ultimately, a strategy and its attendant goals at organisational level are a mere statement of intent. Paving the way to implement goals requires attention being paid to whether these goals are owned by the individuals, in this case teachers as the most critical internal stakeholders, who will put them into action.

Strategic human resources management

There is a well-established literature in the business arena that deals with the notion of integrating human resources issues within the scope of strategic management (see, for example, Boxall and Purcell, 2011; Rudman, 2002). In fact, the successful implementation of any strategic plan depends on the quality of staff, and the motivation and commitment of people in the organisation to support its strategic direction – thus a core principle of effective human resources management is mutuality – of cause and of responsibility. Mutuality of interest between the organisation and its people is one of the essentials to be achieved along the way to achieving the organisation's objectives. In educational terms, this mutuality translates into the need for goals to be fundamentally concerned with pedagogical and academic purposes.

Several writers in this field stress the idea that human resources management can be nothing but *strategic* (Macky and Johnson, 2000). Rudman (2002) states that, 'Human resources strategies exist to ensure that the culture, values and structure of the organisation and the quality, motivation and commitment of its members contribute fully to the achievement of its objectives' (p. 7). Hence, one of the key areas in which an organisation must be effectively resourced to implement strategy is in relation to human resources. This point is well made by Robinson et al. (2009) in relation to an educational leader's need to balance goal setting with appropriate and *aligned* strategic resourcing. These authors say that in order to have an impact on improving teaching and learning, strategic resourcing in schools should have some specific features:

- Resources (both physical and human) need to be secured with pedagogical goals in mind.
- Once secured, resources should be closely aligned to pedagogical goals.
- Recruiting and developing staff may be essential to achieve strategic alignment between goals and resources.
- Seeking expertise externally may be an essential to the alignment process necessary to achievement of pedagogical goals.

These aspects of alignment, also referred to as *integration* in the generic literature, are inherent in the view that strategic human resources management is 'the means of aligning the management of human resources with the strategic content of the business' (Rudman, 2002, p. 11). The focus on strategic resourcing in the BES on school leadership (Robinson et al., 2009) reinforces the primacy of people in all endeavours to implement strategy. Boxall and Purcell (2011) intimate that 'people capability' in actually carrying out strategic processes is reflected in the executive decision-making of organisations and hence the recruitment and development of leaders is a crucial strategic human resources concern. This focus on people capability is also strikingly evident in the approach to strategic school management proposed by Miles and Frank (2008) which centres strategy on staff and student resources. They present three organising principles for a strategic school, calling them the 'big three' guiding resource strategies. These are (1) investing in teaching quality, (2) creating individual attention and personal learning environments for students and (3) using student time strategically to focus on core academics. It is interesting to note that in this approach, resources are consistently aligned to achieve teaching and learning objectives through the careful analysis of the needs of the people in the organisation.

The literature tells us that strategic human resources management is a top-level leadership activity concerned with analysing needs and setting broad direction and strategy. Some educational leadership literature suggests that there is still much to be learnt about aligning goals and resources strategically. For example, Robinson et al. (2009) contend that:

> We need to learn more about the knowledge and skills that leaders require in order to link the recruitment and allocation of resources to specific pedagogical goals. ... This dimension [strategic resourcing] needs greater conceptual development, particularly with respect to how budgeting and staff appointments link to goal setting (p. 99).

It could be argued that there is a wealth of knowledge about the management of strategy and planning that already offers guidance related to the concerns expressed above. It is timely for education sector practitioners and researchers to look both within and beyond the field and see what they might learn from tried and true approaches to strategic management. What will continue to distinguish education purpose from business purpose is the pedagogical and academic foundation for goal-setting and strategic human resources management.

The nature and scope of strategic management

Educational leaders who are committed to providing the most effective environment for student achievement could seriously consider the advantages offered by a strategic management approach to change and improvement. There is a considerable body of knowledge and skills associated with strategic management and it is most effectively accomplished when strategic thinking, strategic analysis, strategic planning and strategic review are being practised in an integrated way. At the heart of strategic management is the notion of planning for both the short and long terms. Strategy is the long-term direction of the organisation and is often associated with the term strategic leadership. Strategic management, according to Johnson and Scholes (2002) is the management of the process of strategic decision-making. It is concerned with deciding on strategy and planning how that strategy will be put into effect. These authors have depicted the nature of strategic management activity in a model which illustrates the key elements and the interrelationships between them.

The model (Figure 8.1) consisting of the elements that constitute strategic activity (Johnson and Scholes, 2002) depicts the iterative nature of strategic activity with the core activities being threefold:

1. The establishment of a strategic position which requires understanding and analysing the environment; clarifying expectations and purposes of the organisation; and assessing the resources and capabilities that the organisation can commit to achieving its strategic direction.
2. Making strategic choices (based on being fully informed about its strategic position) which involves institution-wide corporate level strategies; and units developing their own business-level strategies; and consideration of what needs to be developed and how, in order for the organisation and its parts to achieve their chosen strategy.
3. Turning strategy into action which depends on effective management of change; motivation and support that enables the implementation of changes; and careful organisation of the structures and processes that will sustain the changes.

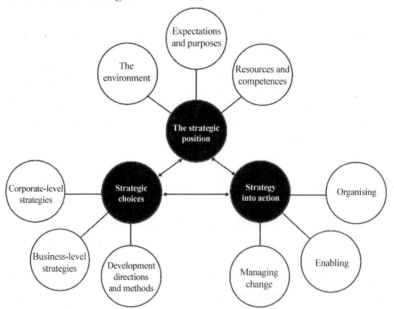

Figure 8.1 *A model of the elements of strategic management (source: G. Johnson and K. Scholes, 2002, p. 17, Exploring Corporate Strategy, Texts and Cases, reproduced with the permission of Pearson Education)*

The elements of the model are interlinked, and do not necessarily follow a clear path which is a feature of strategic management. So, in practice, many activities may occur simultaneously, or as Johnson and Scholes (2002) describe it: 'One way of understanding a strategy better is to implement it, so strategic choices and strategy into action may overlap. Similarly, an understanding of the strategic position may be built up from the experience of strategy in action' (p. 353).

Organisations that embrace strategic management are not content to stay as they are and recognise that the external environment has an impact on strategy that cannot be ignored. Understanding the strategic position and the expectations and influence of stakeholders is fundamental to a shift in thinking that moves the leadership focus from an internal perspective that is operational to an external and much wider perspective that is strategic. In essence this shift is known as strategic thinking.

Strategic thinking

Strategic management activity is most effective when it is accompanied by *strategic thinking*. This management requirement is similar to the notion of establishing a strategic position for the organisation as depicted in the Johnson and Scholes (2002) model, which points to the need for the organisation to understand its own capabilities by being aware of its resources and competences. It also needs to be aware of external environmental issues that may impact on its present and future aspirations and it needs to have and to articulate clearly its own expectations and purposes.

There are several things that thinking strategically demands. First, it demands an appreciation of change forces that impact on education, a proactive stance and a considerable degree of openness to learning from the world of business. Secondly, a mindshift is necessary to accept the view that the voice of the key external stakeholder – the customer – must be heard. Thirdly, the development or affirmation of a generic strategy to frame or guide thinking about both current and future priorities is essential.

Some of the major factors that have been impacting as change forces on education since the beginning of this decade are, for example:

- market-driven competitiveness;
- technological change;
- diversity and equity issues;
- nationally driven curriculum change; and
- emphasis on professional accountability.

As a consequence of developments associated with these factors, teachers and leaders in education settings have experienced the new realities of change which are unlikely to diminish in either scope or speed in the future. They can be either reactive or proactive in relation to internal and external imperatives to change. A reactive stance implies that one waits for change to be demanded. In this scenario the response is made only when internal problems grow to crisis dimensions or when external demands are unable to be selectively managed because there is no anticipation of the need to plan to meet such contingencies. A proactive stance implies readiness to deal in a systematic way with internal problems and is a considered approach to external demands guided by strategic thinking and forward planning. Strategic thinking about the organisation's strategic position opens up new possibilities, new concepts and also a new language associated with strategic management. Some educators are still extremely uncomfortable with words and ideas drawn from business practice that have been imported to the world of education. Nevertheless, educational leaders need to understand and respond to the new challenges that are created by external change forces. Access to a range of strategic management tools, which have been adapted for educational organisations, will help them to do this.

Strategy formulation

Bryson (1995) asserts that every organisation already has a strategy – that is, some pattern or logic that permeates everything the organisation stands for. He says that a strategy may be thought of as a 'pattern of purposes, policies, programs, actions, decisions, and/or resource allocations that defines what an organisation is, what it does, and why it does it' (p. 130). These overarching strategies are a fundamental response to the challenges an organisation faces and are therefore an extension of the 'mission, forming a bridge between the organisation and its environment' (p. 130). In Bryson's view, strategy formulation involves:

- highlighting what is good about the existing pattern;
- reframing or downplaying what is bad about it; and
- adding whatever new bits are needed to complete the picture.

Bryson reminds us that the organisation's culture is critically important during the process of strategy formulation because it affects how strategic issues are framed, discussed and decided. In a culture where defensive behaviour limits the capacity of the organisation to deal with complex problems, no amount of strategic environment scanning or stakeholder consultation will overcome implementation problems. As Argyris (1990) says, in spite of sound planning processes and new structures many organisations find themselves crippled by counterproductive defensive routines that inhibit learning when they introduce strategic change. If an organisation can create a culture in which organisational learning can occur it is securing its long-term health and effectiveness.

Developing a generic strategy

Educational institutions are, in the main, non-profit service organisations and the key service they provide is delivery of the curriculum. Although many aspects of the curriculum (the processes and learning outcomes of peda-gogy) are largely specified, for example in schools, there are many opportunities for creatively designing learning strategies, creating learning resources and creating the mix of resources and programmes/qualifications that are offered.

If strategic thinking is adopted, then a primary task is to identify the over-all or generic strategy adopted by the organisation for its current operation and to regularly review the appropriateness of this strategy when envision-ing the future. Strategy is the organisation's commitment to a position of strength embracing the notion of competitiveness and is a strategic concept adapted from the work of Porter (1980). Organisations can choose many strategic positions and one of these is differentiation. This is the creation of something different, special or unique in the marketplace of education. It carries with it the requirement to confirm the position with stakeholders and to then articulate it publicly and promote it vigorously.

The work of Murgatroyd and Morgan (1992) is drawn upon next to illus-trate the kind of strategic frameworks or generic strategies that they have identified in schooling contexts. One strategic framework is not viewed as being better than any other. Each framework is different and this is its strength. There are four such frameworks depicted in Figure 8.2.

1. *A broad basic curriculum strategy.* Schools offering a broad basic cur-riculum would provide a broad-based programme of activity for all students. This would include curriculum, pastoral care, sport and cul-tural activities and after-school activities.
2. *An enhanced basic curriculum strategy.* This strategy requires the school to offer a broad basic curriculum but also to develop some par-ticular aspect of the services it provides as a form of differentiation.

STRATEGIC FRAMEWORK

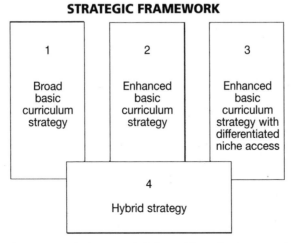

Figure 8.2 *Choosing a strategic framework (adapted from S. Murgatroyd and C. Morgan, 1992,* Total Quality Management and the School, *with the permission of Open University Press)*

3. *An enhanced basic curriculum strategy with differentiated niche access.*
   Schools which choose this strategy offer a broad basic curriculum and
   specialise in a particular field, but they also rely on an element of student selection. This can happen in two ways: (1) by limiting access to
   courses on the basis of student ability, and (2) by limiting access to
   courses by requiring user fees from parents.
4. *A hybrid strategy.* Some schools set out to secure the 'best of all worlds'
   by adopting all of the above strategies. To manage a number of strategies, schools may need to set up separate management entities under a
   broad umbrella if they are determined to proceed this way.

Strategies do not merely emerge or happen – they have to be managed.
Leaders have to be relentless in their commitment to achieving a strategy if
it is to succeed. To activate a strategic framework a school needs to practise
strategic analysis and planning.

Strategic analysis

Strategic choices (Johnson and Scholes, 2002) involve strategic decision-
making based on a sound understanding of the organisation's strategic
position. Engaging in the activity of strategic analysis provides evidence to
confirm the strategic position and guides the choice of corporate and unit-
level strategies that will be incorporated in strategic plans. Strategic decisions
are guided by three fundamental questions. Answering these questions
requires an activity called environmental scanning which involves the collection and analysis of evidence (related to internal and external factors) that
impact on the future of the school. The questions in a strategic journey are:

- Where are we going?
- Where do we want to go?
- How will we be able to tell when we have arrived?

Using analysis to make strategic choices

At the heart of strategic management is *strategic analysis* that provides the
essential data to inform strategic decision-making. The three components of
strategic analysis involve looking at the environment, the internal resources
and the culture and values of the organisation (Fidler, 1996). Four well-tried
analysis tools imported from the business world are presented below.

1. Stakeholder analysis

Before one can begin any type of analysis related to establishing the organisation's strategic position, a preliminary exercise is a stakeholder analysis to

determine who needs to be communicated with and consulted in the process of strategy formulation and planning. A first step in meeting this challenge is the identification of the organisation's stakeholders. Bryson's (1995) definition of a stakeholder is pertinent. In his view, 'A stakeholder is defined as any person, group, or organisation that can place a claim on an organisation's attention, resources, or output or is affected by that output' (p. 27). The analysis should recognise both external stakeholders and internal stakeholders.

2. SWOT analysis

A basic tool for strategic environmental scanning is known as a SWOT analysis. The term SWOT is an acronym for **S**trengths, **W**eaknesses, **O**pportunities and **T**hreats. Internal scanning involves looking within the organisation to assess capability to take a particular strategic position and hence internal strengths and weaknesses are the focus. The external environment is scanned to determine opportunities and threats related to the organisation's future. It is a tool often effectively used by a school board of trustees responsible for planning strategically. It may also be utilised by a senior management team with stakeholder groups. Morden (2007) suggests using the SWOT analysis in relation to understanding the condition in which the organisation currently finds itself. He refers to this as *corporate appraisal*, where internal scanning is undertaken to appraise the strengths of the organisation and to identify performance gaps. A parallel process called *financial appraisal* is also recommended by Morden as a diagnostic exercise to analyse capacity to introduce change – that is, what the organisation is capable of achieving and to pinpoint financial problem areas and analyse the implications of these for the strategic plan.

3. PEST analysis

Another form of analysis suggests that organisations should be outward and forward looking in the way they scan the environment. This tool – the PEST analysis – can be employed to analyse the pressures on the organisation that come from several fronts:

- Political;
- Economic;
- Social; and
- Technological.

Again, this provides a framework for understanding the environment and understanding the organisation's position in relation to its present capability and future intent.

4. Portfolio analysis

A way of analysing the strengths and weaknesses of a portfolio of products in relation to market forces based on the ideas of the Boston Consulting Group (BCG) has been proposed by many strategic management writers (see for example Morden, 2007). If the curriculum programmes that a school or higher education institution offers are viewed as services rather than products, then a BCG type of matrix could be used to analyse these services as strong or weak and having market value in terms of being required or demanded by stakeholders. Based on the BCG business model, curriculum programmes can be classified as stars, cash cows, problem children or dogs. The strength of curriculum service is judged along a horizontal continuum of service strength and this is balanced by a vertical continuum that judges the service on the criteria of requirements and demands. It is fundamentally a resource-based analysis tool.

Curriculum portfolio analysis (Figure 8.3) should not be used as the sole means of analysing an educational organisation's position when strategic decisions have to be made about the mix of curriculum services to be offered. However, it is a useful tool for examining the viability of curriculum programmes, checking perceptions and raising awareness of potential and problems. It allows planners to assemble all elements of curriculum services (the portfolio) in a manner that enables decision-makers to judge dimensions of strategic importance. In essence, portfolio analysis could be viewed as a consultative decision-making tool for making judgements about the programmes that are a priority to retain and those that (usually because of expense) the organisation believes they can dispense with. In assigning programmes a place in the portfolio matrix the following meanings apply to the terms in each quadrant:

> Stars are judged as programmes that are high profile curriculum/service strengths. They are highly sought after, have 'leading edge' status and enhance the reputation of the organisation. In the case of star programmes, usually the institution has considerable teacher expertise and has had success with the programme for some time. (It should be noted that stars have a heavy need for resources to maintain their successful delivery.)

> Cash cows are well established programmes at the heart of the curriculum mix offered. They appear to be strong but somewhat threatened by trends that predict low future importance but are still considered most worthy although investment for growth is not warranted. Institutions usually ride on the reputation of these programmes that have minimal need for resourcing.

> Problem children are programmes in new areas of opportunity and the institution may have little or no experience or internal expertise to draw on in these areas. Yet, the development of programmes in these areas could be essential for survival or for image-building. Challenges for

leaders are related to the high investment such new endeavours call for and deciding what to invest in.

Dogs are the old areas of heavy investment and the viability and desirability of such programmes is questionable. While reasonable to resource, the question of whether costs justify limited benefits must be asked. The key decisions needed are about whether such programmes should be eliminated and resources used elsewhere.

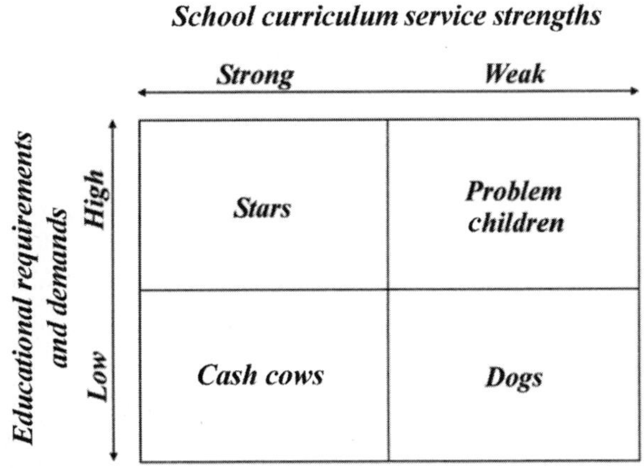

School curriculum service strengths

Figure 8.3 *Curriculum portfolio analysis*

All organisations should identify and retain their stars and cash cows. In relation to dogs and problem children, some decisions are aided when they are linked to a strategy. As Morden (2007) suggests, the portfolio analysis leads to an organisation adopting one of four particular strategies in relation to the future of the service or product:

1. Build – a strategy that shows a willingness to improve the service and resource it adequately to ensure that it survives.
2. Hold – a strategy for preserving long-term commitment (most often applied to cash cows to prolong their capacity to earn resources for the organisation).
3. Harvest – a strategy for achieving the best short-term return on investment.
4. Divest – a strategy for selling-off or closing down and reinvesting the resources in more economically secure areas.

Using the curriculum portfolio analysis tool creates opportunities to engage all people for whom curriculum viability issues are relevant in appropriate consultation when making decisions about the future mix of curriculum services to be offered (Cardno, 2001b; Foskett, 2002).

   All of the tools suggested above contribute to scanning the environment for trends that could impact on the organisation's future. They also allow the organisation to revisit its own goals and consider the expectations of stakeholders. Finally, analysis should also look inwards at the organisation's resources and capability to engage in the strategic choices that are made. An important element of effective planning is alignment between strategies planned at the executive level and their implementation at an operational level where the core work of the organisation takes place.

Strategic and operational planning

Mintzberg (1994) poses a remarkable set of questions when he asks:

> What is the relationship between planning and strategy? Is strategy making simply a process of planning, as the proponents of planning have so vigorously insisted? Or, at the other extreme, is strategic planning simply another oxymoron, like progressive conservative or jumbo shrimp (or civil engineer?). In other words, should strategy always be planned, never be planned, or sometimes be planned? Or should it relate to planning in some other way? (p. 5)

While Mintzberg's inimitable identification of the tension between strategy (and its 'flying high' implication) and planning (with its 'pinning down' demand) provides a memorable reminder of the challenges inherent in this task, it is a task that is nevertheless worth considering. As Mintzberg later states, planning can mean different things to different people in different circumstances. It has elements of all of the following in how it is understood:

- planning is future thinking;
- planning is controlling the future;
- planning is decision-making; and
- planning is a formalised procedure to produce an articulated result, in the form of an integrated system of decisions.

It is this fundamental aim of integrating decisions from bottom up, top down, and across the organisation that gives strategic leadership its important management dimension. The challenge for leaders at the top end of the organisation is to ensure that those who manage the work of others within the organisation have the means to motivate and enable the commitment of individuals to be translated into aligned and integrated action. Hence, effective educational leaders need to be concerned about creating conditions that make workplace relationships productive: that is, capable of producing the results the organisation aspires to.

Differences between strategic and operational plans

There are considerable differences between strategic and operational plans in terms of focus, span, the elements that constitute them, the amount of detail included and the locus of responsibility for devising and implementing them. The summary in Table 8.1 identifies these differences. Both types of plans are needed. The strategic plan with its wider and longer-term focus is a mechanism for leaders to use in a process of reinforcing and reforging commitment to what the organisation values. Flowing from these priorities are the working goals which in the case of educational organisations need to be strongly secured to educational purposes. To implement goals, annual objectives determine the work to be done, by whom, by when and with what resourcing support. Cycles of consistent and systematic planning incorporate a focus on financial management at both strategic and operational levels. Long-range planning that incorporates strategic human resources management principles (Macky and Johnson, 2000) and skilled budgeting and staff management (Miles and Frank, 2008) contribute to effective strategic and operational planning in a framework of strategic management.

Table 8.1 Differences between strategic and operational plans

Strategic plans are:	Operational plans are:
• about strategy	• about implementing strategy
• focused on the future	• focused on the present
• long term (3–10 years)	• short term (1–3 years)
• a governance responsibility in collaboration with the chief executive officer and stakeholders	• the responsibility of the principal and staff
• about what will be different	• about what is already established
• a single succinct document that refers to vision, guiding values, critical strategic issues and goals, and associated initiatives with target dates	• several detailed documents that link to strategic initiatives and school goals and specify objectives, outcomes, actions, responsibility, time frames and budget implications

Strategic planning

With its roots in military usage, this term implies that a grand design underpins the organisation's plans. It incorporates the notion of developing an approach that is consistent with an organisation's vision for the future. In modern business terms, strategy also denotes a scheme of action that will distinguish the organisation from its competitors and give it a 'competitive edge' in the marketplace. The growth of understanding around marketing schools in a competitive environment has given rise to many schools utilising the concept of differentiation. Used as a marketing strategy, differentiation can create a unique school image (Foskett, 2002).

Plans are aligned when at the highest level of an organisation there is a clear indication of being knowledgeable about system-level policy and strategy that must be taken into account in developing institution-level strategic initiatives. Concurrently, the institute's own vision, guiding values and institutional goals may generate further, local strategic initiatives. In turn, at the middle management level department and unit heads need to plan in a way that is aligned with institution-wide strategic initiatives and goals. This implies that communication of direction and emphasis is essential at the outset of planning and throughout the implementation of the plan. Strategic planning is normally an executive-level responsibility (for example, in schools this would be in the domain of the board of trustees and senior management). It takes into account environmental scanning knowledge that can inform the plan. This knowledge is drawn from several data sources through the activities of strategic analysis and review, and includes, for example:

- system-wide information about legislation and policy changes;
- professional information on trends and issues;
- results of curriculum analysis and forecasting;
- results of SWOT or PEST analysis meetings;
- results of community or stakeholder group surveys; and
- recommendations from a range of reviews of practice.

The span of a strategic plan varies from organisation to organisation. Some typically span three to five years, others have a 10-year horizon. The strategic plan is directly linked to the operational plan that is about implementation of specific strategic initiatives drawn into annual or three-year business or management plans on an incremental basis. In terms of the Johnson and Scholes (2002) model of iterative strategic activity, the strategic plan is the culmination of strategic choices that are made for the whole organisation and its parts. This level of planning then has to be operationalised which is the next stage of turning strategy into action. Strategic plans provide the blueprint for this action.

Several components are associated with strategising and planning which are often seen as inseparable activities (Johnson and Scholes, 2002). However, in order to implement strategy, planning is required. A hierarchy of planning begins at the strategic level and cascades through to an operational level that is actualised through action plans. The components of plans are the goals (sometimes called aims) which are broken down into working objectives or targets to be reached in the shorter term. By stating an outcome or expected result, the objective can be evaluated in terms of how well it has been achieved. The components of planning have generally been assigned common meanings across a very wide range of endeavours, from military manoeuvres to personal aspirations; however, when used in a strategic management context, there is general agreement about the nature of each of these components that work together to create strategic alignment in relation to an organisation's strategic and operational planning practice.

A strategic plan should be a short, succinct document containing four essential elements, each about a page or less in length. These are the vision and mission, the guiding values, the critical strategic issues and the strategic initiatives that generate strategic goals.

Vision and mission in planning

In relation to strategic management, a vision statement indicates a future state for the organisation. It is not about the present, but about what will be – and what will be different. It refers to a future ideal state for the organisation. Vision statements are written to guide planning over a long span of time – usually looking five to 10 years ahead.

The vision statement is a brief overview of where the organisation needs to be. It should:

- state the time-horizon for the strategic plan;
- state what will be different (not revisit what is already being done);
- state dissatisfaction with the status quo (when appropriate); and
- be written either as a narrative or in bullet points.

A mission statement is different from a vision statement in that it should capture the essence of the organisation's purpose as it is now. Mission statements often refer to values. These are sometimes listed or they may be integrated in a descriptive statement. The audience of a mission statement are the stakeholders. In educational contexts these are both external and internal to the organisation.

Guiding values

Every decision, from generic strategy to the way in which day-to-day practice is carried out, should be linked to the expressed values that guide the organisation to be what it is. These guiding values act as a touchstone, allowing both strategic and operational decisions to be weighed against their 'fit' with the espoused values.

Critical strategic issues

As a consequence of strategic analysis activity the organisation must identify and then prioritise the issues that it is imperative to take note of for the future. This is usually documented as a list, prioritised in relation to the significance of the issue in terms of continuing to meet the current goals and aspirations to meet new goals.

Strategic initiatives

This final element shows what specific initiatives will have to be implemented to address a strategic issue. For example, if an issue with enrolment trends connected to the building of a new educational institution in the community has been identified through environmental scanning, then this part of a strategic plan should document what the planners intend. The template provided (Figure 8.4) can be used to generate goals for implementing a strategic initiative. It involves breaking down the initiative into specific goals and then specifying for each goal how its achievement will be measured. The noting of a time frame for implementing an initiative is a signal as to when this item needs to be operationalised. It will then be transferred to an operational (annual management or business) plan and assigned as a responsibility in the job description of the nominated person.

Strategic goals

These are a linking mechanism between vision and planning and expand on a mission statement by encapsulating the purpose of the organisation.

- Goals are written as descriptive statements of intent and are to be found in institutional documents such as the organisation's charter, or a prospectus or similar document that conveys what the organisation intends to achieve.
- Goals are generally long-term and unchanging intents; they are not normally revised but may be added to, especially if the mission of the organisation changes.
- If they need to be amended (as a consequence of radical reform, for example) they require some form of strategic review.
- Goals are actioned through objectives. These break down goals into manageable chunks for inclusion in operational plans.

Operational planning

These plans allow an organisation to put strategy into action (Johnson and Scholes, 2002) and the implementation of these plans relies on skilled management occurring at all leadership levels throughout the organisation. Here the relationships between people who are accountable for implementing change and those they lead are critical. Change must be managed, people must be enabled to participate in change and the changes must be organised to have a positive impact. In turn, the close monitoring of the changes and formal periodic review of change outcomes lead back to the starting point of strategic activity and inform the organisation's strategic positioning in an ongoing way. Operational plans are most effective when they are documented in landscape orientation and contain reference to goals, objectives, outcomes, actions, responsibility, budget and time.

Plan goals

Selected strategic goals provide the basis for operational planning.

Plan objectives

Objectives move goals into action.

- These are derived from goals and should be linked to achievement of a particular goal.
- They are short-term statements of intent, are usually set annually and are subject to regular review.
- Objectives specify the detail of what is going to be achieved.
- This may include way-points or targets that are observable and measurable.
- Specific responsibility for achieving the objective should be assigned to the appropriate person(s).
- Consideration of budget (financial resources) is required.
- *SMART* objectives meet the following criteria:
  - *Specific:* they are written 'tightly' about specific, identifiable aspects of development;
  - *Measurable:* they must be measurable to determine whether the intention has been carried out to achieve a desirable result (measures can be quantifiable or descriptive);
  - *Attainable:* they must be realistic, that is, the outcomes must be reasonably attainable yet sufficiently challenging to be both manageable and developmental;
  - *Results oriented:* they must link with strategic and performance accountabilities and should focus on achievement of a result – a demonstrable outcome; and
  - *Time-bound:* they must have a time span specified.
- Objectives are written in a format starting with the word 'To ...' and are therefore stated as an intention of what is to be done, for example:
  - To review and rewrite the programme.
  - To raise Year 3 reading ages by two years beyond chronological age as the minimum achievement standard.

STRATEGIC INITIATIVES AND GOALS

Strategic initiative:

Strategic goal(s)	Measure(s)	Time frame	Responsibility
1			
2			
3			

Figure 8.4 Template for strategic initiatives and goals

Plan outcomes

Outcomes indicate what needs to be achieved to show that an objective has been reached.

- Outcomes are measurable and are generally embedded in an objective when it is written in a descriptive mode.
- Outcomes are often written with a measure stated as a performance indicator.
- Targets (which are commonly quantitative) are often specified as part of, or steps towards achieving an outcome.
- Outcomes are always written as a result statement to show that an action has been completed, a target has been met, or an intent achieved, for example:
  - Charter is rewritten.
  - Eighty per cent of 7-year-olds are reading at Reading Age 9 level or above.

Plan actions

The recording of key actions that must occur in the implementation stage allows planners to consider who will be responsible for these actions. This also leads to consideration about the cost of the actions.

Plan responsibilities

Noting who will be responsible for taking action and meeting the outcomes of objectives is a key planning task. Assigning responsibilities to staff members should be directly linked to recording these in individual job descriptions as part of the performance appraisal process.

Plan budget

Plans have financial implications. Hence, a budget must be allocated to enable the implementation of actions.

Plan dates

It is important to clearly indicate time frames for reaching an objective. Sometimes it is necessary to assign dates to specific actions as well.

When all of the above components are brought together in plans, then an organisation can be confident that it has articulated its vision, values and purpose and has clear goals that chart direction. Translating goals into objectives and outcomes provides a clear route back towards achieving goals and presents ways of incrementally measuring and monitoring plan achievement. A template for effective operational planning is provided (Figure 8.5).

Strategic review

When it is recognised that the notion of strategy and its management is closely linked to concepts of quality and marketing through a common focus on stakeholder expectations and stakeholders' views about the quality of service provided (Foskett, 2002), then the importance of reviewing both strategy and its implementation is confirmed. In the context of education, some form of external review applies to most educational organisations as part of the organisation's accountability to external stakeholders and government. This may take the form of school inspections such as those that occur within the framework of the Office for Standards in Education (Ofsted) inspections in the UK (Brundrett and Rhodes, 2011). In New Zealand, for example, all early childhood services and schools are subject to periodic external reviews conducted by the Education Review Office (ERO). Internal review of quality is an expectation linked to external review. In fact, in the case of New Zealand the connection between strategic planning and self-review in schools is well established, as the following statement from the ERO demonstrates: 'Strategic planning provides the context for self review. A strategic plan is a management document that sets a direction for the school – taking into account its charter, its resources, the community, and what it wishes for its students' (Education Review Office, 2000b, p. 3).

Furthermore, in the case of New Zealand, internal review feeds into a system of external validation of internal self-review results and follow-on improvement actions. Tertiary system reviews in the polytechnic sector, for example, are undertaken by the Institute of Technology/Polytechnic Quality (ITPQ) agency in conjunction with an institutional self-assessment process. In the compulsory sector, schools are required to engage in a system of school self-review with periodic external reviews undertaken by the ERO. Similarly, early childhood services are also required to engage in both internal and external review processes. The expectation is that self-review in the early childhood sector will be aligned with strategic planning and used to inform external evaluations (Education Review Office, 2009b).

Review activity should span all levels of planning and implementation of plans to provide a comprehensive evaluation of quality of provision that can, in turn, contribute to the redevelopment of strategy as part of the internal environment analysis phase that establishes strategic position (Johnson and Scholes, 2002). For example, a school's policy and programme for self-review should include reference to the regular activity of *strategic review*.

OPERATIONAL PLAN TEMPLATE

INSTITUTIONAL OR DEPARTMENT GOAL:

OBJECTIVES	OUTCOMES	ACTIONS	RESPONSIBILITY	BUDGET	DATE

Figure 8.5 Operational plan template

While the review of the school's annual management plan will contribute to a review of the strategies selected for implementation in a particular year, the principal and board should also conduct a formal strategic review of the whole strategic plan on a regular basis. It is often effective to conduct strategic review at the time of election of new members to a board. Strategic review practices are also evident when an educational organisation establishes a relationship with the community in which feedback is both sought and welcomed. A critical aspect of developing effective stakeholder relationships is the inclusion of a stakeholder perspective in judging the strategic achievement of the organisation. After all, strategy should ultimately be driven by the desire to serve the organisation's stakeholders.

The purpose of such review should be to establish what has been achieved from the previous strategic plan and to update the plan at the same time by drawing on the results and recommendations of other levels of review. Surveys of internal and external stakeholders, to establish satisfaction with the direction the organisation is taking, are useful in this context. The literature on service quality (see, for example, Joseph et al., 2005) provides useful guidance on gathering evidence of stakeholder perceptions using gap analysis to determine what customers consider is important and their evaluation of the organisation's performance in relation to this.

Levels of planning and review

While it is acknowledged that there are no specific educational models for strategic management, an understanding of the many levels of planning and review is a first step along the way to the development of a viable model. Table 8.2 uses an example from New Zealand to provide an overview of the linkages between the various levels of planning and review that constitute a strategic management approach to change and improvement. A strategic manager needs to be aware that none of these levels are fixed forever. The levels, however, show not only the links and relationships between the various levels of planning and review, but also illustrate the likelihood for change. Levels 1 to 3 are least likely to change and certainly with no regularity. Levels 4 and 5 need regular updating and Levels 6 to 9 require constant monitoring and adjustment.

Including others in strategic change

Strategic management is a key leadership task because its aim is change and improvement. It encompasses the identification of strategic initiatives; with an eye on the future but with feet firmly planted in the present in order to manage the implementation of plans that will keep the organisation on track.

It is a dynamic and collaborative process requiring the active involvement of many people with and through whom a leader achieves strategic change (Cardno, 1998c). Hence, a fundamental challenge for educational leaders will always be the management of the participation of stakeholders in the organisation's planning of its priorities for success. As Bryson (1995) asserts, planning strategically is a collective endeavour:

> The tasks of leadership for strategic planning are complex and many. Unless the organisation is very small, no single person or group can perform them all. Effective strategic planning is a collective phenomenon, typically involving sponsors, champions, facilitators, teams, task forces, and others in various ways at various times. (p. 227)

Table 8.2 Levels of strategic management planning and review

	Levels of planning	Levels of review (mechanisms)
1	Government strategy	External review
		Financial audit
2	Vision/values	Strategic review
		(Charter review)
3	Charter	Strategic review
		(Charter review)
4	Policy	Strategic review
		(Policy review)
5	Strategic plan	Strategic review
		(Stakeholder review)
6	Management plan	Self-review
		(Operations review)
7	Middle management plan	Self-review
		(Curriculum review)
8	Individual teacher plan	Self-review
		(Performance review)
9	Teaching plan	Self-review
		(Student assessment)

There are several important issues that educational leaders must consider in embarking on a strategic journey.

- An organisation cannot successfully be all things to all people. Once strategy is determined, the organisation must work to educate all its stakeholders in this strategy to create a sense of ownership.
- The consent of those directly involved with implementing the strategy must be secured. This means that all those involved in implementing

change should participate in discussion that leads to agreement about the additional commitments that change inevitably creates.

- All aspects of the organisation should be geared to supporting or reflecting the chosen strategy. This means that staffing, finance, professional development, marketing and management plans and decisions should be closely linked from institution-wide level through to middle management level and to the level of individual teachers.
- The strategy must be realistically related to available expertise and resources and strongly supported by commitment to it at all levels of governance, management and teaching.

There is nothing so powerful as a plan that is both a vision and a blueprint for concerted effort. There is also nothing more disappointing than an unrealistic plan that is doomed to failure through poor resourcing and lack of genuine commitment. The very exercise of thinking and planning strategically for educational purposes and priorities is a way of developing an organisational learning culture in the school that is inclusive of all stakeholders. In a very positive sense, the development or the review of a strategic plan can provide the ideal opportunity to test and harness commitment to core guiding values and the goals that flow from these. It provides opportunities for gathering data about stakeholders' views and for consultation with the institution's community. A more negative perception of the employment of a strategic management approach is that organisational strategy is a controlling device. It may be viewed as 'an activity designed to help executives make their world more manageable' (Argyris, 1990, p. 138). If leaders were able to use productive reasoning in the process of analysing the external environment and internal capabilities and testing options, then they would be opening up possibilities for organisational learning to occur in tandem with strategic management.

Successful strategic management relies on the organisation being able to build productive relationships with its stakeholders throughout an ongoing, cyclic and systematic process. Research shows that when purposes and goals are contested, and leadership dilemmas arise, leadership skills are tested in terms of enabling dialogue to occur in ways that open up rather than close down opportunities for learning and change. Therefore, a precursor to building productive relationships is engagement in conversations that are collaborative and productive (Cardno, 1998c, 2007) and open to learning (Robinson et al., 2009). When leaders approach strategic decision-making in an inclusive way it is part of relationship building with all those who have a stake in the organisation achieving goals that are mutually aligned to meet the needs of students, teachers, leaders and the wider community.

REFERENCES

Adair, J. (1986) *Effective Teambuilding*. London: Pan Books.

Adair, J. (1997) 'Effective teambuilding', in M. Crawford, L. Kydd and C. Riches (eds), *Leadership and Teams in Educational Management*. Buckingham: Open University Press. pp. 179–88.

Argyris, C. (1977) 'Double-loop learning in organizations', *Harvard Business Review*, 55(5): 115–25.

Argyris, C. (1985) *Strategy, Change and Defensive Routines*. Boston, MA: Pitman.

Argyris, C. (1990) *Overcoming Organizational Defenses: Facilitating Organisational Learning*. Boston, MA: Allyn and Bacon.

Argyris, C. (1992) *On Organisational Learning*. Cambridge, MA: Blackwell.

Argyris, C. (1993) *Knowledge for Action: A Guide to Overcoming Barriers to Organizational Change*. San Francisco, CA: Jossey-Bass.

Argyris, C. and Schön, D.A. (1974) *Theory into Practice: Increasing Professional Effectiveness*. San Francisco, CA: Jossey-Bass.

Argyris, C. and Schön, D. (1978) *Organizational Learning: A Theory of Action Perspective*. Reading, MA: Addison-Wesley.

Argyris, C. and Schön, D. (1996) *Organizational Learning II: Theory, Method and Practice*. Reading, MA: Addison Wesley.

Armstrong, M. (2000) *Performance Management: Key Strategies and Practical Guidelines*. 2nd edn. London: Kogan Page.

Barth, R.S. (2006) 'Improving relationships within the schoolhouse', *Educational Leadership*, 63(6): 8–13.

Begley, P.T. (1999) 'Practitioner and organizational perspectives on values in administration', in P.T. Begley (ed.), *Values and Educational Leadership*. Albany, NY: State University of New York Press. pp. 3–7.

Belbin, M. (1993) *Team Roles at Work*. London: Butterworth.

Belbin, M.R. (2010) *Management Teams: Why They Succeed or Fail*. 3rd edn. London: Butterworth-Heinneman.

Bell, L. (1992) *Managing Teams in Secondary Schools*. London: Routledge.

Bell, L. (2002) 'Strategic planning and school management: full of sound and fury, signifying nothing?', *Journal of Educational Administration*, 40(5): 407–24.

Bennett, N., Woods, P., Wise, C. and Newton, W. (2007) 'Understandings of middle leaders in secondary schools: a review of empirical research', *School Leadership and Management*, 27(5): 453–70.

Blase, J. and Blase, J. (2000) 'Effective instructional leadership: teachers' perspectives on how principals promote teaching and learning in schools', *Journal of Educational Administration*, 38(2): 130–41.

Bohm, D. (1965) *The Special Theory of Relativity.* New York: W.A. Benjamin.

Bolman, L.G. and Deal. T.E. (2008) *Reframing Organisations: Artistry, Choice and Leadership.* 4th edn. San Francisco, CA: Jossey-Bass.

Boreham, N. and Morgan, C. (2004) 'A sociocultural analysis of organisational learning', *Oxford Review of Education*, 30(3): 307–25.

Bottery, M. (2004) *The Challenges of Educational Leadership.* London: Paul Chapman Publishing.

Bowman, E.H., Singh, H. and Thomas, H. (2002) 'The domain of strategic management: history and evolution', in A. Pettigrew, H. Thomas and R. Whittington (eds), *Handbook of Strategy and Management.* Thousand Oaks, CA: Sage. pp. 31–51.

Boxall, P. and Purcell, J. (2011) *Strategy and Human Resource Management.* 3rd edn. Basingstoke, Hampshire: Palgrave Macmillan.

Bridges, E.M. (1967) 'A model for shared decision making in the school principalship', *Educational Administration Quarterly*, 3: 49–61.

Bridges, E.M. (1992) *The Incompetent Teacher.* Lewes: Falmer Press.

Brundrett, M. (1998) 'What lies behind collegiality, legitimation or control?', *Educational Management and Administration*, 26(3): 305–16.

Brundrett, M. and Rhodes, C. (2011) *Leadership for Quality and Accountability in Education.* Abingdon: Routledge.

Bryk, A. and Schneider, B. (2003) 'Trust in schools: a core resource for school reform', *Educational Leadership*, 60(6): 40–4.

Bryman, A. (2007) 'Effective leadership in higher education', *Studies in Higher Education*, 32(6): 693–710.

Bryson, J.M. (1995) *Strategic Planning for Public and Non-profit Organisations.* San Francisco, CA: Jossey-Bass.

Bush, T. (2003) *Theories of Educational Leadership and Management.* 3rd edn. London: Sage.

Bush, T. (2009) 'Leadership development', in T. Bush, L. Bell and D. Middlewood (eds), *The Principles of Educational Leadership and Management.* London: Sage.

Bush, T. (2011) *Theories of Educational Leadership and Management.* 4th edn. London: Sage.

Bush, T. and Middlewood, D. (2005) *Leading and Managing People in Education.* London: Sage.

Bush, T., Bell, L. and Middlewood, D. (2010) 'Introduction: new directions in educational leadership', in T. Bush, L. Bell and D. Middlewood (eds), *The Principles of Educational Leadership and Management.* London: Sage. pp. 3–12.

Cardno, C. (1990) *Collaborative Management in New Zealand Schools.* Auckland: Longman Paul.

Cardno, C. (1996) 'Problem-based management development – a team approach', *International Studies in Educational Administration*, Winter: 46–56.

Cardno, C. (1998a) 'Making a difference by managing dilemmas', *Research Information for Teachers, SET One* (13). Wellington: New Zealand Council for Educational Research.

Cardno, C. (1998b) 'Teams in New Zealand schools', *Leading & Managing*, 4(1): 47–60.

Cardno, C. (1998c) 'Working together: managing strategy collaboratively', in D. Middlewood and J. Lumby (eds), *Strategic Management in Schools and Colleges*. London: Paul Chapman Publishing. pp. 105–19.

Cardno, C. (1999) 'Problem-based methodology in leadership development: interventions to improve dilemma management', *New Zealand Journal of Educational Administration*, 14: 44–51.

Cardno, C. (2001a) 'Managing dilemmas in appraising performance: an approach for school leaders', in D. Middlewood and C. Cardno (eds), *Managing Teacher Appraisal and Performance: A Comparative Approach*. London: RoutledgeFalmer. pp. 143–59.

Cardno, C. (2001b) 'The strategic management of schools: expectations and challenges for principals', *Secondary Principals Association of New Zealand Journal*, April: 9–13.

Cardno, C. (2002) 'Team learning: opportunities and challenges for school leaders', *School Leadership & Management*, 22(2): 211–23.

Cardno, C. (2003) *Action Research: A Developmental Approach*. Wellington: New Zealand Council for Educational Research.

Cardno, C. (2005) 'Leadership and professional development: the quiet revolution', *International Journal of Educational Management*, 19(4): 292–306.

Cardno, C. (2006) 'Leading change from within: action research to strengthen curriculum leadership in a primary school', *School Leadership and Management*, 26(5): 453–71.

Cardno, C. (2007) 'Leadership learning: the praxis of dilemma management', *International Studies in Educational Administration*, 35(2): 33–50.

Cardno, C. (2010) 'Focusing educational leadership on creating learning conditions that sustain productive relationships: the case of a New Zealand primary school', *Leading & Managing*, 16(1): 37–54.

Cardno, C. and Fitzgerald, T. (2005) 'Leadership learning: a development initiative for experienced New Zealand principals', *Journal of Educational Administration*, 43(3): 316–29.

Cardno, C. and Piggot-Irvine, E. (1997) *Effective Performance Appraisal: Integrating Accountability and Development in Staff Appraisal*. Auckland: Longman.

Cardno, C. and Reynolds, B. (2009) 'Resolving leadership dilemmas in New Zealand kindergartens: an action research study', *Journal of Educational Administration*, 47(2): 206–26.

Childs-Bowen, D., Moller, G. and Scrivner, J. (2000) 'Principals: leaders of leaders', *National Association of Secondary School Principals Bulletin*, 84(616): 27–34.

Coleman, M. and Bush, T. (1994) 'Managing with teams', in T. Bush and J. West-Burnham (eds), *The Principles of Educational Management*. Harlow: Longman. pp. 265–84.

Cranston, N., Ehrich, L.C. and Kimber, M. (2006) 'Ethical dilemmas: the "bread and butter" of educational leaders' lives', *Journal of Educational Administration*, 44(2): 106–21.

Cuban, L. (1988) *The Management Imperative and the Practice of Leadership in Schools*. Albany, NY: State University of New York Press.

Cuban, L. (2001) *How Can I Fix It? Finding Solutions and Managing Dilemmas: An Educator's Road Map*. New York: Columbia University, Teachers College Press.

Darling-Hammond, L. and Richardson, N. (2009) 'Teacher learning: what matters?', *Educational Leadership*, 66(5): 46–53.

Davies, B.J. and Davies, B. (2004) 'Strategic leadership', *School Leadership & Management*, 24(1): 29–38.

Day, C. (1999) *Developing Teachers: The Challenges of Lifelong Learning*. London: Falmer Press.

Dempster, N., Alen, J. and Gatehouse, R. (2009) 'Professional learning for experienced educational leaders: research and practice', in N.C Cranston and L.C. Ehrich (eds), *Australian School Leadership Today*. Sydney: Australian Academic Press. pp. 314–32.

Dempster, N. and Berry, V. (2003) 'Blindfold in a minefield: principals' ethical decision-making', *Cambridge Journal of Education*, 33(3): 457–77.

Department for Education and Skills (2004) *National Standards for Headteachers*. Nottingham: Department for Education and Skills.

Dick, B. and Dalmau, T. (1999) *Values in Action: Applying the Ideas of Argyris and Schön*. 2nd edn. Brisbane: Interchange.

Dimmock, C. (1999a) 'Principals and school restructuring: conceptualising challenges as dilemmas', *Journal of Educational Administration*, 37(5): 441–62.

Dimmock, C. (1999b) 'The management of dilemmas in school restructuring', *School Leadership & Management*, 19(1): 97–113.

Dimmock, C. and Walker, A. (2005) *Educational Leadership: Culture and Diversity*. London: Sage.

Donmoyer, R. and Wagstaff, J.G. (1990) 'Principals can be effective managers and instructional leaders', *National Association of Secondary School Principals Bulletin*, 74(525): 20–9.

Drucker, P. (1955) *The Practice of Management*. London: Heinemann.

Drucker, P. (1966) *The Effective Executive*. New York: Harper and Row.

Druskat, V.U. and Wolff, S.B. (2001) 'Building the emotional intelligence of groups', *Harvard Business Review*, March, 80–90.

Dunham, J. (1995) *Developing Effective School Management*. London: Routledge.

Ebbeck, M. and Waniganayake, M. (2003) *Early Childhood Professionals: Leading Today and Tomorrow*. Sydney: MacLennan and Petty.

Education Review Office (2000a) *In-Service Training for Teachers in New Zealand Schools*. Wellington: Education Review Office.

Education Review Office (2000b) *Self Review in Schools,* July. Wellington: Education Review Office.

Education Review Office (2009a) *Managing Professional Learning and Development in Secondary Schools*. Wellington: Education Review Office.

Education Review Office (2009b) *Implementing Self-review in Early Childhood Services*, January. Wellington: Education Review Office.

Ellett, C.D. and Teddlie, C. (2003) 'Teacher evaluation, teacher effectiveness and school effectiveness: perspectives from the USA', *Journal of Personnel Evaluation in Education*, 17(1): 101–28.

Fauske, J.R. (2002) 'Preparing school leaders: understanding, experiencing, and implementing collaboration', *International Electronic Journal for Leadership in Learning*, 6(6).

Fidler, B. (1996) *Strategic Planning for School Improvement*. London: Pitman Publishing.

Fidler, B. and Atton, T. (2004) *The Challenges of Contemporary School Leadership*. London: RoutledgeFalmer.

Filan, G.L. and Seagren, A.T. (2003) 'Six critical issues for midlevel leadership in postsecondary settings', *New Directions for Higher Education*, 124: 21–31.

Foskett, N. (2002) 'Marketing', in T. Bush and L. Bell (eds), *The Principles and Practice of Educational Management*. London: Paul Chapman Publishing. pp. 241–57.

Gardiner, L.F. (2002) 'Research on learning and student development and its implications', in R.M. Diamond (ed.), *Field Guide to Academic Leadership*. San Francisco, CA: Jossey-Bass. pp. 89–110.

Goldring, E., Porter, A, Murphy, J., Elliott, S. and Cravens, X. (2009) 'Assessing learning-centred leadership: connections to research, professional standards and current practices', *Leadership and Policy in Schools*, 8: 1–36.

Goleman, D. (1996) *Emotional Intelligence: Why It Can Matter More than IQ*. New York: Bantam Books.

Goleman, D. (1998) *Working with Emotional Intelligence*. London: Bloomsbury.

Goleman, D., Boyzatis, R. and McKee, A. (2002) *The New Leaders: Transforming the Art of Leadership into the Science of Results*. London: Little, Brown.

Goodwin, G.F., Burke, C.S., Wildman, J.L. and Salas, E. (2009) 'Team effectiveness in complex organisations: an overview', in E. Salas, G.F. Goodwin and C.S. Burke (eds), *Team Effectiveness in Complex Organisations*. New York: Psychology Press. pp. 3–16.

Government of New Zealand (1989) *The Education Act*. Wellington: Government Printer.

Government of New Zealand (2001) *Education Standards Act: Public Act 88*. Available at http//www/knowledge-basket.co.nz/gpprint/docs/acts/2001088P.

Govier, T. (1998) *Dilemmas of Trust*. Quebec: McGill-Queen's University Press.

Gronn, P. (1997) 'Leading for learning: organizational transformation and the formation of leaders', *Journal of Management Development*, 16(4): 274–83.

Gronn, P. (2003) *The New Work of Educational Leaders: Changing Leadership Practice in an Era of School Reform*. London: Paul Chapman Publishing.

Gronn, P. (2008) 'The future of distributed leadership', *Journal of Educational Administration*, 46(2): 141–58.

Gronn, P. (2009) 'Where to next for educational leadership?', in T. Bush, L. Bell and D. Middlewood (eds), *The Principles of Educational Leadership and Management*. 2nd edn. London: Sage. pp. 70–85.

Guskey, T.R. (2000) *Evaluating Professional Development*. Thousand Oaks, CA: Corwin Press.

Hallinger, P. and Heck, R. (1998) 'Exploring the principal's contribution to school effectiveness', *School Effectiveness and School Improvement*, 8(4): 309–24.

Hallinger, P. and Heck, R. (2010) 'Leadership for learning: does collaborative leadership make a difference in school improvement?', *Educational Management Administration & Leadership*, 38(6): 654–78.

Hammersley-Fletcher, L. and Kirkham, G. (2007) 'Middle leaders in primary school communities of practice: distribution or deception', *School Leadership and Management*, 27(5): 423–35.

Harris, A. (2005) 'Leading from the chalk-face: an overview of school leadership', *Leadership*, 1(1): 73–87.

Haydon, G. (2007) *Values for Educational Leadership*. London: Sage.

Heck, R.H., Johnsrud, L.K. and Rosser, V.J. (2000) 'Administrative effectiveness in higher education: improving assessment procedures', *Research in Higher Education*, 47(6): 663–84.

Hensey, M. (2001) *Collective Excellence: Building Effective Teams.* 2nd edn. Danvers, MA: American Society of Civil Engineers.

Hersey, P. and Blanchard, K.H. (1982) *Management of Organizational Behaviour.* Englewood Cliffs, NJ: Prentice Hall.

Hodgkinson, C. (1991) *Educational Leadership: The Moral Art.* New York: State University of New York Press.

Hoy, A.W. and Hoy, W.K. (2009) *Instructional Leadership: A Research-based Guide to Learning in Schools.* Boston, MA: Allyn and Bacon.

Hoy, W.K. and Miskel, C.G. (2001) *Educational Administration: Theory, Research and Practice.* 2nd edn. New York: McGraw-Hill.

Hoy, W.K. and Miskel, C.G. (2005) *Educational Administration: Theory, Research and Practice.* 7th edn. New York: McGraw-Hill.

Hoy, W.K. and Miskel, C.G. (2008) *Educational Administration: Theory, Research and Practice.* 8th edn. Boston, MA: McGraw-Hill.

Hoy, W.K. and Tarter, C.J. (2008) *Administrators Solving the Problems of Practice: Decision-making Concepts, Cases and Consequences.* Boston, MA: Pearson Education.

Hunt, J.G. (2004) 'What is leadership?', in J. Antonakis, A.T. Ciancilolo, and R.J. Sternberg (eds), *The Nature of Leadership.* Thousand Oaks, CA: Sage. pp. 19–47.

Jenni, R.W. and Mauriel, J. (2004) 'Co-operation and collaboration: reality or rhetoric?', *International Journal of Leadership in Education,* 7(2): 181–95.

Johnson, G. and Scholes, K. (2002) *Exploring Corporate Strategy: Texts and Cases.* 6th edn. Harlow: Pearson Education.

Joseph, M., Yakhou, M. and Stone, G. (2005) 'An educational institution's quest for service quality: customers' perspective', *Quality Assurance in Education,* 13(1): 66–82.

Knowles, M.S. (1980) *The Modern Practice of Adult Education.* New York: Adult Education Company.

Lashway, L. (2006) 'The effects of leadership', in S.C. Smith and P.K Piele (eds), *School Leadership: Handbook for Excellence in Student Learning.* Thousand Oaks, CA: Corwin Press. pp. 38–49.

Latham, G.P. and Locke, E.A. (2006) 'Enhancing the benefits and overcoming the pitfalls of goal setting', *Organizational Dynamics,* 35(4): 332–40.

Leithwood, K. (1998) 'Team learning processes', in K. Leithwood and K. Seashore Louis (eds), *Organisational Learning in Schools.* Lisse: Swets and Zeitlinger. pp. 203–17.

Leithwood, K. and Riehl, C. (2005) 'What we know about successful school leadership', in K. Leithwood and C. Reihl (eds), *A New Agenda: Directions for Research on Educational Leadership.* New York: Teachers College Press. pp. 22–47.

Leithwood, K., Jantzi, D. and Steinbach, R. (1998) 'Leadership and other conditions which foster organisational learning in schools', in K. Leithwood and K. Seashore Louis (eds), *Organisational Learning in Schools: Contexts of Learning.* Lisse: Swets and Zietlinger. pp. 67–90.

Leithwood, K., Jantzi, D. and Steinbach, R. (1999) *Changing Leadership for Changing Times.* Buckingham: Open University Press.

Leithwood. K., Seashore Louis, K., Anderson, S. and Wahlstrom, K. (2004) *Review of Research: How Leadership Influences Student Learning.* New York: The Wallace Foundation.

Limerick, D. and Cunnington, B. (1993) *Managing the New Organisation: A Blueprint for Strategic Networks and Alliances*. Chatswood: Business and Professional Publishing.

Macky, K. and Johnson, G. (2000) *The Strategic Management of Human Resources in New Zealand*. Sydney: McGraw-Hill.

MacNeill, N. and Cavanagh, R. (2006) 'Principals' pedagogic leadership', *The Australian Educational Leader*, 4: 38–48.

Manz, C.C. and Neck, C.P. (1997) 'Teamthink: beyond the groupthink syndrome in self-managing work teams', *Team Performance Management*, 3(1): 18–31.

Marshall, S., Adams, M. and Cameron, A. (2000) 'In search of academic leadership', in L. Richardson and J. Lidstone (eds), *Flexible Learning for a Flexible Society*. ASET-HERDSA Conference Proceedings.

Middlewood, D. (1998) 'Strategic management in education: an overview', in D. Middlewood and J. Lumby (eds), *Strategic Management in Schools and Colleges*. London: Paul Chapman Publishing. pp. 1–17.

Miles, K.H. and Frank, S. (2008) *The Strategic School: Making the Most of People, Time, and Money*. Thousand Oaks, CA: Corwin Press and National Association of Secondary School Principals.

Mintzberg, H. (1994) *The Rise and Fall of Strategic Planning*. New York: Macmillan.

Morden, T. (2007) *Principles of Strategic Management*. Aldershot: Ashgate.

Moss Kanter, R. (1983) *The Change Masters: Corporate Entrepreneurs at Work*. London: Unwin Hyman.

Mulford, W., Silins, H. and Leithwood, K.A. (2004) *Educational Leadership for Organisational Learning and Improved Student Outcomes*. Dordrecht: Springer.

Murgatroyd, S. and Morgan, C. (1992) *Total Quality Management and the School*. Milton Keynes: Open University Press.

Murphy. C. (2003) 'The rewards of academic leadership', *New Directions for Higher Education*, 124: 87–93.

Murphy, D. (2007) *Professional School Leadership: Dealing with Dilemmas*. Edinburgh: Dunedin Academic Press.

Napier, R.A. and Gershenfeld, M.K. (1988) *Making Groups Work: A Guide for Group Leaders*. Boston, MA: Houghton Mifflin.

Neck, C.P. and Manz, C.C. (1994) 'From groupthink to teamthink: towards the creation of constructive thought patterns in self-managing workteams', *Human Relations*, 48(5): 537–57.

New Zealand Ministry of Education (2008) *Kiwi Leadership for Principals: Principals as Educational Leaders*. Wellington, NZ: Ministry of Education.

Notman, R. and Henry, A. (2009) 'The human face of principalship: a synthesis of case study findings', *Journal of Educational Leadership, Policy and Practice*, 1(24): 37–52.

O'Neill, J. (1997) 'Managing through teams', in T. Bush and D. Middlewood (eds), *Managing People in Education*. London: Paul Chapman Publishing. pp. 76–92.

Owens, R.G. (2004) *Organizational Behaviour in Education: Adaptive Leadership and School Reform*. 8th edn. Boston, MA: Pearson.

Parliament of New Zealand (1988a) *Tomorrow's Schools: The Reform of Education Administration in New Zealand*. Wellington: Government Printer.

Parliament of New Zealand (1988b) *Before Five: Early Childhood Care and Education in New Zealand*. Wellington: Government Printer.

Parliament of New Zealand (1989) *Learning for Life: Education and Training beyond the Age of Fifteen*. Wellington: Government Printer.

Pew, S. (2007) 'Andragogy and pedagogy as foundational theory for student motivation in higher education', *Student Motivation*, (2): 14–25.

Pont, B., Nusche, D. and Moorman, H. (2008) *Improving School Leadership. Volume 1: Policy and Practice*. Paris: Organisation for Economic Co-operation and Development.

Porter, M. (1980) *Competitive Strategy*. New York: Free Press.

Preedy, M., Glatter, R. and Wise, C. (2003) 'Strategic leadership challenges', in M. Preedy, R. Glatter, and C. Wise (eds), *Strategic Leadership and Educational Improvement*. London: Paul Chapman Publishing. pp. 1–16.

Preskill, H. and Torres, R.T. (1999) *Evaluative Inquiry for Learning in Organizations*. Thousand Oaks, CA: Sage.

Pritchard, R.J. and Marshall, J.C. (2002) 'Professional development in "healthy" vs. "unhealthy" districts: top 10 characteristics based on research', *School Leadership & Management*, 22(2): 113–41.

Ramsden, P. (1998) *Learning to Lead in Higher Education*. London: Routledge.

Razik, T.A. and Swanson, A.D. (1995) *Fundamental Concepts of Educational Leadership and Management*. Englewood Cliffs, NJ: Prentice Hall.

Robinson, V., Hohepa, M. and Lloyd, C. (2009) *School Leadership and Student Outcomes: Identifying What Works and Why. Best Evidence Synthesis Iteration [BES]*. Wellington: Ministry of Education.

Robinson, V.M.J. (1993) *Problem-based Methodology: Research for the Improvement of Practice*. Oxford: Pergamon Press.

Robinson, V.M.J. (1995) 'Organisational learning as organisational problem-solving', *Leading and Managing*, 1(1): 63–78.

Robinson, V.M.J. (2007) 'School leadership and student outcomes: identifying what works and why', *Australian Council for Educational Leaders Monograph*, 41.

Robinson, V.M.J. (2008) 'Forging the links between distributed leadership and educational outcomes', *Journal of Educational Administration*, 46(2): 241–56.

Robinson, V.M.J. (2010) 'From instructional leadership to leadership capabilities: Empirical findings and methodological challenges', *Leadership and Policy in Schools*, 9: 1–26.

Rodd, J. (2006) *Leadership in Early Childhood*. 3rd edn. Crows Nest, NSW: Allen and Unwin.

Rudman, R. (2002) *Human Resources Management in New Zealand*. 4th edn. Auckland: Prentice-Hall.

Schein, E.H. (2010) *Organizational Culture and Leadership*. 4th edn. San Francisco, CA: Jossey-Bass.

Schön. D.A. (1993) *The Reflective Practitioner*. New York: Basic Books.

Scott, G., Coates, H. and Anderson, M. (2008) *Learning Leaders in Times of Change: Academic Leadership Capabilities for Australian Higher Education*. Perth: University of Western Sydney and Australian Council for Educational Research.

Seashore Louis, K., Leithwood, K., Wahlstrom, K.L. and Anderson, S.E. (2010) *Learning from Leadership: Investigating the Links to Improved Student Learning*. New York: The Wallace Foundation.

Senge, P. (1990) *The Fifth Discipline: The Art and Practice of the Learning Organisation*. New York: Doubleday.

Senge, P. (2006) *The Fifth Discipline: The Art and Practice of the Learning*

Organisation (revised and updated). London: Random House.

Senge, P., Cambron-McCabe, N., Lucas, T., Smith, B., Dutton, J. and Kleiner, A. (2000) *Schools that Learn*. New York: Doubleday.

Senge, P.M., Kleiner, A., Roberts, C, Ross, R.B. and Smyth, B.J. (1994) *The Fifth Discipline Fieldbook: Strategies and Tools for Building a Learning Organization*. New York: Doubleday.

Simon, H. (1973) 'The structure of ill-structured problems', *Artificial Intelligence*, 4, 181–201.

Sinnema, C.E.L. and Robinson, V.J.M. (2007) 'The leadership of teaching and learning: Implications for teacher evaluation', *Leadership and Policy in Schools*, 6: 319–43.

Smith, R. (2005) 'Departmental leadership and management in chartered and statutory universities: a case of diversity', *Educational Management Administration & Leadership*, 33(4): 449–64.

Southworth, G. (2004) *Primary School Leadership in Context: Leading Small, Medium and Large Sized Schools*. London: RoutledgeFalmer. pp. 97–118.

Spillane, J.P. and Diamond, J.B. (2007) 'Taking a distributed perspective', in J.P. Spillane and J.B. Diamond (eds), *Distributed Leadership in Practice*. New York: Teachers College Press. pp. 1–15.

Starratt, R. (2003) *Centering Educational Administration: Cultivating Meaning, Community, Responsibility*. Mahwah, NJ: Lawrence Erlbaum Associates.

Stein, M.K. and Nelson, B.S. (2003) 'Leadership content knowledge', *Educational Evaluation and Policy Analysis*, 25(4): 423–48.

Stott, K. and Walker, A. (1992) *Making Management Work*. Hong Kong: Simon and Schuster.

Sun, P.Y.T. and Scott, J.L. (2003) 'Exploring the divide – organizational learning and learning organization', *The Learning Organization*, 10(4): 202–15.

Tannenbaum, R. and Schmidt, W.H. (1973) 'How to choose a leadership pattern', *Harvard Business Review*, 51(May–June): 162–80.

Timperley, H., Wilson, A., Barrar, H. and Fung, I. (2007) *Teacher Professional Learning and Development. Best Evidence Synthesis (BES)*. Wellington: Ministry of Education.

Tschannen-Moran, M. (2001) 'Collaboration and the need for trust', *Journal of Educational Administration*, 39(4): 308–31.

Tschannen-Moran, M. (2004) *Trust Matters: Leadership for Successful Schools*. San Francisco, CA: Jossey-Bass.

Tschannen-Moran, M. and Hoy, W.K. (2000) 'A multidisciplinary analysis of the nature, meaning and measurement of trust', *Review of Educational Research*, 70(4): 547–93.

Tuckerman, B.W. (1965) 'Development sequences in small groups', *Psychology Bulletin*, 63 (6): 384–99.

Voogt, J.C., Lagerweij, N.A.J., and Seashore Louis, K. (1998) 'School development and organizational learning: towards an integrative theory', in K. Leithwood and K. Seashore Louis (eds), *Organisational Learning in Schools: Contexts of Learning*. Lisse: Swets and Zeitlinger. pp. 327–58.

Vroom, V.H. and Yetton, P.W. (1973) *Leadership and Decisionmaking*. Pittsburgh, PA: University of Pittsburgh Press.

Walker, A. and Stott, K. (1993) 'The work of senior management teams: some pointers to improvement', *Studies in Educational Administration*, 58: 33–40.

Wallace, M. and Huckman, L. (1999) *Senior Management Teams in Primary Schools: The Quest for Synergy.* London: Routledge.

Waters, T.J., Marzano, R.J. and McNulty, B. (2004) 'Leadership that sparks learning', *Educational Leadership*, 61(7): 48–51.

Weber, J.R. (1987) 'Instructional leadership: a composite working model', *ERIC Digest 17.* University of Oregon, Clearing House on Educational Management.

Weingart, L.R. and Cronin, M.A. (2009) 'Teams research in the 21st century: a case for theory consolidation', in E. Salas, G.F. Goodwin and C.S. Burke (eds), *Team Effectiveness in Complex Organisations.* New York: Psychology Press. pp. 509–24.

West-Burnham, J. (2009) *Developing Outstanding Leaders: Professional Life Histories of Outstanding Headteachers.* Nottingham: National College for School Leadership.

Wheeler, D.W. (2002) 'Chairs as institutional leaders', in R.M. Diamond (ed.), *Field Guide to Academic Leadership.* San Francisco, CA: Jossey-Bass. pp. 451–68.

White, D. (2008) 'Pedagogical leadership: under the microscope', *The Australian Educational Leader*, 30(3): 17–20.

Wildy, H., Clarke, S. and Cardno, C. (2009) 'Antipodean perspectives on enhancing the quality of school leadership: views from Australia and New Zealand', in A.W. Wiseman (ed.), *Educational Leadership: Global Contexts and International Comparisons, International Perspectives on Education and Society.* Vol. 11. Bingley: Emerald Group Publishing. pp. 153–189.

Woodall, J. and Winstanley, D. (1998) *Management Development: Strategy and Practice.* Oxford: Blackwell.

Woods, P.A. and Gronn, P. (2009) 'The contribution of distributed leadership to a democratic organizational landscape', *Educational Management Administration & Leadership*, 37(4): 430–51.

Yukl, G.A. (2002) *Leadership in Organizations.* 5th edn. Upper Saddle River, NJ: Prentice-Hall.

Zaccaro, S.J., Heinen, B. and Shuffler, M. (2009) 'Team leadership and team effectiveness', in E. Salas, G.F. Goodwin and C.S. Burke (eds), *Team Effectiveness in Complex Organisations.* New York: Psychology Press. pp. 83–112.

INDEX

LEADING AND MANAGING SCHOOLS

Edited by **Helen O'Sullivan** *University of Dublin Trinity College* and **John West-Burnham**

School leadership and management are fundamental components of school improvement. This is the first study of its kind to relate the principles of effective leadership to the broad spectrum of school life in Ireland.

A key resource for school leaders in their personal and professional study, this book critically appraises issues in leading and managing schools. The editors bring together an array of renowned scholars to inform and stimulate the debate on the future of leadership development in Irish schools.

Each author explores different perspectives and sets a framework for rethinking school leadership and management and an agenda for future research. The book includes in-depth discussions of a broad spectrum of issues encountered by practitioners, such as:

- justice and equality as cornerstones of any educational system and the challenges they pose for those in leadership positions;
- principles of good governance;
- the key positions of accountability and leadership of change.

Inspiring and informative in its style, the authors bring together a range of perspectives on every aspect of school leadership and management, from well known contributors such as Michael Fullan, Ciaran Sugrue and Marty Linsky, creating a unique and rich canvas. Focusing on national and international perspectives this book adds to the growing canon of international studies of school leadership.

CONTENTS

READERSHIP

Practitioners, scholars and students of educational leadership and management; also policy makers in Ireland

April 2011 • 200 pages
Cloth (978-0-85702-395-7) • **£75.00** / **Paper (978-0-85702-396-4)** • **£24.99** / **Electronic (978-1-4462-0944-8)** • **£24.99**

ALSO AVAILABLE FROM SAGE

LEADING AND MANAGING PEOPLE IN EDUCATION

Tony Bush and **David Middlewood** both at *University of Warwick*

'In my view this book is to be highly recommended, to students, to academics and to managers. Its strengths of style, comparative perspective, and dealing with up-to-date issues make it a valuable text' – *ESClate*

'Leading and Managing People in Education is a completely revised and updated version of one of the most influential books in the field. Bush and Middlewood are two of the best, and best known, writers on this topic today. This is one of those rare texts that is capable of being used by both academics and practitioners since it contains that unusual combination of a wealth of scholarship combined with lifetimes of experience in educational leadership and management. School leaders, advisers, University lecturers, and those engaged in courses of further study will all welcome this text. I have no doubt that it will become of the best known and most widely purchased works in the field' – *Mark Brundrett, Professor of Education at the University of Hull*

Building upon the success of the highly regarded and best selling text ManagingPeople in Education this new book covers leadership and management at all human resource levels, and spans the whole spectrum of educational institutions.

It is based on the most up -to- date research and literature on this topic and directly meets the needs of practising leaders and managers in education, as well as postgraduate students in educational leadership.

CONTENTS
PART ONE: LEADING AND MANAGING PEOPLE: SETTING THE SCENE \ The Context for Leadership and Management in Education \ Leading and Managing People for Performance \ The Importance of Support Staff in Schools and Colleges \ PART TWO: KEY CONCEPTS UNDERPINNING EDUCATIONAL LEADERSHIP \ Organizational Cultures \ Organization Structures and Roles \ Staff Motivation and Job Satisfaction \ Leading and Managing for Equal Opportunities \ Leading and Managing through Teams \ PART THREE: LEADING AND MANAGING KEY PROCESSES \ Staff Recruitment and Selection \ Induction and Retention \ Mentoring and Coaching \ Performance Appraisal and Review \ Staff and Organizational Learning

EDUCATION LEADERSHIP FOR SOCIAL JUSTICE

2005 • 232 pages

Cloth (978-0-7619-4407-2) • £75.00 / Paper (978-0-7619-4408-9) • £24.99 / Electronic (978-1-84860-056-0) • £24.99

ALSO AVAILABLE FROM SAGE